Lecture Notes in Computer Science 4966

Commenced Publication in 1973
Founding and Former Series Editors:
Gerhard Goos, Juris Hartmanis, and Jan van Leeuwen

Bernhard Beckert Reiner Hähnle (Eds.)

Tests and Proofs

Second International Conference, TAP 2008
Prato, Italy, April 9-11, 2008
Proceedings

Volume Editors

Bernhard Beckert
University of Koblenz-Landau
Dept. of Computer Science
Universitätsstrasse 1, 56072 Koblenz, Germany
E-mail: beckert@uni-koblenz.de

Reiner Hähnle
Chalmers University of Technology
Dept. of Computer Science and Engineering
41296 Göteborg, Sweden
E-mail: reiner@cs.chalmers.se

Library of Congress Control Number: 2008924177

CR Subject Classification (1998): D.2.4-5, F.3, D.4, C.4, K.4.4, C.2

LNCS Sublibrary: SL 2 – Programming and Software Engineering

ISSN 0302-9743
ISBN-10 3-540-79123-X Springer Berlin Heidelberg New York
ISBN-13 978-3-540-79123-2 Springer Berlin Heidelberg New York

Springer is a part of Springer Science+Business Media

springer.com

Printed in Germany

Typesetting: Camera-ready by author, data conversion by Scientific Publishing Services, Chennai, India
Printed on acid-free paper SPIN: 12255030 06/3180 5 4 3 2 1 0

Preface

This volume contains the research papers, invited papers, and abstracts of tutorials presented at the Second International Conference on Tests and Proofs (TAP 2008) held April 9–11, 2008 in Prato, Italy.

TAP was the second conference devoted to the convergence of proofs and tests. It combines ideas from both areas for the advancement of software quality.

To prove the correctness of a program is to demonstrate, through impeccable mathematical techniques, that it has no bugs; to test a program is to run it with the expectation of discovering bugs. On the surface, the two techniques seem contradictory: if you have proved your program, it is fruitless to comb it for bugs; and if you are testing it, that is surely a sign that you have given up on any hope of proving its correctness. Accordingly, proofs and tests have, since the onset of software engineering research, been pursued by distinct communities using rather different techniques and tools.

And yet the development of both approaches leads to the discovery of common issues and to the realization that each may need the other. The emergence of model checking has been one of the first signs that contradiction may yield to complementarity, but in the past few years an increasing number of research efforts have encountered the need for combining proofs and tests, dropping earlier dogmatic views of their incompatibility and taking instead the best of what each of these software engineering domains has to offer.

The first TAP conference (held at ETH Zurich in February 2007) was an attempt to provide a forum for the cross-fertilization of ideas and approaches from the testing and proving communities. For the 2008 edition we found the Monash University Prato Centre near Florence to be an ideal place providing a stimulating environment.

We wish to sincerely thank all the authors who submitted their work for consideration. And we would like to thank the Program Committee members as well as additional referees for their great effort and professional work in the review and selection process. Their names are listed on the following pages.

In addition to the contributed papers, the program included three excellent keynote talks. We are grateful to Michael Hennell (LDRA Ltd., Cheshire, UK), Orna Kupferman (Hebrew University, Israel), and Elaine Weyuker (AT&T Labs Inc., USA) for accepting the invitation to address the conference.

Two very interesting tutorials were part of TAP 2008: "Parameterized Unit Testing with Pex" (J. de Halleux, N. Tillmann) and "Integrating Verification and Testing of Object-Oriented Software" (C. Engel, C. Gladisch, V. Klebanov, and P. Rümmer). We would like to express our thanks to the tutorial presenters for their contribution. Extended abstracts of the tutorials are included in this proceedings volume.

It was a team effort that made the conference so successful. We are grateful to the Conference Chair and the Steering Committee members for their support. And we particularly thank Christoph Gladisch, Beate Körner, and Philipp Rümmer for their hard work and help in making the conference a success. In addition, we gratefully acknowledge the generous support of Microsoft Research Redmond, who financed an invited speaker.

April 2008

Bernhard Beckert
Reiner Hähnle

Organization

Conference Chair

Bertrand Meyer	ETH Zurich, Switzerland

Program Committee Chairs

Bernhard Beckert	University of Koblenz, Germany
Reiner Hähnle	Chalmers University, Gothenburg, Sweden

Program Committee

Bernhard Aichernig	TU Graz, Austria
Michael Butler	University of Southampton, UK
Patrice Chalin	Concordia University Montreal, Canada
T. Y. Chen	Swinburne University of Technology, Australia
Yuri Gurevich	Microsoft Research, USA
Dick Hamlet	Portland State University, USA
William Howden	University of California at San Diego, USA
Daniel Jackson	MIT, USA
Karl Meinke	KTH Stockholm, Sweden
Peter Müller	Microsoft Research, USA
Tobias Nipkow	TU München, Germany
Andrea Polini	University of Camerino, Italy
Robby	Kansas State University, USA
David Rosenblum	University College London, UK
Wolfram Schulte	Microsoft Research, USA
Natasha Sharygina	CMU & University of Lugano, Switzerland
Betti Venneri	University of Florence, Italy
Burkhart Wolff	ETH Zurich, Switzerland

Additional Referees

Michele Boreale
Roberto Bruttomesso
Myra Cohen
John Colley
Mads Dam
Andrew Edmunds
Viktor Kuncak
Rupak Majumdar
Karol Ostrovsky
Edgar Pek
Rosario Pugliese
Steffen Schlager

Steering Committee

Yuri Gurevich	Microsoft Research, USA
Bertrand Meyer	ETH Zurich, Switzerland

Organizing Committee

Christoph Gladisch	University of Koblenz, Germany
Philipp Rümmer	Chalmers University, Gothenburg, Sweden

Sponsoring Institutions

Microsoft Research Redmond, USA
Chalmers University of Technology, Gothenburg, Sweden
University of Koblenz-Landau, Germany
ETH Zurich, Switzerland

Table of Contents

Invited Talks

Research Papers

Tutorials

The First Thirty Years: Experience with Software Verification

Michael Hennell

Technical Director
LDRA ltd
Portside, Monks Ferry
Cheshire, CH41 5LH
UK
Michael.hennell@ldra.com

The author started systematic testing in the early seventies, formed LDRA Ltd in 1975, and having stayed in business ever since has acquired considerable experience. The verification tool market is small, mainly embedded systems, and strongly customer driven. Other markets still believe that black-box testing does the job!

In the past the requirements were humble, basically, to measure the effectiveness of test data. Programs were largely simple and very carefully written. They probably had a strong mathematical basis.

Then came requirements for metrics and structured programming verification. At this point there also came ambiguity, false expectations and confusion. How do you measure the metric, what does it mean, how can the metrics be compounded, etc.? As more people become involved carelessness entered the game and so programming rules came important, followed by data flow analysis, information flow analysis computational analysis and other defect finding techniques.

Programs originally were small (less than 20k LOC), held in one file and implemented in a language which had few defects but even then, as now the compilers were rubbish.

Today projects are huge, millions of lines of code, held in thousands of files. The files are themselves big (4 million lines in one file), and can have highly complex inter file structures. The user's knowledge of the system can be minimal: they may even be unable to find where all the bits are stored. The implementation languages are appalling but can be patched. In fact they can be transformed into 1st class languages by recent programming rules.

Programmers frequently resent the fact that the tools are criticising their product. This means that the verification tools work in a doubly hostile environment, i.e., the users resent having to use the tools and the tools attempt to analyse an ill-defined language (that implemented by the compiler).

Verification is a non-productive and potentially costly activity and hence it is unattractive to software producers. The aim is to get verification over, with the minimum of pain and cost. Therefore the tendency is to ship it out to low cost countries and provide the minimum of management control (preferably none). This is possible because a modern test tool requires no specialist skills. If there

B. Beckert and R. Hähnle (Eds.): TAP 2008, LNCS 4966, pp. 1–3, 2008.

is a regulatory authority then there might be a conflict but nothing that can't be patched with documents.

The requirement today is for tools which work at the speed of light, have a low entry cost, can be used by unskilled labour and which generate minimum levels of pain. The tools must also be highly dependable. The application area for tools on the other hand is highly complex, multiple unspecified dialects of badly defined languages with widely different execution platforms and environments. In summary, there is variable syntax and widely different semantics.

The verification market is customer led but the customers are fearful and largely not well informed. This means that any use of sophisticated methods needs to be surreptitious to quell the fear factor.

The future will probably produce tools which automatically repair the software although this moves the tools into another category in terms of risk and assessment.

The emphasis is moving from technical defects towards application defects. Currently this involves tracing requirements through the phases to unit tests. The result is a stream of automatically generated documents showing the successful verification of the derived requirements with complete traceability. Unit test tools now not only totally automatically generate the drivers but can also automatically generate the test data. Soon no doubt they will also confirm the tests so that no human interaction is required.

The whole subject of verification is however bedevilled by un-scientific nonsense, examples:

- "Testing cannot show the absence of errors": it can, see e.g. mutation testing. Note also that a test can constitute a formal proof of correctness.
- "A proof replaces the need for testing": it doesn't, a proof confirms that possibly misconceived pre-conceptions are consistently applied.

Where does the mystique associated with MCDC come from? A minor (but worthwhile) extension to branch coverage has become almost a religion. Statements about horrendous extra costs incurred, for example. A program with multiple conditions can be trivially rewritten without them in which case do the costs still accrue? If not where do they go? Claims are also made that MCDC does not detect faults. Since a trivial exercise shows that it can why are these statements made? Experiments in which it is claimed that MCDC found no faults in a particular project are interesting (in a minor way) but prove nothing. It is possible that the programmers or designers were particularly good or used some other technique to remove any faults. What is inescapable is that some possible faults will be exposed.

Statements are also made about the relative costs of techniques, but the comparisons are nonsensical and if based on data then the data is old and irrelevant. When researchers quote comparisons, e.g. method x is cheaper than testing what is meant? Any form of testing, for example modern Dynamic Analysis to a specific metric or just some gentle hacking of test data?

In reality some programs cannot be tested, and some concepts cannot be verified by testing. Some programs cannot be proved, and some concepts cannot be proved. The trick is to discern which is the appropriate way to go for a specific project. Some of the current thinking is frightening, one company elected to replacing unit testing with the use of a formal method, arguing on the basis of one project in which both methods were used that they are equivalent. Unfortunately the certification body identified one type of fault which was now missed and that company had to do additional work. The question now is what else was missed?

Notation is another barrier to progress, each little research group jealously guards its own definitions and view of the world, even terms like testing and formal methods are not universally meaningful.

The realisation that no verification technique is wholly reliable or convincing is leading to a change of thinking. The emphasis is on using complementary techniques which provide some degree of independence in verification activities.

The way forward, surely, is to bring together the techniques at our disposal and on a project by project basis choose those techniques which in combination yield a cost-effective demonstration that the implemented system is the one required and that system is fault free. Each technique needs to be subjected to a careful critical analysis so the strengths and weaknesses can be identified. In particular which faults or defects are identified and which ones are not?

This means that more and more mathematically based concepts will be incorporated into verification tools.

How can academe help? By providing a framework by means of which we can make sensible scientifically based comparisons and measurements of verification techniques. The days of "here is a wonderful method wot I invented and it finds all yer faults" should be long gone.

Finally for the young, believe nothing in the literature without critical analysis. Software Engineering has delivered very little which is useful!

Vacuity in Testing

Thomas Ball[1] and Orna Kupferman[2]

[1] Microsoft Research
tball@microsoft.com
[2] Hebrew University
orna@cs.huji.ac.il

Abstract. In recent years, we see a growing awareness to the importance of assessing the quality of specifications. In the context of model checking, this can be done by analyzing the effect of applying mutations to the specification or the system. If the system satisfies the mutated specification, we know that some elements of the specification do not play a role in its satisfaction, thus the specification is satisfied in some *vacuous* way. If the mutated system satisfies the specification, we know that some elements of the system are not *covered* by the specification. Coverage in model checking has been adopted from the area of testing, where coverage information is crucial in measuring the exhaustiveness of test suits. It is now time for model checking to pay back, and let testing enjoy the rich theory and applications of vacuity. We define and study vacuous satisfaction in the context of testing, and demonstrate how vacuity analysis can lead to better specifications and test suits.

1 Introduction

The realization that hardware and software systems can, and often do, have bugs brought with it two approaches for reasoning about the correctness of systems. In *testing*, we execute the system on input sequences and make sure its behavior meets our expectation. In *model checking*, we formally prove that the system satisfies its specification.

Each input sequence for the system induces a different execution, and a system is correct if it behaves as required for all possible input sequences. Checking all the executions of a system is an infeasible task. Testing can be viewed as a heuristic in which the execution of only some input sequences is checked [4]. It is therefore crucial to measure the exhaustiveness of the input sequences that are checked. Indeed, there has been an extensive research in the testing verification community on *coverage metrics*, which provide such a measure. Coverage metrics are used in order to monitor progress of the verification process, estimate whether more input sequences are needed, and direct simulation towards unexplored areas of the system. Coverage metrics today play an important role in the system validation effort [22]. For a survey on the variety of metrics that are used in testing, see [13,20,23].

Since testing suits are typically not exhaustive, the verification community welcomed the idea of model checking, where the system is formally proven to be

B. Beckert and R. Hähnle (Eds.): TAP 2008, LNCS 4966, pp. 4–17, 2008.

correct with respect to all input sequences [12]. In the last few years, however, there has been growing awareness to the importance of suspecting the system and the specification of containing an error also in the case model checking succeeds. The main justification of such suspects are possible errors in the (often not simple) modeling of the system or of the behavior.

Early work on "suspecting a positive answer" concerns the fact that temporal logic formulas can suffer from antecedent failure [2]. For example, verifying a system with respect to the specification $\varphi = AG(req \rightarrow AF grant)$ ("every request is eventually followed by a grant"), one should distinguish between satisfaction of φ in systems in which requests are never sent, and satisfaction in which φ's precondition is sometimes satisfied. Evidently, the first type of satisfaction suggests some unexpected properties of the system, namely the absence of behaviors in which the precondition was expected to be satisfied.

In [3], Beer et al. suggested a first formal treatment of vacuity. As described there, vacuity is a serious problem: "our experience has shown that typically 20% of specifications pass vacuously during the first formal-verification runs of a new hardware design, and that vacuous passes always point to a real problem in either the design or its specification or environment" [3]. The definition of vacuity according to [3] is based on the notion of subformulas that do not affect the satisfaction of the specification. Consider a model M satisfying a specification φ. A subformula ψ of φ *does not affect* (the satisfaction of) φ in M if M also satisfies all formulas obtained by modifying ψ arbitrarily. In the example above, the subformula *grant* does not affect φ in a model with no requests. Now, M satisfies φ vacuously if φ has a subformula that does not affect φ in M. A general method for vacuity definition and detection was presented in [17] and the problem was further studied in [1,6,7]. It is shown in these papers that for temporal logics such as LTL, the problem of vacuity detection is in PSPACE — not harder than model checking.

When the system is proven to be correct, and vacuity has been checked too, there is still a question of how complete the specification is, and whether it really covers all the behaviors of the system. It is not clear how to check completeness of the specification. Indeed, specifications are written manually, and their completeness depends entirely on the competence of the person who writes them. The motivation for a completeness check is clear: an erroneous behavior of the system can escape the verification efforts if this behavior is not captured by the specification. In fact, it is likely that a behavior not captured by the specification also escapes the attention of the designer, who is often the one to provide the specification.

Measuring the exhaustiveness of a specification in model checking ("do more properties need to be checked?") has a similar flavor as measuring the exhaustiveness of a test suit in testing ("do more input sequences need to be checked?"). Nevertheless, while for testing it is clear that coverage corresponds to activation during the execution on the given input sequence, it is less clear what coverage should correspond to in model checking. Indeed, all reachable parts of the system may be visited during the model-checking process, regardless of the role they play in the satisfaction of the specification. Early work on coverage metrics in model checking [15] adopted the idea of *mutation testing*, developed in the context of software testing [5]. The metric in [15], later followed by [8,9,10], is based on *mutations* applied to the model of the system. Essentially, a state in the model of the system is covered by the specification if modifying the value of a variable in the state renders the specification untrue. In [11], the authors took the adoption of coverage from testing to model-checking one step forward and adjusted various coverage metrics that are used in testing to the model-checking setting. For example, branch coverage in testing checks that the test suits has led to an execution of all branches. Accordingly, branch coverage in model checking, studies the effect of disabling branches on the satisfaction of the specification.

In this paper we adopt the research that has been done on vacuity in the model-checking community to the setting of testing. Essentially, as in model checking, a test suit T passes a specification vacuously if we can modify the specification to one that would be harder to satisfy, and still T passes. We define and study vacuity for three settings of testing. The first setting considers the expected extension of LTL vacuity in the context of model checking. Thus, we check whether a given test suit could have passed even a stronger specification.

The second setting is that of *run-time verification*: we assume the specification is a monitor that is executed in parallel to the system, and an input sequence passes the test if the monitor does not get stuck on it [14]. Thus, the properties we are checking are safety properties, and the monitor gets stuck when a violation of the safety property has been detected. Our definition of vacuity in this setting refers to the transitions of the monitor: a test suit passes vacuously if it passes also with a monitor with fewer transitions.

The third setting is that of *software checking*: we assume the system is a procedure that terminates, and the specification is Boolean function, to which we feed both the input to the systems and its output. For example, the system may be a procedure that sorts a list of numbers, and the specification is a function that, given two lists, checks that a second list is the first list, sorted. We model both the system and the specification in a simple programming language. Our definition of vacuity refers to branches in the specification: a test suit passes vacuously if it does not branch-cover the specification, i.e., not all branches of the specification procedure are executed on the process of checking the test suit.

Our vacuity check is complementary to coverage checking. The rational behind vacuity checking in testing is that the structure of the specification is often different from the structure of the system: they may be designed by different designers, and the specification may refer to properties that are irrelevant in the system (for example, the output list being a permutation of the input list, in the case of sorting). Thus, there are cases in which all elements of the system have been covered, and still some elements of the specification are not covered, causing the test suit to pass vacuously. As we demonstrate in our examples, an attempt to cover all elements of the specification can then reveal bugs. In addition, we show that in most cases, the complexity of detecting a vacuous pass does not exceed that of testing. In particular, in the case of a deterministic specification, vacuity checking can be easily combined with the testing process.

2 Vacuity in Model Checking

In this section we describe the basic definitions of vacuity. We model a system by a sequential circuit (*circuit*, for short) $\mathcal{C} = \langle I, O, S, \theta, \delta, \rho \rangle$, where I is a set of input signals, O is a set of output signals, S is a set of states, $\theta : 2^I \rightarrow S$ is an initialization function that maps every input assignment (that is, assignment to the input signals) to a state, $\delta : S \times 2^I \rightarrow S$ is a transition function that maps every state and input assignment to a successor state, and $\rho : S \rightarrow 2^O$ is an output function that maps every state to an output assignment (that is, an assignment to the output signals).[1]

Note that the interaction between the circuit and its environment is initiated by the environment. Once the environment generates an input assignment $i \in 2^I$, the circuit starts reacting with it from the state $\theta(i)$. Note also that the circuit is deterministic and receptive. That is, $\theta(s)$ and $\delta(s, i)$ are defined for all $s \in S$ and $i \in 2^I$, and they suggest a single state.

Given an input sequence $\xi = i_0, i_1, \ldots \in (2^I)^\omega$, the *execution* of $\mathcal{C}$ on ξ is the path π_ξ that $\mathcal{C}$ traverses while reading ξ. Formally, $\pi_\xi = s_0, s_1, \ldots \in S^\omega$, where $s_0 = \theta(i_0)$ and for all $j \geq 0$, we have $s_{j+1} = \rho(s_j, i_j)$. The *computation* of $\mathcal{C}$ on ξ is then the word $w_\xi = w_0, w_1, \ldots \in (2^{I \cup O})^\omega$ such that for all $j \geq 0$, we have $w_j = i_j \cup \rho(s_j)$. The language of $\mathcal{C}$, denoted $L(\mathcal{C})$ is union of all its computations. We sometimes refer also to executions and computations of $\mathcal{C}$ on finite words.

A specification to a system can be given either in terms of an LTL formula over atomic propositions in $I \cup O$ (we will consider also specifications given in terms of a *monitor* over the alphabet $2^{I \cup O}$; this setting, however, was not yet studied in the context of vacuity). We assume the reader is familiar with the syntax and the semantics of LTL. We recall the definition of vacuity in model checking.

Consider a circuit $\mathcal{C}$ and an LTL formula φ that is satisfied in $\mathcal{C}$. In the *single-occurrence* approach to LTL vacuity [17], we check that each of the occurrences of a subformula of φ has played a role in the satisfaction of φ in $\mathcal{C}$. Each occurrence σ of a subformula ψ of φ has a *polarity*. The polarity is positive if σ appears under an even number of negations, and is negative is σ appears under an odd number of negations. When the polarity of σ is positive, replacing σ with $false$ results in a formula that is harder to satisfy. Dually, when the polarity is negative, replacing σ with *true* results in a formula that is harder to satisfy. Let $\perp_\sigma$ stand for $false$ if the polarity of σ is positive, and stand for *true* if the polarity is negative.

We say that an occurrence σ of a subformula of φ *does not affect the satisfaction of* φ *in* $\mathcal{C}$ if $\mathcal{C}$ also satisfies the formula $\varphi[\sigma \leftarrow \perp_\sigma]$, in which σ is replaced by the most challenging replacement. For example, if $\varphi = G(\neg req \vee Fack)$, then

[1] Typically, $S = 2^C$ for a set C of control signals. Here, we are not going to refer to the control signals, and hide them in the notation.

$\varphi[req \leftarrow \bot_{req}] = GFack$ and $\varphi[ack \leftarrow \bot_{ack}] = G\neg req$. A specification φ is *vacuously satisfied in* $\mathcal{C}$ (in the single-occurrence approach) if φ has an occurrence of a subformula that does not affect its satisfaction in $\mathcal{C}$.

The *multiple-occurrence* approach to LTL vacuity in model checking considers LTL formulas augmented with universal quantification over atomic propositions. Recall that an LTL formula over a set AP of atomic propositions (typically $AP = I \cup O$) is interpreted over computations of the form $w = w_0, w_1, w_2, \ldots$, with $w_j \in 2^{AP}$. The path then satisfies a formula of the form $\forall x.\varphi$, where φ is an LTL formula and x is an atomic proposition, if φ is satisfied in all the computations that agree with w on all the atomic propositions except (maybe) x. Thus, $w \models \forall x.\varphi$ iff $w' \models \varphi$ for all $w' = w'_0, w'_1, w'_2, \ldots$ such that $w'_j \cap (AP \setminus \{x\}) = w_j \cap (AP \setminus \{x\})$ for all $j \geq 0$. As with LTL, a circuit $\mathcal{C}$ satisfies $\forall x.\varphi$ if all computations of $\mathcal{C}$ satisfy $\forall x.\varphi$.

We say that a subformula ψ of φ *does not affect the satisfaction of* φ *in* $\mathcal{C}$ if $\mathcal{C}$ also satisfies the formula $\forall x.\varphi[\psi \leftarrow x]$, in which ψ is replaced by a universally quantified proposition [1]. Intuitively, this means that $\mathcal{C}$ satisfies φ even with the most challenging assignments to ψ. Finally, a specification φ is *vacuously satisfied in* $\mathcal{C}$ (in the multiple-occurrence approach) if φ has a subformula that does not affect its satisfaction in $\mathcal{C}$.

3 Vacuity Checking in Testing

In the context of testing, we have two types of vacuous satisfaction. Consider a system $\mathcal{C}$, a specification $\mathcal{S}$, and a test suit T such that all the input sequences in T result in computations of $\mathcal{C}$ that satisfy $\mathcal{S}$.

- **Strong vacuity** is independent of T, and it coincides with vacuity in model checking. That is, some element of $\mathcal{S}$ does not affect the satisfaction of $\mathcal{S}$ in $\mathcal{C}$. As in model checking, strong vacuity suggests that $\mathcal{C}$ and $\mathcal{S}$ should be re-examined: some behavior that the specifier expect cannot happen.
- **Weak vacuity** depends on T and it refers to the role that the elements of $\mathcal{S}$ play in the fact that T passes. Weak vacuity suggest that either there is strong vacuity or that more tests are needed.

We define and study vacuity for three settings of testing. The first setting considers the expected extension of LTL vacuity in the context of model checking. Thus, we check whether a given test suit could have passed even a stronger specification.

The second setting is that of *run-time verification*: we assume the specification is a monitor that is executed in parallel to the system, and an input sequence passes the test if the monitor does not get stuck on it [14]. Thus, the properties we are checking are safety properties, and the monitor gets stuck when a violation of the safety property has been detected. Our definition of vacuity in this setting refers to the transitions of the monitor: a test suit passes vacuously if it passes also with a monitor with fewer transitions.

The third setting is that of *software checking*: we assume the system is a procedure that terminates, and the specification is Boolean function, to which we feed both the input to the systems and its output. For example, the system may be a procedure that sorts a list of numbers, and the specification is a function that, given two lists, checks that a second list is the first list, sorted. We model both the system and the specification in a simple programming language. Our definition of vacuity refers to branches in the specification: a test suit passes vacuously if it does not branch-cover the specification, i.e., not all branches of the specification procedure are executed on the process of checking the test suit.

3.1 Vacuity in LTL Specifications

We first consider specifications in LTL. Verification of a circuit $\mathcal{C}$ with respect to an LTL formula φ amounts to checking that for all infinite sequences $\xi \in (2^I)^\omega$, the execution of $\mathcal{S}$ on the computation of ξ satisfies φ. Model checking of $\mathcal{C}$ with respect to φ is done by checking that the language of $\mathcal{C}$ is contained in that of an automaton accepting exactly all the models of φ. Technically, this is reduced to checking the emptiness of the product of $\mathcal{C}$ with an automaton accepting exactly all the models of $\neg\varphi$ [21]. One computational challenge is to cope with the exponential size of the automaton, which, in the worst case, is exponential in the length of the formula. The computational bottleneck, however, relies in the size of $\mathcal{C}$, which is typically much larger than φ. The alternative that testing suggests is to examine a vector $T \subseteq (2^I)^\omega$ of *lasso-shaped* input sequences. That is, each input sequence in T is of the form $u.v^\omega$, for $u, v \in (2^I)^*$. We say that T *passes* φ in $\mathcal{C}$ if for all $\xi \in T$, the computation w_ξ of $\mathcal{C}$ satisfies φ. We define the length of T, denoted $\|T\|$, as $\sum_{\xi \in T} |\xi|$.

As with vacuity in model checking, we say that an occurrence σ of a subformula of φ *does not affect* φ in $\mathcal{C}$ and T if $w_\xi \models \varphi[\sigma \leftarrow \bot_\sigma]$ for all input sequences ξ in T. Similarly, we say that a subformula ψ of a specification φ *does not affect* φ in $\mathcal{C}$ and T if w_ξ satisfies $\forall x.\varphi[\psi \leftarrow x]$ for all input sequences ξ in T. We then say that T passes φ vacuously in $\mathcal{C}$ in the single-occurrence approach if some occurrence of a subformula of φ does not affect φ in $\mathcal{C}$ and T, and say that T passes φ vacuously in $\mathcal{C}$ in the multiple-occurrence approach if some subformula of φ does not affect φ in $\mathcal{C}$ and T.

Theorem 1. *The problem of deciding whether T passes φ vacuously in $\mathcal{C}$ is in PTIME in the single-occurrence approach and is in PSPACE in the multiple-occurrence approach.*

Proof. In the single-occurrence approach, we go over all occurrences σ of subformulas of φ and model-check $\varphi[\sigma \leftarrow \bot_\sigma]$ in all computations w_ξ, for all $\xi \in T$. Since LTL model checking for a single path can be done in PTIME [18], the whole check is in PTIME.

In the multiple-occurrence approach, we go over all subformulas ψ of φ and model-check $\forall x.\varphi[\psi \leftarrow x]$ in all computations w_ξ, for all $\xi \in T$. Now each check requires PSPACE, and so does the whole check. □

We note that the lower bounds in Theorem 1 are open. In the single-occurrence approach, the challenge has to do with the open problem of the complexity of

LTL model-checking with respect to a single path (known PTIME upper bound, only an NLOGSPACE lower bound [18]). In the multiple-occurrence approach, the challenge has to do with the open problem of the complexity of LTL vacuity detection (known PSPACE upper bound, only an NPTIME lower bound [1]).

3.2 Vacuity in Run-Time Verification

We now turn to study specifications given by monitors. A *monitor* for a circuit $\mathcal{C} = \langle I, O, S, \theta, \delta, \rho \rangle$ is an automaton $\mathcal{S} = \langle 2^{I \cup O}, Q, Q_0, M \rangle$, where Q is a set of states $Q_0 \subseteq Q$ is a set of initial states, and $M : Q \times 2^{I \cup O} \to 2^Q$ is a transition function that maps a state and a letter to a set of possible successor states. We refer to the transitions of $\mathcal{S}$ as relations and write $M(s, \sigma, s')$ to indicate that $s' \in M(s, \sigma)$. Note that while $\mathcal{S}$ has no acceptance condition, it may be that $M(s, \sigma) = \emptyset$, in which case $\mathcal{S}$ gets stuck.[2] A word $w \in (2^{I \cup O})^*$ is accepted by $\mathcal{S}$ if $\mathcal{S}$ has a run on w that never gets stuck. The language of $\mathcal{S}$, denoted $L(\mathcal{S})$, is the set of words that $\mathcal{S}$ accepts. All safety properties can be translated to monitors [16,19].

The complexity considerations in the setting of model checking safety properties are similar to these in LTL model checking. Verification of $\mathcal{C}$ with respect to $\mathcal{S}$ amounts to checking that for all infinite sequences $\xi \in (2^I)^\omega$, the execution of $\mathcal{S}$ on the computation of ξ never gets stuck. Model checking of $\mathcal{C}$ with respect to $\mathcal{S}$ is done by checking that the language of $\mathcal{C}$ is contained in that of $\mathcal{S}$. Technically, this is reduced to checking the emptiness of the product of $\mathcal{C}$ with an automaton that complements $\mathcal{S}$. One computational challenges is to cope with the complementation of $\mathcal{S}$, which involves an exponential blow up. The computational bottleneck, however, relies in the size of $\mathcal{C}$, which is typically much larger than $\mathcal{S}$. The alternative that testing suggests is to examine a vector $T \subseteq (2^I)^*$ of finite prefixes of input sequences. We say that T *passes* $\mathcal{S}$ in $\mathcal{C}$ if for all $\xi \in T$, the computation w_ξ of $\mathcal{C}$ is accepted by $\mathcal{S}$.

We first describe the algorithm for checking whether T passes $\mathcal{S}$ in $\mathcal{C}$. The algorithm is a simple membership checking algorithm for monitors, applied to all input sequences in T. Given an input sequence $\xi = i_0, i_1, \ldots, i_{n-1} \in (2^I)^n$, we define the product of its computation in $\mathcal{C}$ with $\mathcal{S}$ as a sequence $\langle s_0, R_0 \rangle, \langle s_1, R_1 \rangle, \ldots, \langle s_{n-1}, R_{n-1} \rangle \in (S \times 2^Q)^n$ as follows. Intuitively, $s_0, \ldots, s_{n-1}$ is the execution of $\mathcal{C}$ on ξ, and R_j, for $0 \leq j \leq n-1$, is the set of states that $\mathcal{C}$ can be in after reading the prefix of the computation on ξ up to the letter i_j. Formally, $s_0 = \theta(i_0)$ and $R_0 = Q_0$, and for all $0 \leq j \leq n+1$, we have $s_{j+1} = \rho(s_j, i_{j+1})$ and $R_{j+1} = M(R_j, i_j \cup \rho(s_j))$. The pairs $\langle s_j, R_j \rangle$ can be constructed on-the-fly, and the computation w_ξ is accepted by $\mathcal{S}$ if $R_j \neq \emptyset$ for all $0 \leq j \leq n-1$.

Assume that T passes $\mathcal{S}$. The traditional approach to coverage checks that all the transitions of $\mathcal{C}$ have been taken during the execution of $\mathcal{C}$ on the input

[2] Readers familiar with Büchi automata would notice that a monitor is a *looping* Büchi automaton – a Büchi automaton in which all states are accepting. Here, we execute $\mathcal{C}$ on finite words.

sequences in T. Here, we consider vacuity, which corresponds to coverage in the specification. Consider a transition $\langle s, \sigma, s' \rangle \in M$. Let $\mathcal{S}_{\langle s,i,s' \rangle}$ denote the monitor obtained from $\mathcal{S}$ by removing the transition $\langle s, i, s' \rangle$ from M. We say that $\langle s, i, s' \rangle$ *does not affect* $\mathcal{S}$ in $\mathcal{C}$ and T if T also passes $\mathcal{S}_{\langle s,i,s' \rangle}$ in $\mathcal{C}$. We then say that T *passes* $\mathcal{S}$ *vacuously* in $\mathcal{C}$ if some transition of $\mathcal{S}$ does not affect its pass.

Theorem 2. *The problem of checking whether T passes $\mathcal{S}$ vacuously in $\mathcal{C}$ is NLOGSPACE-complete.*

Proof. We start with the upper bound. Consider a circuit $\mathcal{C} = \langle I, O, S, \theta, \delta, \rho \rangle$, a monitor $\mathcal{S} = \langle 2^{I \cup O}, Q, Q_0, M \rangle$, and a test suit $T \subseteq (2^I)^*$. Consider an input sequence $\xi \in T$ and a transition $\langle s, i, s' \rangle \in M$. It is easy to see that the problem of deciding whether ξ is accepted by $\mathcal{S}_{\langle s,i,s' \rangle}$ is in NLOGSPACE. Indeed, an algorithm that guesses an accepting run has to store the location in ξ, as well as the states in S and Q are currently visited. Since NLOGSPACE is closed under complementation, we conclude that the problem of deciding whether ξ is rejected by $\mathcal{S}_{\langle s,i,s' \rangle}$ is also in NLOGSPACE.

Now, given a transition $\langle s, i, s' \rangle$, the problem of deciding whether $\langle s, i, s' \rangle$ affects $\mathcal{S}$ in $\mathcal{C}$ and T can be solved in NLOGSPACE. Indeed, by definition, $\langle s, i, s' \rangle$ affects $\mathcal{S}$ in $\mathcal{C}$ and T if there is $\xi \in T$ such that ξ is rejected by $\mathcal{S}_{\langle s,i,s' \rangle}$, and the algorithm can guess such an input sequence $\xi \in T$ and check in NLOGSPACE that it is rejected by $\mathcal{S}_{\langle s,i,s' \rangle}$. Again we apply the closure of NLOGSPACE under complementation, and conclude that the problem of deciding whether a given transition does not affect $\mathcal{S}$ in $\mathcal{C}$ and T can be solved in NLOGSPACE. Thus, an algorithm for checking whether T passes $\mathcal{S}$ vacuously in $\mathcal{C}$ guesses a transition $\langle s, i, s' \rangle$ in M, and checks in NLOGSPACE that it does not affect $\mathcal{S}$ in $\mathcal{C}$ and T.

Hardness in NLOGSPACE can be easily proven by a reduction from reachability. □

We note that the straightforward algorithm for the problem requires polynomial time: it goes over all transitions $\langle s, i, s' \rangle$ and input sequences $\xi \in T$, and checks whether w_ξ is accepted by $\mathcal{S}_{\langle s,i,s' \rangle}$. The algorithm concludes that T passes $\mathcal{S}$ vacuously in $\mathcal{C}$ iff there is a transition $\langle s, i, s' \rangle$ for which the answer is positive for all input sequences.

Remark 3. When $\mathcal{S}$ is deterministic, things are much simpler, and it is easy to extend the algorithm for checking whether T passes $\mathcal{S}$ in $\mathcal{C}$ so that it also checks whether the pass is vacuous. Indeed, checking whether T passes is done by executing the input sequences in T. When we execute an input sequence $\xi \in T$, we mark the transitions in M that have been traversed during the monitoring of w_ξ. The test suit T then passes vacuously if not all transitions have been marked. □

The idea behind weak vacuity is that the structure of the specification is often different from the structure of the system. Hence, a test suit may cover all the transitions of the system, yet may not cover all the transitions of the specification. Adding to the test suit input sequences that cover the specification may reveal errors. We demonstrate this in Example 1 below.

Example 1. Consider the circuit $\mathcal{C}$ and its specification $\mathcal{S}$ appearing in Figure 1. We assume that $I = \{req\}$ and $O = \{ack\}$. The specification $\mathcal{S}$ corresponds to the LTL formula $\psi = G(req \rightarrow (ack \vee X(ack \vee Xack)))$. For convenience, we describe the input and output assignments by Boolean assertions. Note that a single assertion may correspond to several assignment, and thus a single edge in the figure may correspond to several transitions. For example, the self loop in state q_0 of $\mathcal{S}$, which is labeled $\neg req \vee ack$, stands for the three transitions $\langle q_0, \{\ \}, q_0\rangle$, $\langle q_0, \{ack\}, q_0\rangle$, and $\langle q_0, \{req, ack\}, q_0\rangle$. It is not hard to see that $\mathcal{S}$ does not satisfy ψ (and $\mathcal{S}$). For example, an input sequence of the form $req, \neg req, \neg req, \neg req, \neg req, \ldots$ would loop forever in s_0 and s_2 and the first request is never acknowledged.

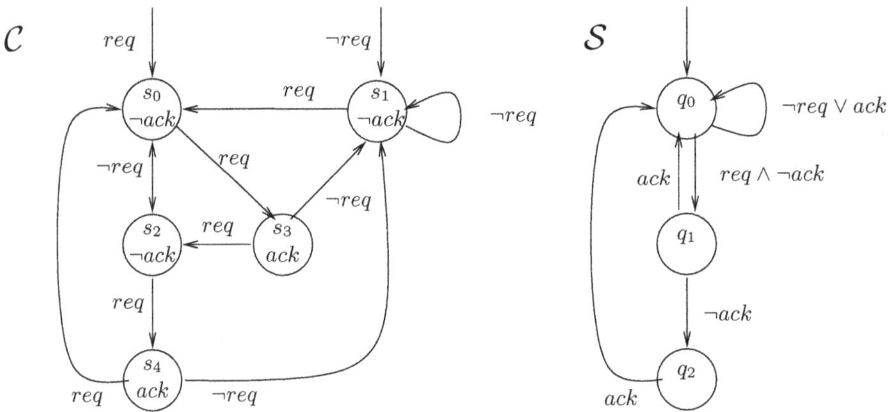

Fig. 1. A system and its monitor

Below we describe the behavior of $\mathcal{C}$ and $\mathcal{S}$ on a test suit $T = \{\xi_1, \xi_2 . \xi_3\}$, as follows.

- $\xi_1 = req, req, req, \neg req, req, \neg req$. The execution of $\mathcal{C}$ on ξ_1 is $\pi_1 = s_0, s_3\ , s_2$, s_0, s_3, s_1, and the run of $\mathcal{S}$ on the induced computation traverses the following sequence of transitions: $\langle q_0, \{req\}, q_1\rangle$, $\langle q_1, \{req, ack\}, q_0\rangle$, $\langle q_0, \{req\}, q_1\rangle$, $\langle q_1, \{\ \}, q_2\rangle$, $\langle q_2, \{req, ack\}, q_0\rangle$, $\langle q_0, \{\ \}, q_0\rangle$.
- $\xi_2 = \neg req, \neg req, req, \neg req, req, req$. The execution of $\mathcal{C}$ on ξ_2 is $\pi_2 = s_1$, s_1, s_0, s_2, s_4, s_0, and the corresponding run of $\mathcal{S}$ is $\langle q_0, \{\ \}, q_0\rangle$, $\langle q_0, \{\ \}, q_0\rangle$, $\langle q_0, \{req\}, q_1\rangle$, $\langle q_1, \{\ \}, q_2\rangle$, $\langle q_2, \{req, ack\}, q_0\rangle$, $\langle q_0, \{req\}, q_1\rangle$.
- $\xi_3 = req, \neg req, req, \neg req$. The execution of $\mathcal{C}$ on ξ_3 is $\pi_3 = s_0$, s_2, s_4, s_1, and the corresponding run of $\mathcal{S}$ is $\langle q_0, \{req\}, q_1\rangle$, $\langle q_1, \{\ \}, q_2\rangle$, $\langle q_2, \{req, ack\}, q_0\rangle$, $\langle q_0, \{\ \}, q_0\rangle$.

Note that all runs are accepting, thus T passes $\mathcal{S}$ in $\mathcal{C}$. Moreover, all the transitions of $\mathcal{C}$ have been taken during the execution of T. Thus, T covers $\mathcal{C}$, which indicates that T satisfies some quality criteria.

Consider the transition $\langle q_2, \{ack\}, q_0\rangle$ of $\mathcal{S}$. The transition does not affect $\mathcal{S}$ in $\mathcal{C}$ and T. Indeed, it was not traversed in the three runs. We claim that there is strong vacuity with respect to the transition $\langle q_2, \{ack\}, q_0\rangle$, and that detecting this strong vacuity is likely to reveal the bug. To see why, note that no computation of $\mathcal{C}$ generates the letter $\{ack\}$. Thus, acknowledgments are issued only with requests. Thus, if a request is not acknowledged immediately, another request is needed in order to issue an acknowledgement. This information should urge the designer to test $\mathcal{C}$ with respect to an input vector with a single request, which would reveal the bug. Note that the transitions $\langle q_0, \{req, ack\}, q_0\rangle$ and $\langle q_1, \{req\}, q_2\rangle$ also do not affect $\mathcal{S}$ in $\mathcal{C}$ and T, and in fact there is strong vacuity also with respect to them. □

3.3 Vacuity in Software Checking

We now turn to consider the third setting, of terminating software procedures. We assume the system is a procedure P that terminates, and the specification is a Boolean function $\mathcal{S}$ to which we feed both the input and output of P. Given an input v to P, the Boolean value $\mathcal{S}(v, P(v))$ indicates whether P satisfies the specification modeled by $\mathcal{S}$. For the definition of vacuity, we adopt the standard *branch coverage* metric: all branches of $\mathcal{S}$ should be executed.

We consider procedures in a simple programming language, with branches induced by the *if-then-else*, *case*, and *while* statements. For a Boolean function $\mathcal{S}$ and a branch b, let $\mathcal{S}_b$ denote the function obtained from $\mathcal{S}$ by replacing the statement guarded by b by "return(*false*)". Given a procedure P, we say that a branch b of $\mathcal{S}$ *does not affect* $\mathcal{S}$ *in* P if $\mathcal{S}(v, P(v)) = \mathcal{S}_b(v, P(v))$ for all input vectors v. Then, given a procedure P, a specification $\mathcal{S}$ for it, and a test suit T, we say that a branch b *does not affect* $\mathcal{S}$ *in* P *and* T if $\mathcal{S}$ agrees with $\mathcal{S}_b$ on all the inputs in T. That is, for all $v \in T$, we have that $\mathcal{S}(v, P(v)) = \mathcal{S}_b(v, P(v))$. Finally, T passes $\mathcal{S}$ vacuously in P if some branch of $\mathcal{S}$ does not affect its pass.

Deciding whether a branch b does not affect $\mathcal{S}$ in P and T can be done by testing T with respect to $\mathcal{S}_b$. Since, however, $\mathcal{S}$ is deterministic, it is easy to combine the testing of T with a vacuity check: whenever a branch of $\mathcal{S}$ is taken, we mark it, and T passes $\mathcal{S}$ vacuously in P if we are done testing T and some branch is still not marked. Clearly, such a branch does not affect $\mathcal{S}$ in P and T.

Note that finding a bug in P amounts to covering a branch in $\mathcal{S}$ in which false is returned. Thus, an attempt to cover all branches is at least as challenging as finding a bug. We therefore seek to cover all "hopeful branches" – these that can be taken in an execution of $\mathcal{S}$ that returns *true*. In the rest of this section we describe two examples that demonstrate the effectiveness of vacuity checking in this setting.

Example 2. Consider the sorting program appearing in Figure 2. We use the operator :: to denote concatenation between elements or lists. For a list of the form $x :: y :: tail$, where x and y are numbers and $tail$ is a list of numbers, the procedure sorts the list by sorting x and y and then recursively sorting $y :: tail$ (in case $x \leq y$) or $x :: tail$ (in case $y < x$).

sort(*list*):
  case *list* is
    nil $\rightarrow nil$
    $x :: nil$ $\rightarrow x :: nil$
    $x :: y :: tail$ $\rightarrow$ if $x \leq y$ then return($x ::$ **sort**($y :: tail$))
        else return($y ::$ **sort**($x :: tail$))

Fig. 2. A buggy sorting procedure

The Boolean function **sorted** in Figure 3 is a specification for the sorting procedure. It gets as input two lists of numbers and returns true iff the second list is a permutation of the first list, and the second list is sorted. For that, it calls two Boolean functions, each checking one condition.

sorted($list, list'$):
  if **permutation**($list, list'$) and **sort_check**($list'$) then return($true$)
    else return($false$)

Fig. 3. A specification for the sorting procedure

In our example, it not hard to see that the procedure **sort** is correct with respect to input vectors v of length n for which, for all $2 \leq i \leq n$, the prefix of length i contains all the smallest $i - 1$ numbers in v. For example, the procedure correctly sorts $4 :: 1 :: 2 :: 3$ or $3 :: 1 :: 2 :: 5 :: 4$. Note that these two vectors branch cover **sort**, which indicates that a test suit consisting of them satisfies some quality criteria. Still the procedure sort is buggy. For example, it fails on $3 :: 1 :: 2$.

Assume now that the Boolean function **permutation**($list, list'$) distinguishes between cases where the first and last elements of $list$ are switched in $list'$ and cases it does not. Then, at attempt to cover a branch that considers the first case would reveal the bug. Indeed, no input (of length at least three) in which the biggest number is first and the smallest number is last, would be correctly sorted by **sort**. □

Example 2 shows how vacuity checking is useful in cases the specification checks properties that are not referred to by the system. In Example 3 below we show how vacuity checking is useful also in cases the specification need not check additional properties, yet the structure of the system and the specification is different.

Example 3. The procedure **convert** in Figure 4 gets as input a string over 0 and 1. Its goal is to replace all substrings of the form 01 by 21. It is, however, buggy: by leaving a 00 head as is, **convert** ignores cases in which the second 0 is followed by 1. For example, the output of convert on 011001 is 211001, where the correct output is 211021.

```
convert(list):
  case list is
    nil             → return(nil)
    1 :: tail       → return(1 :: convert(tail))
    0 :: 1 :: tail  → return(2 :: 1 :: convert(tail))
    0 :: 0 :: tail  → return(0 :: 0 :: convert(tail))
```

Fig. 4. The procedure **convert** replaces a substring 01 by 21

The specification **check**, appearing in Figure 5, gets as input the original string $list$ and the output $list'$ of **convert** and it outputs true iff $list'$ is indeed obtained from $list$ by replacing all substrings of the form 01 by 21. Note that while **check** looks complicated, one cannot simplify it.

```
check(list, list'):
  case (list, list') is
    (nil, nil)                             → return(true)
    (0 :: nil, 0 :: nil)                   → return(true)
    (1 :: tail, 1 :: tail')                → check(tail, tail')
    (0 :: 0 :: tail, 0 :: 0 :: tail')      → check(0 :: tail, 0 :: tail')
    (0 :: 1 :: tail, 2 :: 1 :: tail')      → check(tail, tail')
    (0 :: 0 :: 1 :: tail, 0 :: 2 :: 1 :: tail') → check(tail, tail')
    else                                   → return(false)
```

Fig. 5. A specification for **convert**

The input 0110001 branch covers **convert**, and **convert** is correct with respect to it. Indeed, **convert**(0110001) = 2110021, and **check**(0110001, 2110021) is true. On the other hand, (0110001, 2110021) does not branch cover **check**. In fact, **check** suffers from both strong and weak (with respect to $T = \{0110001\}$) vacuity.

Let us start with strong vacuity. We claim that the branch $b = (0 :: 0 :: 1 :: tail, 0 :: 2 :: 1 :: tail')$ does not affect S in P. That is, replacing the right hand side of b by "return(*false*)" results in a function that agrees with **check** on all inputs generated by **convert**. To see this, note that in order to cover b, the input $list$ must contain a substring 001 that was correctly converted to 021. Let us analyze all the possible suffixes of 001 in which **convert** was called.

- **convert**$(0 :: 0 :: 1 :: tail)$. Then, the output would have been buggy.
- **convert**$(0 :: 1 :: tail)$. Then, as the letter before $0 :: 1 :: tail$ was 0, our 001 substring must be a suffix of a 0001 substring (if it had been a suffix of a

1001 substring, we would have found ourselves in the previous case). Then, **convert**(0001) has first converted the 00 prefix to 00 and has then converted the 01 suffix to 21. While **convert** is correct, the $(0 :: 0 :: tail, 0 :: 0 :: tail')$ branch of **check** must be applied to the 00 prefix of the substring, and then the $(0 :: 1 :: tail, 0 :: 2 :: tail')$ branch is applied to the 01 suffix, thus b is not taken.
- **convert**$(1 :: tail)$. Then, as the letters before the $1 :: tail$ were 00, the previous application of **convert** has converted the 00 to 00, and is buggy.

Detecting the strong vacuity is helpful, as it is likely to lead the programmer to think why the designer of the specification has come up with a specification that is more complicated than his simple **convert** procedure.

We now move to weak vacuity. The branch $(0 :: nil, 0 :: nil)$ is not covered by T. While it is easy to add an input vector with which $(0 :: nil, 0 :: nil)$ is covered, the fact it is not covered by a test suit that branch-covers **convert** should raise a question mark, as again it means the specifier had a good reason to distinguish between a last 0 and an internal 0, something the programmer failed to do. □

References

1. Armon, R., Fix, L., Flaisher, A., Grumberg, O., Piterman, N., Tiemeyer, A., Vardi, M.Y.: Enhanced vacuity detection for linear temporal logic. In: Hunt Jr., W.A., Somenzi, F. (eds.) CAV 2003. LNCS, vol. 2725, pp. 368–380. Springer, Heidelberg (2003)
2. Beatty, D., Bryant, R.: Formally verifying a microprocessor using a simulation methodology. In: Proc. 31st Design Automation Conf, pp. 596–602. IEEE Computer Society, Los Alamitos (1994)
3. Beer, I., Ben-David, S., Eisner, C., Rodeh, Y.: Efficient detection of vacuity in ACTL formulas. Formal Methods in System Design 18(2), 141–162 (2001)
4. Bening, L., Foster, H.: Principles of verifiable RTL design – a functional coding style supporting verification processes. Kluwer Academic Publishers, Dordrecht (2000)
5. Budd, T.: Mutation analysis. In: PhD thesis, Yale University, New Haven (1979)
6. Bustan, D., Flaisher, A., Grumberg, O., Kupferman, O., Vardi, M.Y.: Regular vacuity. In: Borrione, D., Paul, W. (eds.) CHARME 2005. LNCS, vol. 3725, pp. 191–206. Springer, Heidelberg (2005)
7. Chechik, M., Gurfinkel, A.: Extending extended vacuity. In: Hu, A.J., Martin, A.K. (eds.) FMCAD 2004. LNCS, vol. 3312, pp. 306–321. Springer, Heidelberg (2004)
8. Chockler, H., Kupferman, O.: Coverage of implementations by simulating specifications. In: Proceedings of 2nd IFIP Int. Conf. on Theoretical Computer Science. IFIP Conf. Proceedings, vol. 223, pp. 409–421. Kluwer Academic Publishers, Dordrecht (2002)
9. Chockler, H., Kupferman, O., Kurshan, R.P., Vardi, M.Y.: A practical approach to coverage in model checking. In: Berry, G., Comon, H., Finkel, A. (eds.) CAV 2001. LNCS, vol. 2102, pp. 66–78. Springer, Heidelberg (2001)
10. Chockler, H., Kupferman, O., Vardi, M.Y.: Coverage metrics for temporal logic model checking. In: Margaria, T., Yi, W. (eds.) TACAS 2001. LNCS, vol. 2031, pp. 528–542. Springer, Heidelberg (2001)

11. Chockler, H., Kupferman, O., Vardi, M.Y.: Coverage metrics for formal verification. In: Geist, D., Tronci, E. (eds.) CHARME 2003. LNCS, vol. 2860, pp. 111–125. Springer, Heidelberg (2003)
12. Clarke, E.M., Grumberg, O., Peled, D.: Model checking. MIT Press, Cambridge (1999)
13. Dill, D.L.: What's between simulation and formal verification? In: Proc. 35th Design Automation Conf, pp. 328–329. IEEE Computer Society, Los Alamitos (1998)
14. Havelund, K., Rosu, G.: Efficient monitoring of safety properties. Software Tools for Technology Transfer 6(2), 18–173 (2004)
15. Hoskote, Y., Kam, T., Ho, P.-H., Zhao, X.: Coverage estimation for symbolic model checking. Proc. 36st Design Automation Conf., 300–305 (1999)
16. Kupferman, O., Vardi, M.Y.: Model checking of safety properties. Formal Methods in System Design 19(3), 291–314 (2001)
17. Kupferman, O., Vardi, M.Y.: Vacuity detection in temporal model checking. Software Tools for Technology Transfer 4(2), 224–233 (2003)
18. Markey, N., Schnoebelen, P.: Model Checking a Path. In: Amadio, R.M., Lugiez, D. (eds.) CONCUR 2003. LNCS, vol. 2761, pp. 251–265. Springer, Heidelberg (2003)
19. Sistla, A.P.: Safety, liveness and fairness in temporal logic. Formal Aspects of Computing 6, 495–511 (1994)
20. Tasiran, S., Keutzer, K.: Coverage metrics for functional validation of hardware designs. IEEE Design and Test of Computers 18(4), 36–45 (2001)
21. Vardi, M.Y., Wolper, P.: Reasoning about infinite computations. Information and Computation 115(1), 1–37 (1994)
22. Verisity. Surecove's code coverage technology. (2003), `http://www.verisity.com/products/surecov.html`
23. Zhu, H., Hall, P.V., May, J.R.: Software unit test coverage and adequacy. ACM Computing Surveys 29(4), 366–427 (1997)

What Can Fault Prediction Do for YOU?

Elaine J. Weyuker and Thomas J. Ostrand

AT&T Labs - Research, Florham Park, NJ 07932
{weyuker,ostrand}@research.att.com

Abstract. It would obviously be very valuable to know in advance which files in the next release of a large software system are most likely to contain the largest numbers of faults. This is true whether the goal is to validate the system by testing or formally verifying it, or by using some hybrid approach. To accomplish this, we developed negative binomial regression models and used them to predict the expected number of faults in each file of the next release of a system. The predictions are based on code characteristics and fault and modification history data. This paper discusses what we have learned from applying the model to several large industrial systems, each with multiple years of field exposure. It also discusses our success in making accurate predictions and some of the issues that had to be considered.

1 Introduction

The main focus of our research for the past several years has been the development of statistical models to predict the location of faults in the next release of a large, long-lived software system. Our goal was to help testers prioritize their testing efforts by directing them to the files likely to contain the largest number of faults, so they could test those files first and most comprehensively. Of course, it is necessary for the entire system to be tested, but if priority is given to the most fault-prone files, then faults should be found more quickly leaving resources for more comprehensive testing. This should make the resulting system more dependable, and perhaps also more economical to produce.

If a large system is to be validated using formal verification, it may not be possible to provide that level of validation for every file of the system, and so a subset of files may be targeted for formal verification. Typically, the most *important* files would be selected to be verified, where importance is determined by system requirements. The use of our prediction models might provide an additional basis for selecting files for formal verification.

It is important to emphasize how this research differs from classical software testing research, and even test prioritization algorithms. Traditionally, the goal of software testing research is to develop algorithms or strategies to create test suites that will expose many faults, or to design metrics to assess the effectiveness of test case selection or generation algorithms.

The current research is orthogonal to those goals, and intended to be used in conjunction with a test case selection method. It aims at identifying which files

B. Beckert and R. Hähnle (Eds.): TAP 2008, LNCS 4966, pp. 18–29, 2008.

to focus on. Once that is determined using our prediction algorithms, it is still necessary to develop appropriate test suites based on either the software code or the specifications, or some combination of the two.

Although our statistical models can be very useful to testers in helping them focus attention on parts of the software system, it is also distinct from much of the research in the area of test case prioritization. The goal of most test case prioritization algorithms is to select a subset of an existing set of test cases to rerun. This is usually done during the so-called *regression testing* phase when parts of the test suite are being rerun to assure that changes made to the system, either to fix identified bugs or add new functionality, have not introduced new faults (and caused the system to regress). Since it is sometimes too expensive to rerun the entire test suite, test case prioritization algorithms aim at identifying those test cases that are most likely to be relevant to the code changes, in the sense of being able to expose any faults caused by the recent changes. Our research is also fundamentally different from that type of research. Our goal is to help the tester to decide which files to emphasize during testing but there is no pre-existing test suite that we are prioritizing by sorting. Thus we are prioritizing which files to test rather than which specific test cases to reuse or test first.

In this paper we will provide an overview of our approach and summary of our findings. Each of the predictions was made using a negative binomial regression model. More details about the statistical model used can be found in [20,21]. The model was generally used to identify the 20% of the files of the system predicted to contain the largest numbers of faults. This was accomplished by predicting the number of faults expected to occur in the next release for each file of the system, and then sorting those numbers in decreasing order.

Although we could obviously use the predictions to identify any percentage of the files, we have found that the 20% of the files targeted generally contain the vast majority of the faults and is a small enough percentage to permit focused intensive scrutiny. The goal is to help the quality assurance team to prioritize their efforts, not to limit the amount of work done.

The whole process is possible because in practice we typically observe a Pareto-like distribution of faults, in which a relatively small percentage of files contain the majority of the faults. If there were a more or less uniform distribution of faults, then it would not even be meaningful to speak about identifying the most fault-prone files.

We have now applied our approach to six different large software systems, with different functionality, development paradigms, implementation languages, and levels of maturity. As we shall demonstrate, the results are strikingly similar. Those results will be described in Section 3.

2 The Basis for Prediction

The first issue we had to consider was whether in fact there was a Pareto-like distribution of faults, and, if so, what factors most prominently influence whether or not a file is likely to be faulty. In order to determine that, we did a preliminary study using a large inventory control system which at the time consisted of twelve releases and had been in the field for about 3 years. We first observed that there was a very non-uniform distribution of faults across files, with the concentration becoming more acute as the system matured. For example, we observed that for the first release, all of the identified faults were contained in 40% of the files. For the release that occurred about a year later, all of the faults were concentrated in just 16% of the files. After two years, the identified faults were all contained in just 11% of the files, and after three years they were all contained in just 7% of the files. The goal of this research, therefore, is to try to identify which files are the ones that account for all or most of the faults.

We considered a number of different file attributes as well as development process and file modification characteristics and selected those that seemed to be most closely associated with files that proved to be problematic in future releases. Initially our study focused on identifying characteristics most closely associated with files that had the highest fault densities in terms of faults per thousands of lines of code (KLOCs). This had been studied by an earlier research group [8]. However, after discussing the matter with some of our system test group we decided that identifying files with the highest numbers of faults was more useful in practice.

The types of characteristics considered were the size of the file in KLOCs, how many releases the file had been in the system, and the programming language in which the file had been written. We also considered the maturity of the overall system in terms of the number of releases, as well as information about the fault and change history of the file. An important issue was to make sure that all characteristics considered could be assessed objectively; i.e. two different observers would answer the question in exactly the same manner. This is important as our goal is to build a tool that can fully automate the prediction process, requiring no expertise of the tool user, and no appreciable overhead. The preliminary study is described in [19].

All of this information was obtained from the integrated version control/ change management system used by each of the six systems studied or from the software code itself. Underlying this modification request system is a database containing a substantial amount of data about every change made to the system, whether initiated because of an observed fault, or because of a planned or unplanned enhancement, as well as links to the actual code in each file of the system at any given point in the system's history.

From the codebase we were able to extract such information as the size of the file and the programming language in which it was written. The database contains a description of why the change is being initiated written in English, which files were modified as a result of the *modification request* (MR), whether the file was new to that release, and if not, if it was modified in previous releases, the actual code that was added, deleted or modified, the development stage at which the MR was initiated, the developer who made the change, how old the

Table 1. System Information for Case Study Subjects and Percentage of Faults in Top 20% of Files

System	Number of Releases	Years	KLOC	Pctg Faults Identified
Inventory	17	4	538	83%
Provisioning	9	2	438	83%
Voice Response	-	2+	329	75%
Maintenance Support A	35	9	442	83%
Maintenance Support B	35	9	384	94%
Maintenance Support C	26	7	327	84%

file is in terms of the number of releases it has been in the system, a severity rating as well as a great deal of other information.

Some of this information proved to be useful in building predictive models, and other information proved not to be. For example, although we initially thought that the severity rating would be a potentially interesting predictive factor, it in fact proved not to be. For the systems we studied, severity could range from 1 meaning that the fault had to be fixed immediately, to a severity of 4 which means that the fault was largely cosmetic. We thought that we were particularly interested in identifying files that would not only contain the largest numbers of faults, but also the most critical ones as assessed by the severity rating. What we observed was that the overwhelming majority of reported faults were classified as Severity 3 for every system considered. For many releases there were no Severity 1 faults reported at all. Therefore severity proved not to be a useful factor.

We found the most relevant characteristics to be the size of the file (KLOCs), whether this was the first release the file was in the system, whether the file was changed in earlier releases, and if so, how many changes were made to that file, whether there were faults in the file in earlier releases, and if so, how many faults occurred in earlier releases, and the programming language used to implement the file. These factors were weighted appropriately and used as part of both custom-built and standardized prediction models.

3 Empirical Studies

We begin this section by providing information about each of the six software systems that have been the subjects of our empirical studies. In Table 1 we see a summary of the longevity (in terms of both the number of releases included in the relevant study and number of years the system was in the field), the size of the system in KLOCs, and the success of the predictions in terms of the average percentage of actual detected faults that occurred in the 20% of the files identified by our prediction model as likely to contain the largest numbers of faults. In each case the percentage shown is averaged across all of the releases of the system studied.

We see that each of the systems is substantial in size, containing hundreds of thousands of lines of code. We studied systems for which we had data ranging from two years to nine years, representing both relatively young and evolving systems as well as very stable and mature systems. These systems were very different from the point of view of functionality and programming languages used, as well as the development paradigm used when building the system. The first three systems listed were developed and maintained by one large international corporation, and the three maintenance support systems were written and maintained by another large international company. The latter three systems were stand-alone subsystems of a very large maintenance support system. They were originally written as independent systems which were later integrated into this much larger system.

We note that the Voice Response system has a dash in the column indicating the number of releases included in the study. We followed this system for a total of 27 months in the field. This system used a different development paradigm than any of the others, using what they referred to as "continuous" releases. This means there was no regular release schedule. Since this was the fundamental unit for prediction in our model in the sense that we predicted which would be the most faulty files *in the next release of the system*, it was necessary to devise a notion of a synthetic release in this study. The details of how that was dealt with are described in [4]. This may explain why the prediction results were less accurate than than those obtained for the other five systems studied.

What we see in each case, is that the prediction models we developed were very effective at targeting the proper files. For each of the systems, including the Voice Response system, the vast majority of actual faults detected during testing or once the system was in the field, were contained in the 20% of the files identified as likely to be most faulty by the models.

4 Automating the Process

For the first three systems, we built customized prediction models. In each case we used a negative binomial regression model. Since the results obtained for these systems were all very encouraging, we felt it was time to consider how we might automate the process, by seeing whether we could build a general prediction model. We recognized that without a fully automatic tool, we were not going to be able to attract users, and the critical step in this automation would be the development of a model based not on the characteristics of the particular system that was the study subject, but rather based on the things we had learned by studying the three earlier systems. We had already begun the automation of the data extraction portion of a tool which was relatively straightforward, but without the generalized model, automation would not be possible.

We considered a variety of different models and were pleased to observe that the results obtained using an automatable model actually exceeded the results obtained using the customized model. Details of this study are described in [21].

The subject system for that study was the first maintenance support system (Maintenance Support System A in Table 1). We were especially interested in seeing how our prediction models would behave on this system because it had several interesting characteristics which distinguished it from the three earlier systems we had studied.

Perhaps the most important difference from the earlier systems studied was that it was written and maintained by a different company. Each company has its own corporate culture, we felt, and we wondered whether or not the model designed based on the three systems previously studied at AT&T would be applicable to this new system built by another corporation. In addition, System A was much more mature than the earlier systems studied, having been in the field for nine years with 35 separate releases. We wondered whether or not the model would be suitable for the later releases. Finally, the basic functionality of the system, and the languages used were different from those used in the earlier systems.

A look at Table 1 confirms that the general (non-customized) model was very effective for predicting the location of faults in System A. We have now applied this model to Systems B and C and see that the results are similarly effective.

5 Methodological Issues

This research has been ongoing for about six years. Our ultimate goal is to build an industrial-grade fully automated tool that will be widely used by software testers to help prioritize their testing efforts to yield highly dependable systems economically. It might also be used by software developers to help them determine whether or not a file should be re-architected, or by people trying to determine an appropriate subset of files to formally verify.

In this section we outline the steps needed to perform this research thereby indicating to the reader why it has taken so long to get to this point, and why each of the steps are necessary if we hope to transfer this research to practice. This might help clarify why some very interesting published research never goes farther than the small research community of which it is a part.

We have found that a program such as the one outlined below is a central part of the research if a primary goal of the project is to ultimately impact the way software is engineered.

The three things that are essential when performing research that will eventually be transferred to practitioners are making sure that the practitioners are *aware* of what you are doing, making sure that they think it is *relevant* to their tasks, and making sure that the ultimate form is *usable* by practitioners. In order to accomplish this, here are some of the steps that we followed.

- We spoke with practitioners to determine if our goal was worthwhile and to identify projects that might serve as potential study subjects. This addressed the issue of making sure practitioners were aware of the work, and also making sure it was relevant. This also provided us with projects that might serve as subjects of future empirical studies to validate our research.
- We presented preliminary findings to practitioners to get their feedback. This again addressed both awareness and relevance.

- We have performed six large empirical studies to date. They were very time consuming and difficult to do. We believe that performing these studies was essential for convincing practitioners of the relevance of the work. When doing large empirical studies, you have to be prepared for the fact that not every study will turn out to be helpful. Projects sometimes get cancelled or your main contact point with the project may leave or be transferred to another project, leaving you without access to necessary data. However, the more instances of the application of your research to real projects that you can present, the more likely other projects are to take the risk of using your technology. These point are helpful in making practitioners aware of the research and assessing relevance.
- We published results of our studies aimed at both researchers and practitioners. Again this aids in making practitioners aware of the research.
- We invited a statistician to participate in this research.
- We are building a fully-automated tool requiring no expertise to use, and costing little in the way of overhead for use. We believe that such a tool is essential for wide-spread adoption of our research, and have completed much of the implementation of the tool. The tool addresses the issue of usability. Even if a technique can be shown to be very useful, if it requires the users to have highly specialized expertise, or requires extensive overhead, it is unlikely that it will be used.

One very difficult issue that often derails the assessment of interesting software engineering research is the unavailability of a first subject system on which to perform an empirical study. This can be very difficult both for academic researchers and for people working in industrial research environments. Although the company might be producing many large software systems which would be ideal candidates for study, the industrial researcher may be entirely unaware of these projects' existence or have no access to them.

The more an industrial research center provides the opportunity to do academic-style research, and provides autonomy for researchers, the more divorced researchers often are from their potential "customers": the practitioners who could actually *use* their research. Although it is wonderful to work in a research center without the requirement that a development organization believes, a priori, the work to be worthwhile, it can also be a two-edged sword. We work in such an environment, and can attest to how intellectually stimulating it is, however it does often mean that there is a physical isolation from potential customers of your research and projects to study.

In addition, since most research is not in a sufficiently mature state to be useful to a project at the time an empirical study is to begin (which is why the empirical study is being done in the first place) it is often difficult to convince a project to be a subject because they see no direct benefit, and expect to have to spend valuable time which is frequently in very short supply.

Our experience is that the best way to gain access to production software systems is to have created ongoing relationships with practitioners, even though this may require serious effort and travel on the researcher's part. This might involve volunteering to help with such things as test case development, test planning and other tasks that might need doing when a project is getting near a release date. It requires developing mutual trust and respect for each other. It requires that the researcher understand the time constraints faced by developers and testers. It is helpful to make it clear that you understand the risk these practitioners are taking by participating in an empirical study.

To get our first subject system, we approached a testing manager with whom we had had an earlier relationship. We promised to intrude very little, by asking very few questions, and promising to look at the data without ever changing it in any way. Because we had volunteered to help the test manager's group on an earlier project, she knew that we understood the realities of their environment. When asked by a project to help with the collection of metrics, we readily volunteered to take on this responsibility.

Once we had performed the first empirical study, we presented our findings at an in-house conference for practitioners. This gave us very valuable feedback, and more importantly, it ultimately provided us with access to the system used in our second empirical study.

6 Related Work

In this section we describe related research performed by other groups. This will help provide context for our results. During the time that we have been involved in doing this research, there has been increasing interest in the field. We believe, however, that our research is different in several fundamental ways.

A number of research groups have performed studies which, like our preliminary study [19], aim at identifying properties of software files or modules that are associated with the most faulty entities. These studies do not involve the development of statistical models or make predictions. [1,3,7,8,10,11,15,16,19,22].

More closely related to the current work is research that develops predictive models that predict some characteristic of the software in the future, although often they do not predict which files in a system will contain the largest numbers of faults by producing a sorted list of the files based on the predicted numbers of faults in the next release. Papers that do make predictions include [2,6,9,12,13,14,18,23].

In this section we provide an overview of the research that is most closely related to ours, and point out differences in the methods used, specific goals, or results obtained.

Arisholm and Briand [2] defined a prediction model for one mid-size Java system (110 KLOCs), using data from three releases. They used stepwise logistic regression, and made predictions for one future release. Logistic regression classifies entities, in this case as either fault-prone or not fault-prone. In contrast we used the negative binomial regression model which predicted a specific number of faults that were likely to be contained in each file in the next release of the system. In this way we were able to sort the files and make predictions about which would be included in the worst $N\%$ of the files.

Denaro and Pezze [6] also used logistic regression to make predictions. They relied on static software metrics to constructed a number of models, and selected those models that came the closest to correctly identifying the system's most faulty modules. They used the open source Apache system for their studies, using data from Apache version 1.3 to make predictions for Apache version 2.0. They stated that their best models required 50% of the modules to be selected to include 80% of the faults that actually were detected in Version 2.0.

Graves et al. [9] studied a large telecommunications system, considering approximately two years worth of data. They did a preliminary study that was similar to ours to identify characteristics associated with faulty modules, and used what they learned to build models to predict the number of faults that would be in the next version of each module. Their models were based solely on the fault history of the system. They worked at the module level, with each module averaging over 30 files.

Khoshgoftaar et al. [13] used binary decision trees as the means for classifying software modules as being in one of two categories: fault-prone or not fault-prone. They defined fault-prone to mean that the module contained five or more faults and used a mix of static software metrics and execution time metrics to build their models. Their study was performed on a large industrial telecommunications system, for which they built the necessary decision tree using the first release and evaluated their predictions using three additional releases. Success was measured in terms of misclassification rates.

Succi et al. [23] built models to predict which classes of two small C++ projects would be fault-prone. Their models were based on the size of the class and some of Chidamber and Kemerer's object-oriented metrics [5]. They found that for the models they developed, they needed to include from 43% to 48% of the classes to include 80% of the faults.

Nagappan et al. [17] used a variety of code metrics to make predictions about about some Microsoft software systems. They limited attention to failures observed post-release. Although they found a set of metrics that worked well for each particular system, they found that metrics were not general in the sense that the set of metrics that made accurate predictions for one system, typically were not useful for making predictions in other systems.

Some of the most important differences between our research and the above-mentioned relevant papers include:

- We have validated our models by making predictions for six different systems. Most other research groups have made predictions for just a single system. By considering multiple systems, we are able to study the extent to which there are similarities between systems in spite of differences in languages, functionality, and other characteristics. By validating these similarities we were able to develop a non-custom prediction model that allowed us to automate the prediction process, providing a tool that can be used by practitioners.
- We have made predictions for well over one hundred and twenty releases across the six different systems. Most other research groups have made just

a single or a few such predictions. Again this allows us to assess the generality of our model.

- We provide the user with an ordered list of the predicted most faulty files. Most other research groups simply predict whether software entities will or will not contain at least one fault. We are therefore able to assess the effectiveness of our predictions in terms of the percentage of faults included in identified files.
- We have worked at the relatively fine-grained file level. Several other research groups have worked at the coarser module level, where a module typically consists of multiple files, often a substantial number of files. Working at a finer level of granularity facilitates fault localization.
- We have developed models that, on average, accurately identify the most faulty files. Table 1 summarizes our results. Of the relatively few other research groups that tried to predict which files would account for the largest number of faults rather than just categorizing them as likely to contain a fault or not, most were far less accurate.

7 Conclusions

We have described a relatively mature technology that we have developed to predict which files in a large long-lived software system are likely to contain the largest numbers of faults in the next release. We have validated our prediction models by doing a series of six large empirical studies using industrial software systems, averaging over four hundred thousand lines of code per system. We studied several years worth of data for these systems and made predictions for well over one hundred and twenty releases of the systems. We see that for each of the systems to which we have applied our negative binomial regression model, the 20% of the files identified by the model contained the vast majority of the actual detected faults in the systems, typically averaging roughly 83% of the faults.

We have now almost completed the automation of the process with both the data extraction and fault prediction portions of a tool having been implemented. We currently have interest from the team that manages the integrated change management/version control system, and are discussing how our tool can be integrated into that system so that any tester or developer that uses the change management system can take advantage of our fault prediction capabilities. We look forward to the day when this is a standard weapon in the arsenal used by testers to help them prioritize their testing efforts.

In the future, we would like to investigate how this work can be applied to help people doing verification of systems to better target the most appropriate files for formal verification. This might involve both the obvious idea of identifying the files most likely to contain faults as candidates for formal verification, or might involve modifying the definition of what we mean when we talk about faults to target files with other particular characteristics. One might envision, for example, performing some sort of semantic analysis on information in the modification request database to select certain sorts of code entities as potentially worthy of formal verification.

We also expect to continue our examination of other types of predictive models besides the negative binomial regression model, and intend to test the impact of incorporating semantic analysis rules into the selection of what constitutes a fault. In addition, we are interested in studying other ways of assessing the effectiveness of our prediction algorithms beyond determining the percentage of faults included in the identified files.

References

1. Adams, E.N.: Optimizing Preventive Service of Software Products. IBM J. Res. Develop 28(1), 2–14 (Jan, 1984) (1984)
2. Arisholm, E., Briand, L.C.: Predicting Fault-prone Components in a Java Legacy System. In: Proc. ACM/IEEE ISESE, Rio de Janeiro (2006)
3. Basili, V.R., Perricone, B.T.: Software Errors and Complexity: An Empirical Investigation. Communications of the ACM 27(1), 42–52 (1984)
4. Bell, R.M., Ostrand, T.J., Weyuker, E.J.: Looking for Bugs in All the Right Places. In: Proc. ACM/International Symposium on Software Testing and Analysis (ISSTA 2006), July 2006, pp. 61–71. Portland, Maine (2006)
5. Chidamber, S.R., Kemerer, C.F.: A Metrics Suite for Object Oriented Design. IEEE Trans. on Software Engineering 20(6), 476–493 (1994)
6. Denaro, G., Pezze, M.: An Empirical Evaluation of Fault-Proneness Models. In: Proc. International Conf on Software Engineering (ICSE 2002), Miami, USA (May 2002)
7. Eick, S.G., Graves, T.L., Karr, A.F., Marron, J.S., Mockus, A.: Does Code Decay? Assessing the Evidence from Change Management Data. IEEE Trans. on Software Engineering 27(1), 1–12 (2001)
8. Fenton, N.E., Ohlsson, N.: Quantitative Analysis of Faults and Failures in a Complex Software System. IEEE Trans. on Software Engineering 26(8), 797–814 (2000)
9. Graves, T.L., Karr, A.F., Marron, J.S., Siy, H.: Predicting Fault Incidence Using Software Change History. IEEE Trans. on Software Engineering 26(7), 653–661 (2000)
10. Guo, L., Ma, Y., Cukic, B., Singh, H.: Robust Prediction of Fault-Proneness by Random Forests. In: Proc. ISSRE 2004, Saint-Malo, France (Nov. 2004)
11. Hatton, L.: Re examining the Fault Density - Component Size Connection. In: IEEE Software, March/April, pp. 89–97 (1997)
12. Khoshgoftaar, T.M., Allen, E.B., Kalaichelvan, K.S., Goel, N.: Early Quality Prediction: A Case Study in Telecommunications. In: IEEE Software, (Jan 1996) pp. 65–71 (1996)
13. Khoshgoftaar, T.M., Allen, E.B., Deng, J.: Using Regression Trees to Classify Fault-Prone Software Modules. IEEE Trans. on Reliability 51(4), 455–462 (2002)
14. Mockus, A., Weiss, D.M.: Predicting Risk of Software Changes. In: Bell Labs Technical Journal, April-June 2000, pp. 169–180 (2000)
15. Moller, K.-H., Paulish, D.J.: An Empirical Investigation of Software Fault Distribution. In: Proc. IEEE First International Software Metrics Symposium, Baltimore, May 21-22, 1993, pp. 82–90 (1993)
16. Munson, J.C., Khoshgoftaar, T.M.: The Detection of Fault-Prone Programs. IEEE Trans. on Software Engineering 18(5), 423–433 (1992)

17. Nagappan, N., Ball, T., Zeller, A.: Mining Metrics to Predict Component Failures. In: Nagappan, N., Ball, T. (eds.) Proc. Int. Conf. on Software Engineering, May 2006, pp. 452–461. Shanghai, China (2006)
18. Ohlsson, N., Alberg, H.: Predicting Fault-Prone Software Modules in Telephone Switches. In: IEEE Trans. on Software Engineering, 22th edn., 12, December 1996, pp. 886–894 (1996)
19. Ostrand, T., Weyuker, E.J.: The Distribution of Faults in a Large Industrial Software System. In: Proc. ACM/International Symposium on Software Testing and Analysis (ISSTA2002), Rome, Italy, July 2002, pp. 55–64 (2002)
20. Ostrand, T.J., Weyuker, E.J., Bell, R.M.: Predicting the Location and Number of Faults in Large Software Systems. IEEE Trans. on Software Engineering 31(4) (2005)
21. Ostrand, T.J., Weyuker, E.J., Bell, R.M.: Automating Algorithms for the Identification of Fault-Prone Files. In: Proc. ACM/International Symposium on Software Testing and Analysis (ISSTA 2007), London, England (July 2007)
22. Pighin, M., Marzona, A.: An Empirical Analysis of Fault Persistence Through Software Releases. In: Proc. IEEE/ACM ISESE 2003, pp. 206–212 (2003)
23. Succi, G., Pedrycz, W., Stefanovic, M., Miller, J.: Practical Assessment of the Models for Identification of Defect-prone Classes in Object-oriented Commercial Systems Using Design Metrics. Journal of Systems and Software 65(1), 1–12 (2003)

Equivalence Checking for a Finite Higher Order π-Calculus*

Zining Cao

Department of Computer Science and Technology
Nanjing University of Aero. and Astro.
Nanjing 210016, P.R. China
caozn@nuaa.edu.cn

Abstract. In this paper, we present an algorithm for checking weak context bisimulation over a finite higher order π-calculus, called linear higher order π-calculus. To achieve this aim, we propose a new bisimulation, called linear normal bisimulation, and furthermore prove the equivalence between context bisimulation and linear normal bisimulation for such linear higher order π-calculus. The correctness of this algorithm is also demonstrated. At last, we give a complete inference system for linear higher order π-calculus.

1 Introduction

Higher order π-calculus was proposed and studied intensively in Sangiorgi's dissertation [13]. In higher order π-calculus, processes and abstractions over processes of arbitrary high order can be communicated. Some interesting equivalences for higher order π-calculus, such as barbed equivalence, context bisimulation and normal bisimulation, were presented in [13]. Barbed equivalence can be regarded as a uniform definition of bisimulation for a variety of concurrent calculi. Context bisimulation is a very intuitive definition of bisimulation for higher order π-calculus, but it is heavy to handle, due to the appearance of universal quantifications in its definition. In the definition of normal bisimulation, all universal quantifications disappeared, therefore normal bisimulation is a very economic characterisation of bisimulation for higher order π-calculus. The relation between the three equivalences has been studied in [3,13,14].

In [15,16], Thomsen presented a higher order calculus, called $CHOCS$. Higher order bisimulation was presented for $CHOCS$ as an equivalence relation, which requires bisimilarity rather than identity of the processes emitted in a higher order output action. Higher order bisimulation appears to work well in the calculus $CHOCS$ where restriction is a dynamic binding. For higher order π-calculus, higher order bisimulation seems troublesome because unlike $CHOCS$, restriction is a static binder in higher order π-calculus [13].

* This work was supported by the National Natural Science Foundation of China under Grant 60473036.

B. Beckert and R. Hähnle (Eds.): TAP 2008, LNCS 4966, pp. 30–47, 2008.

Developing efficient algorithms for checking bisimulation equivalences for various process calculi is an important research topic in the development of process theories. An efficient algorithm for checking bisimulation equivalences allows us to automatically verify systems specified in process calculi. There has been a lot of work on bisimulation checking algorithms for CCS and π-calculus [5,6,8].

For higher order π-calculus, the checking algorithm is in general difficult to give. The main problem lies in that universal quantifications appear in the definition of bisimulations for higher order π-calculus. For instance, to state the equality between two processes with higher order input prefixing, one has to state the equality between the residuals under all possible process substitutions. To overcome this problem, we have to seek an efficient characterisation of context bisimulation.

One of aims of this paper is to develop an efficient algorithm for checking context bisimulation equivalence in the higher order π-calculus. To achieve this aim, we first define a finite higher order π-calculus, called linear higher order π-calculus. Roughly speaking, a linear process is a process in which a variable may occur at most once. Then we present a new bisimulation, called linear normal bisimulation, whose definition is a variant of normal bisimulation. We study the relation between linear normal bisimulation and context bisimulation, and prove that weak linear normal bisimulation coincides with both weak context bisimulation and weak higher order bisimulation for a linear higher order π-calculus. Since weak context bisimulation is equivalent to weak normal bisimulation for such a linear higher order π-calculus, all bisimulations appeared in literatures are equivalent to each other. A checking algorithm with respect to weak context bisimulation, WBC, is then proposed for such linear higher order π-calculus. Based on the equivalence between weak linear normal bisimulation and weak context bisimulation, the correctness of WBC is proved for weak context bisimulation.

Providing sound and complete axiomatisations for various equivalence relations has been one of the major research topics in the development of process theories. A complete axiomatization not only allows us to reason about process behaviors by syntactic manipulation, but also helps to understand the properties of the operators used to build complex processes from simpler components. There has been a lot of work on algebra theory for CCS and π-calculus [2,7,9,12].

For the higher order π-calculus, the algebra theory is in general difficult to give. The main problem lies in that universal quantifications appear in the definition of bisimulations for the higher order π-calculus. For instance, to equal two processes with higher order input prefixing, one has to equal the residuals under all possible process substitutions. An easy approach to the axiomatization of higher order π-calculus is to introduce an infinite number of premises, but this rule is obviously of little practical use. Another aims of this paper is to provide a complete inference system for context congruence for linear higher order π-calculus. A complete inference system, named WCE, for context congruence is given in this paper.

This paper is organized as follows: In Section 2 we briefly review higher order π-calculus. In Section 3 we present a linear higher order π-calculus, and define a new bisimulation, called linear normal bisimulation, over this calculus. Furthermore the equivalence between weak linear normal bisimulation and weak context bisimulation is proven. In Section 4 we propose a checking algorithm for weak context bisimulation over linear higher order π-calculus, and furthermore study its correctness. In Section 5 we give an inference system for linear higher order π-calculus. The paper is concluded in Section 6.

2 Higher Order π-Calculus

2.1 Syntax and Labelled Transition System of Higher Order π-Calculus

In this section we briefly recall the syntax and labelled transition system of the higher order π-calculus. We only focus on a second-order fragment of the higher order π-calculus [14], i.e., there is no abstraction in this fragment.

We assume a set N of names, ranged over by $a, b, c, ..., x, y...$ and a set Var of process variables, ranged over by $X, Y, Z, U, ...$ We use $E, F, P, Q, ...$ to stand for processes. The class of processes is denoted as Pr.

We first give the grammar for the higher order π-calculus processes as follows:

$P ::= 0 \mid U \mid \pi_1.P_1 + ... + \pi_n.P_n \mid P_1|P_2 \mid (\nu x)P \mid !P$
π_i is called prefix and can be an input or an output or a tau prefix.
$\pi_i ::= \tau \mid l \mid \bar{l} \mid a(U) \mid \overline{a}\langle P\rangle$

Informally, 0 denotes inaction. Operator $+$ represents the nondeterministic choice. $\tau.P + S$ can perform a tau action, then continues as P. $l.P + S$ can perform a first order input action at name l, then continues as P. $\bar{l}.P + S$ can perform a first order output action at name l, then continues as P. $a(U).P + S$ can receive a process at name a, say E, then continues as $P\{E/U\}$, i.e., the process obtained by replacing each free occurrence of U in P by E. $\overline{a}\langle E\rangle.P + S$ can perform an output action at name a emitting process E, then continues as P. $P_1|P_2$ is a parallel composition of two processes P_1 and P_2. $(\nu a)P$ is the restriction operator, which makes name a local to process P. $!P$ stands, intuitively, for an infinite number of copies of P in parallel.

In each process of the form $(\nu a)P$ the occurrence of a is bound within P. An occurrence of a in a process is said to be free iff it does not lie within the scope of a bound occurrence of a. The set of names occurring free in P is denoted $fn(P)$. An occurrence of a name in a process is said to be bound if it is not free, we write the set of bound names as $bn(P)$. $n(P)$ denotes the set of names of P, i.e., $n(P) = fn(P) \cup bn(P)$. The definition of substitution in process terms may involve renaming of bound names when necessary to avoid name capture.

Higher order input prefix $a(U).P$ binds all free occurrences of U in P. The set of variables occurring free in P is denoted $fv(P)$. We write the set of bound variables as $bv(P)$. A process is closed if it has no free variable; it is open if it may have free variables. Pr^c is the set of all closed processes.

Processes P and Q are α-convertible, $P \equiv_\alpha Q$, if Q can be obtained from P by a finite number of changes of bound names and variables. For example, $(\nu b)(\overline{a}\langle b(U).U\rangle.0) \equiv_\alpha (\nu c)(\overline{a}\langle c(U).U\rangle.0)$.

The actions are given by

$\alpha ::= \tau \mid l \mid \bar{l} \mid a\langle P\rangle \mid \overline{a}\langle P\rangle \mid (\nu\widetilde{b})\overline{a}\langle P\rangle$

We write *Act* for the set of actions. $bn(\alpha)$ represents the set of names bound in α, which is $\{\widetilde{b}\}$ if α is $(\nu\widetilde{b})\overline{a}\langle P\rangle$ and $\emptyset$ otherwise. $n(\alpha)$ denotes the set of names that occur in α.

The operational semantics of higher order processes is given in Table 1.

Table 1. Labelled transition system of higher order π-calculus

$$ALP: \frac{P \xrightarrow{\alpha} P'}{Q \xrightarrow{\alpha} Q'} P \equiv_\alpha Q, P' \equiv_\alpha Q' \qquad TAU: \tau.P \xrightarrow{\tau} P$$

$$OUT1: \bar{l}.P \xrightarrow{\bar{l}} P \qquad IN1: l.P \xrightarrow{l} P$$

$$OUT2: \overline{a}\langle E\rangle.P \xrightarrow{\overline{a}\langle E\rangle} P \qquad IN2: a(U).P \xrightarrow{a\langle E\rangle} P\{E/U\}$$

$$SUM: \frac{P \xrightarrow{\alpha} P'}{P+Q \xrightarrow{\alpha} P'} \qquad PAR: \frac{P \xrightarrow{\alpha} P'}{P|Q \xrightarrow{\alpha} P'|Q} bn(\alpha) \cap fn(Q) = \emptyset$$

$$COM1: \frac{P \xrightarrow{l} P' \quad Q \xrightarrow{\bar{l}} Q'}{P|Q \xrightarrow{\tau} P'|Q'}$$

$$COM2: \frac{P \xrightarrow{(\nu\widetilde{b})\overline{a}\langle E\rangle} P' \quad Q \xrightarrow{a\langle E\rangle} Q'}{P|Q \xrightarrow{\tau} (\nu\widetilde{b})(P'|Q')} \widetilde{b} \cap fn(Q) = \emptyset$$

$$COM3: \frac{P \xrightarrow{\overline{a}\langle E\rangle} P' \quad Q \xrightarrow{a\langle E\rangle} Q'}{P|Q \xrightarrow{\tau} P'|Q'}$$

$$RES: \frac{P \xrightarrow{\alpha} P'}{(\nu a)P \xrightarrow{\alpha} (\nu a)P'} a \notin n(\alpha) \qquad REP: \frac{P|!P \xrightarrow{\alpha} P'}{!P \xrightarrow{\alpha} P'}$$

$$OPEN: \frac{P \xrightarrow{(\nu\widetilde{c})\overline{a}\langle E\rangle} P'}{(\nu b)P \xrightarrow{(\nu b,\widetilde{c})\overline{a}\langle E\rangle} P'} a \neq b, b \in fn(E) - \widetilde{c}$$

2.2 Weak Bisimulations in Higher Order π-Calculus

Context and normal bisimulations were presented in [13,14] to describe the behavioral equivalences for higher order π-calculus. Context bisimulation is an intuitive definition of bisimulation in higher order π-calculus and is regarded as a standard bisimulation for higher order π-calculus. A drawback of context bisimulation is the universal quantifications on input and output actions, which can make it hard, in practice, to use this equivalence. A simpler characterisation of context bisimulation is normal bisimulation, which does not require universal quantifications but contains the replication operator.

Let us review the definition of weak context and normal bisimulations. In the following, we abbreviate $P\{E/U\}$ as $P\langle E\rangle$, and we use $\overset{\widehat{\tau}}{\Longrightarrow}$ to abbreviate the reflexive and transitive closure of $\xrightarrow{\tau}$, and use $\overset{\alpha}{\Longrightarrow}$ to abbreviate $\overset{\widehat{\tau}}{\Longrightarrow}\xrightarrow{\alpha}\overset{\widehat{\tau}}{\Longrightarrow}$.

Definition 1. *A symmetric relation $R \subseteq Pr^c \times Pr^c$ is a weak context bisimulation if $P\ R\ Q$ implies:*

(1) whenever $P \xrightarrow{\tau} P'$, there exists Q' such that $Q \stackrel{\widehat{\tau}}{\Longrightarrow} Q'$ and $P'\ R\ Q'$;

(2) whenever $P \xrightarrow{\alpha} P'$, there exists Q' such that $Q \stackrel{\alpha}{\Longrightarrow} Q'$, and $P'\ R\ Q'$, where α is in the form of l or $\overline{l}$;

(3) whenever $P \xrightarrow{a\langle E\rangle} P'$, there exists Q' such that $Q \stackrel{a\langle E\rangle}{\Longrightarrow} Q'$ and $P'\ R\ Q'$;

(4) whenever $P \xrightarrow{(\nu\widetilde{b})\overline{a}\langle E\rangle} P'$, there exist Q', F, $\widetilde{c}$ such that $Q \stackrel{(\nu\widetilde{c})\overline{a}\langle F\rangle}{\Longrightarrow} Q'$ and for all $C(U)$ with $fn(C(U)) \cap \{\widetilde{b}, \widetilde{c}\} = \emptyset$, $(\nu\widetilde{b})(P'|C\langle E\rangle)\ R\ (\nu\widetilde{c})(Q'|C\langle F\rangle)$. Here $C(U)$ is a process containing a unique variable U.

We write $P \approx_{Ct} Q$ if P and Q are weakly context bisimilar.

Definition 2. *A symmetric relation $R \subseteq Pr^c \times Pr^c$ is a weak normal bisimulation if $P\ R\ Q$ implies:*

(1) whenever $P \xrightarrow{\tau} P'$, there exists Q' such that $Q \stackrel{\widehat{\tau}}{\Longrightarrow} Q'$ and $P'\ R\ Q'$;

(2) whenever $P \xrightarrow{\alpha} P'$, there exists Q' such that $Q \stackrel{\alpha}{\Longrightarrow} Q'$, and $P'\ R\ Q'$, where α is in the form of l or $\overline{l}$;

(3) whenever $P \xrightarrow{a\langle\overline{m}.0\rangle} P'$, there exists Q' such that $Q \stackrel{a\langle\overline{m}.0\rangle}{\Longrightarrow} Q'$ and $P'\ R\ Q'$, where m is a fresh name;

(4) whenever $P \xrightarrow{(\nu\widetilde{b})\overline{a}\langle E\rangle} P'$, there exist Q', F, $\widetilde{c}$ such that $Q \stackrel{(\nu\widetilde{c})\overline{a}\langle F\rangle}{\Longrightarrow} Q'$ and $(\nu\widetilde{b})(P'|!m.E)\ R\ (\nu\widetilde{c})(Q'|!m.F)$, where m is a fresh name.

We write $P \approx_{Nr} Q$ if P and Q are weakly normal bisimilar.

In [15,16], Thomsen presented a higher order bisimulation.

Definition 3. *A symmetric relation $R \subseteq Pr^c \times Pr^c$ is a weak higher order bisimulation if $P\ R\ Q$ implies:*

(1) whenever $P \xrightarrow{\tau} P'$, there exists Q' such that $Q \stackrel{\widehat{\tau}}{\Longrightarrow} Q'$ and $P'\ R\ Q'$;

(2) whenever $P \xrightarrow{\alpha} P'$, there exists Q' such that $Q \stackrel{\alpha}{\Longrightarrow} Q'$, and $P'\ R\ Q'$, where α is in the form of l or $\overline{l}$;

(3) whenever $P \xrightarrow{a\langle E\rangle} P'$, there exists Q' such that $Q \stackrel{a\langle E\rangle}{\Longrightarrow} Q'$ and $P'\ R\ Q'$;

(4) whenever $P \xrightarrow{(\nu\widetilde{b})\overline{a}\langle E\rangle} P'$, there exist Q', F such that $Q \stackrel{(\nu\widetilde{b})\overline{a}\langle F\rangle}{\Longrightarrow} Q'$, $E\ R\ F$ and $P'\ R\ Q'$.

We write $P \approx_{HO} Q$ if P and Q are weakly higher order bisimilar.

3 A Linear Higher Order π-Calculus and Its Bisimulations

In this section, we first give a finite higher order π-calculus. Then to get an bisimulation checking algorithms for this calculus , we present a new bisimulation, called linear normal bisimulation, and study the relation between context bisimulation and this bisimulation.

3.1 Syntax of Linear Higher Order π-Calculus

Firstly, we have to isolate a finite sub calculus in higher order π-calculus. In CCS and π-calculus, sub calculus with inaction, prefix, sum, parallel and restriction operators are finite, but for higher order π-calculus, things are different.

For example, let us see the language of higher order π-calculus with sum, parallel and restriction operators defined by the following grammar:

$P ::= 0 \mid U \mid \pi_1.P_1 + ... + \pi_n.P_n \mid P_1|P_2 \mid (\nu a)P$

$\pi_i ::= \tau \mid l \mid \bar{l} \mid a(U) \mid \overline{a}\langle P\rangle$

We write the set of processes of this higher order π-calculus as Pr_A. The set of all closed processes in Pr_A is denoted as Pr_A^c.

But Pr_A is not finite since the processes in Pr_A may transform to infinite states. Let us see an example: if $W = a(X).(X|X|\bar{a}\langle X\rangle.0)$, $\Omega = (\nu a)(W|\bar{a}\langle W\rangle.0)$, then $\Omega \stackrel{\tau}{\longrightarrow} (\nu a)(W|W|\bar{a}\langle W\rangle.0) \stackrel{\tau}{\longrightarrow} (\nu a)(W|W|W|\bar{a}\langle W\rangle.0) \stackrel{\tau}{\longrightarrow} ...$ is a possible reduction. In fact, the expressive power of Pr_A is equal to Pr. In [11], Parrow has shown that in higher order π-calculus, the replication can be defined by other operators such as higher order prefix, parallel and restriction. For example, $!P$ can be simulated by $R_P = (\nu a)(D|\overline{a}\langle P|D\rangle.0)$, here $D = a(X).(X|\overline{a}\langle X\rangle.0)$. Hence the behavior of any process of higher order π-calculus can be simulated by Pr_A.

Therefore, to get a finite higher order π-calculus, we have to restrict the language of Pr_A. Roughly speaking, we will isolate a class of processes in which a variable may occur at most once. In [13,14], the class of such processes was called *linear calculus*.

Definition 4. *The language of linear higher order π-calculus defined by the following grammar:*

$P ::= 0$

$\mid U$

$\mid \pi_1.P_1 + ... + \pi_n.P_n$ *where* $fv(\pi_i) \cap fv(P_i) = \emptyset$. *Here* π_i *is in the form of* τ, l, $\bar{l}$, $a(U)$ *or* $\overline{a}\langle P\rangle$, *and* $fv(\pi)$ *represents the set of variables occurring free in* π, *which is* $fv(P)$ *if* π *is* $\overline{a}\langle P\rangle$ *and* $\emptyset$ *otherwise.*

$\mid P_1|P_2$ *where* $fv(P_1) \cap fv(P_2) = \emptyset$

$\mid (\nu a)P$

We write the set of processes of linear higher order π-calculus as Pr_L. The set of all closed processes in Pr_L is denoted as Pr_L^c.

For example, $a(X).(b.X + \overline{c}\langle m.X\rangle.0)$, $(\nu a)(\overline{a}\langle m.0\rangle|a(X).(m.0|X))$ and $a(X).\overline{b}\langle c.X\rangle.0 + b(U).(m.U + \overline{c}.U)$ are processes in Pr_L. In addition, since processes in CCS contains no variable, all finite processes in CCS are also in Pr_L.

The labelled transition system of linear higher order processes is defined on Pr_L^c, i.e., all processes appearing in the labelled transition system are closed. The labelled transition system of Pr_L^c is similar to Table 1, except that there is no Rule *REP*.

3.2 Linear Normal Bisimulation

There are several checking algorithms for bisimulation-based equivalence over various process calculi, such as CCS and π-calculus. To generalize them to higher order π-calculus a key issue is how to deal with higher order input and output prefixing, because this is exactly where process variables are introduced. A possible solution is to adopt the following algorithm:

INPUT: If $P\{E/U\} = Q\{E/U\}$ for each process E, then $a(U).P = a(U).Q$.
OUTPUT: If $(\nu\widetilde{b})(P|C\{E/U\}) = (\nu\widetilde{c})(Q|C\{F/U\})$ for each process $C(U)$, then $(\nu\widetilde{b})(\overline{a}\langle E\rangle.P) = (\nu\widetilde{c})(\overline{a}\langle F\rangle.Q)$.

However the problem here is that to apply the above rules we have to inspect an infinite number of premises since there are infinitely many processes, and therefore these rules are of little use.

To obtain an efficient algorithm we need to replace the statements *INPUT* and *OUTPUT* with finitary ones. As the infinity in the rules is caused by the appearance of universal quantifications in the definition of $\approx_{Ct}$, to avoid such universal quantifications, we need a new definition of bisimulation. One may think that normal bisimulation is such a definition since it was proved to be equivalent to weak context bisimulation and there is no universal quantifications in the definition of $\approx_{Nr}$. Unfortunately, normal bisimulation is not such a candidate. If we adopt the definition of $\approx_{Nr}$, the algorithm will be as follows:

INPUT: If $P\{\overline{m}.0/U\} = Q\{\overline{m}.0/U\}$ with a new name m, then $a(U).P = a(U).Q$.
OUTPUT: If $(\nu\widetilde{b})(P|!m.E) = (\nu\widetilde{c})(Q|!m.F)$ with a new name m, then $(\nu\widetilde{b})(\overline{a}\langle E\rangle.P) = (\nu\widetilde{c})(\overline{a}\langle F\rangle.Q)$.

Now the statement *INPUT* is efficient, but replication operators appear in the rule *OUTPUT* which is not an operator in finite process. Hence normal bisimulation cannot be used directly to give the algorithm for higher order input or output prefixing.

Finally, if we adopt the definition of $\approx_{HO}$, the algorithm will be as follows:

INPUT: If $P\{E/U\} = Q\{E/U\}$ for each process E, then $a(U).P = a(U).Q$.
OUTPUT: If $E = F$ and $P = Q$, then $(\nu\widetilde{b})(\overline{a}\langle E\rangle.P) = (\nu\widetilde{b})(\overline{a}\langle F\rangle.Q)$.

It is easy to see that higher order bisimulation is also not a definition that we need because universal quantifications appear in the rule of higher order input prefixing and furthermore $\approx_{HO}$ is not equivalent to $\approx_{Ct}$ for Pr as showed in [13,14].

To give a bisimulation checking algorithm for Pr_L^c, we need to study other bisimulation simpler than context bisimulation. Normal bisimulation is simpler than context bisimulation, but the definition of normal bisimulation contains the replication operator. Therefore we should present a new bisimulation. In the following, we simplify the definition of normal bisimulation and get a new bisimulation, called linear normal bisimulation.

Definition 5. *A symmetric relation $R \subseteq Pr_L^c \times Pr_L^c$ is a weak linear normal bisimulation if $P\ R\ Q$ implies:*

(1) whenever $P \stackrel{\tau}{\longrightarrow} P'$, there exists Q' such that $Q \stackrel{\widehat{\tau}}{\Longrightarrow} Q'$ and $P'\ R\ Q'$;
(2) whenever $P \stackrel{\alpha}{\longrightarrow} P'$, there exists Q' such that $Q \stackrel{\alpha}{\Longrightarrow} Q'$, and $P'\ R\ Q'$, where α is in the form of l or $\overline{l}$;

(3) whenever $P \stackrel{a\langle\overline{m}.0\rangle}{\longrightarrow} P'$, *there exists* Q' *such that* $Q \stackrel{a\langle\overline{m}.0\rangle}{\Longrightarrow} Q'$ *and* $P'\ R\ Q'$, *where* m *is a fresh name;*

(4) whenever $P \stackrel{(\nu\widetilde{b})\overline{a}\langle E\rangle}{\longrightarrow} P'$, *there exist* Q', F, $\widetilde{c}$ *such that* $Q \stackrel{(\nu\widetilde{c})\overline{a}\langle F\rangle}{\Longrightarrow} Q'$, *and* $(\nu\widetilde{b})(P'|m.E)\ R\ (\nu\widetilde{c})(Q'|m.F)$, *where* m *is a fresh name.*

We write $P \approx_{Ln} Q$ *if* P *and* Q *are weakly linear normal bisimilar.*

Weak linear normal bisimulation is a simplification of weak normal bisimulation by eliminating replication operators in the clause (4) of Definition 2. In [13], Sangiorgi showed that if we eliminate replication operators in the definition of $\approx_{Nr}$, the resulting bisimulation, i.e., weak linear normal bisimulation $\approx_{Ln}$, is not equivalent to $\approx_{Ct}$ for the general processes in Pr^c. A counterexample in [13] is: $P \equiv (\nu b)\overline{a}\langle b.b.\overline{c}|\overline{b}\rangle.0$ and $Q \equiv \overline{a}\langle 0\rangle.0$.

It is obvious that in this definition, the universal quantification and the replication operator are all disappeared. Hence we can give a bisimulation checking algorithm for weak linear normal congruence over Pr^c_L. Furthermore, if we can prove the coincidence between weak context bisimulation and this bisimulation for Pr^c_L, then this algorithm also works for weak context bisimulation over Pr^c_L.

Similarly, for processes in Pr^c_L, the definition of weak context bisimulation is the same as Definition 1, except that the clause (4) is replaced with the following clause:

(4') whenever $P \stackrel{(\nu\widetilde{b})\overline{a}\langle E\rangle}{\longrightarrow} P'$, *there exist* Q', F, $\widetilde{c}$ *such that* $Q \stackrel{(\nu\widetilde{c})\overline{a}\langle F\rangle}{\Longrightarrow} Q'$ *and for all* $C(U) \in Pr_L$ *with* $fn(C(U)) \cap \{\widetilde{b}, \widetilde{c}\} = \emptyset$, $(\nu\widetilde{b})(P'|C\langle E\rangle)\ R\ (\nu\widetilde{c})(Q'|C\langle F\rangle)$. *Here* $C(U)$ *is a process containing a unique variable* U.

3.3 Finiteness of Pr^c_L

In this section, we show the finiteness of Pr^c_L, i.e., the transition sequence of a process in Pr^c_L is finite.

Lemma 1. *For any* $P \in Pr^c_L$, *if* $P \stackrel{\alpha}{\longrightarrow} P'$, *then* $P' \in Pr^c_L$.

Proof. Induction on the structure of P. ∎

The depth of processes, which is the maximal number of nested prefix operators, is defined as below:

Definition 6. *The depth of higher order processes in* Pr^c_L, *is defined as below:*

1. $d(0) \stackrel{def}{=} 0$;
2. $d(U) \stackrel{def}{=} 2$;
3. $d(\tau.P) \stackrel{def}{=} 1 + d(P)$;
4. $d(l.P) \stackrel{def}{=} 1 + d(P)$;
5. $d(\overline{l}.P) \stackrel{def}{=} 1 + d(P)$;
6. $d(a(U).P) \stackrel{def}{=} 1 + d(P)$;

7. $d(\overline{a}\langle E\rangle.P) \overset{def}{=} 3 + d(E) + d(P)$;
8. $d(P_1 + P_2) \overset{def}{=} max(d(P_1), d(P_2))$;
9. $d(P_1|P_2) \overset{def}{=} d(P_1) + d(P_2)$;
10. $d((\nu a)P) \overset{def}{=} d(P)$.

Remark 1. We set $d(U) = 2$ because we need $d(U) > d(\overline{m}.0)$, which is used in the proof of Lemma 3. We set $d(\overline{a}\langle E\rangle.P) = 3 + d(E) + d(P)$ because we need $d(\overline{a}\langle E\rangle.P) > d(\tau.(P|m.E)) = 2 + d(E) + d(P)$, which is used in the proofs of Proposition 1 and Proposition 7.

Lemma 2. *For any $P \in Pr_L$, then $d(P\{\overline{m}.0/U\}) + d(E) > d(P\{E/U\})$.*

It is easy to see that after performing a first order action, a process always transforms to a simpler process. For example, in the case of finite CCS and finite π-calculus, if $P \xrightarrow{\alpha} P'$, then $d(P) > d(P')$. This property is useful in proof of completeness of inference system. But for higher order input action, it may make process transform to a more complicated process since it may introduce any complicated process. For instance, $a(U).U \xrightarrow{a\langle b.b.0\rangle} b.b.0 \xrightarrow{b}\xrightarrow{b} 0$, $a(U).U \xrightarrow{a\langle b.b.b.0\rangle} b.b.b.0 \xrightarrow{b}\xrightarrow{b}\xrightarrow{b} 0$. Therefore to ensure the finiteness of Pr_L^c, we have to restrict the process introduced by higher order input action. In the following, we present the concept of normal transition.

Definition 7. *Normal transition*
The transition $P \xrightarrow{\alpha} P'$ is called a normal transition if α is of the form τ, l, $\overline{l}$, $(\nu\widetilde{b})\overline{a}\langle E\rangle$, or $a\langle\overline{m}.0\rangle$, where m is a fresh name.

Lemma 3. *For a normal transition $P \xrightarrow{\alpha} P'$, if α is not a higher order output action, then $d(P) > d(P')$; if α is of the form $(\nu\widetilde{b})\overline{a}\langle E\rangle$ then $d(P) > d(P') + d(E) + 2$.*

The following Proposition states the finiteness of Pr_L^c w.r.t. normal transition.

Proposition 1. *For any $P \in Pr_L^c$, any normal transition sequence of P is finite, i.e., there is no infinite normal transition sequence $P \xrightarrow{\alpha_1}\xrightarrow{\alpha_2} \ldots$.*

Proof. By Lemma 3, if $P \xrightarrow{\alpha} P'$ is a normal transition, then $d(P) > d(P')$. Hence any normal transition sequence of P is finite. ∎

3.4 The Equivalence between Weak Context Bisimulation and Weak Linear Normal Bisimulation for Pr_L^c

In this paper, we aim to present a checking algorithm for weak context congruence over Pr_L^c. To achieve this end, we first prove the equivalence between weak linear normal bisimulation and weak context bisimulation for Pr_L^c.

Lemma 4. *For all $P, Q \in Pr_L^c$, $P \approx_{Ln} Q$ implies*
(1) $\alpha.P + R \approx_{Ln} \alpha.Q + R$
(2) $P|R \approx_{Ln} Q|R$.
(3) $(\nu a)P \approx_{Ln} (\nu a)Q$.
(4) $\overline{a}\langle P\rangle.R + S \approx_{Ln} \overline{a}\langle Q\rangle.R + S$

Proof. Similar to the proof of Theorem 4.4.1 in [13]. ∎

Lemma 5. *For all P, $Q \in Pr_L^c$, $P \approx_{Ct} Q$ implies*
(1) $\alpha.P + R \approx_{Ct} \alpha.Q + R$
(2) $P|R \approx_{Ct} Q|R$.
(3) $(\nu a)P \approx_{Ct} (\nu a)Q$.
(4) $!P \approx_{Ct} !Q$.
(5) $\overline{a}\langle P\rangle.R + S \approx_{Ct} \overline{a}\langle Q\rangle.R + S$

Proof. See the proof of Theorem 4.4.1 in [13]. ∎

To give a bisimulation checking algorithm, we will study the relation between $\approx_{Ln}$ and $\approx_{Ct}$. The following lemma is used in the proof of the equivalence between $\approx_{Ln}$ and $\approx_{Ct}$.

Lemma 6. *For any P, $Q \in Pr_L^c$, $P \approx_{Ct} Q \Rightarrow P \approx_{Ln} Q$.*

The following lemma is a simplified version of factorisation theorem of higher order π-calculus for Pr_L^c.

Lemma 7. *For any $P, E \in Pr_L^c$ with $m \notin fn(P, E)$, it holds that $P\{E/U\} \approx_{Ct} (\nu m)(P\{\overline{m}.0/U\}|m.E)$.*

Proof. The proof is similar to the proof of the factorisation theorem [13,14] with the condition P, $E \in Pr_L^c$. ∎

For example, if $P \stackrel{def}{=} b.Q + \overline{c}\langle a.Q\rangle.0$, then $P = (b.X + \overline{c}\langle a.X\rangle.0)\{Q/X\}$ and, applying the above lemma (and assuming m fresh), $P \approx_{Ct} (\nu m)((b.\overline{m}.0 + \overline{c}\langle a.\overline{m}.0\rangle.0)|m.Q)$.

The following Proposition gives the coincidence between $\approx_{Ct}$ and $\approx_{Ln}$ for our linear higher order π-calculus.

Lemma 8. *For any P, $Q \in Pr_L^c$, $P \approx_{Ln} Q \Rightarrow P \approx_{Ct} Q$.*

Proposition 2. *For any P, $Q \in Pr_L^c$, $P \approx_{Ln} Q \Leftrightarrow P \approx_{Ct} Q$.*

Proof. It is immediate by Lemma 6 and Lemma 8. ∎

4 A Bisimulation Checking Algorithm *WBC* for Pr_L^c

Now we want to describe an algorithm which given two processes P, $Q \in Pr_L^c$, calculates whether $P \approx_{Ct} Q$ or not. As we discussed before, since universal quantifications appear in the definition of weak context bisimulation, it is difficult to give an efficient checking algorithm directly. On the other hand, we have proved the equivalence between $\approx_{Ct}$ and $\approx_{Ln}$, therefore to check $\approx_{Ct}$ over Pr_L^c, it is enough to check $\approx_{Ln}$ over Pr_L^c.

4.1 Normal Transition Graph

In this section, a formal language, normal transition graph (NTG), will be introduced. Traditionally processes are modelled by labelled transition systems (LTS) which are directed graphs in which arcs are labelled by higher order actions. A vertex in an LTS represents a state and the outgoing arcs show the possible actions the process at the state can perform to evolve into the target states. NTGs are graphical representation for higher order processes, where input/output actions and process expressions are retained in the edges.

The formal definition of NTG is as follows:

Definition 8. *A normal transition graph (NTG) is a tuple* (S, s_0, A, E) *where*

(1) S *is a finite set of nodes, which represent higher order processes in* Pr_L^c.

(2) s_0 *is the initial node.*

(3) $A = \{\tau, l, \bar{l}, a?, a! \mid l, a \in$ *channel set* $N\}$ *is a set of actions. Here* $\tau, l, \bar{l}$ *are first order actions,* $a?$ *represents higher order input action through channel* a. $a!$ *represents higher order output action through channel* a.

(4) $E \subseteq S \times A \times S$ *is a finite set of edges. Where* $(s, \alpha, t) \in E$ *if* $s \xrightarrow{\alpha} t$ *and* α *is not a higher order action,* $(s, a?, t) \in E$ *if* $s \xrightarrow{a\langle \overline{m}.0\rangle} t$ *and* m *is a fresh name,* $(s, a!, t) \in E$ *if* $s \xrightarrow{(\widetilde{\nu b})\overline{a}\langle r\rangle} p$, $t = (\widetilde{\nu b})(p|m.r)$ *and* m *is a fresh name.*

An example NTG is shown in Fig. 1.

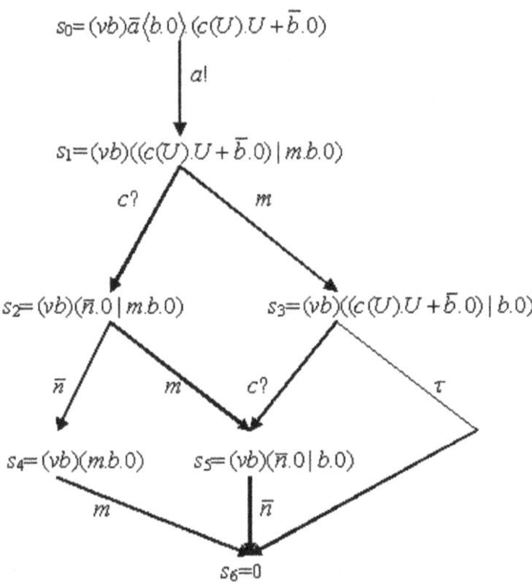

Fig. 1. A normal transition graph

In this figure, $s_0 = (\nu b)\overline{a}\langle b.0\rangle.(c(U).U + \overline{b}.0)$ is the initial node of the system. On the edge from s_0 to s_1, action $a!$ output process $b.0$. At s_1, the system can choose to change to s_2 by performing higher order input $c?$ or change to s_3 by performing first order action m. Similarly, action m makes s_2 transform to node s_5, action τ makes s_3 become s_6 and action $\overline{n}$ makes s_5 become s_6.

Proposition 3. *For any $P \in Pr_L^c$, the normal transition graph of P is finite.*

Proof. It is easy by induction on the structure of P and using Lemma 3: for any α, if $P \xrightarrow{\alpha} P'$ is a normal transition, then $d(P) > d(P')$ if α is not a higher order output action, or $d(P) > d(P') + d(E) + 1$ if α is of the form $(\nu\widetilde{b})\overline{a}\langle E\rangle$. ∎

4.2 The Algorithm *WBC*

In this section we presented an algorithm WBC for checking linear normal bisimulation over Pr_L^c as follows:

$$
\begin{array}{l}
bisim(P,Q) = \\
\qquad if\ P = 0\ and\ Q = 0\ then\ return(true) \\
\qquad else\ b := \bigwedge_{\alpha \in NA(P,Q)} match_\alpha(P,Q) \\
\qquad return(b) \\
match_{\alpha \in \{\tau, l, \overline{l}\}}(P,Q) = \\
\qquad if\ P \xrightarrow{\alpha}\ and\ Q \overset{\widehat{\alpha}}{\not\Longrightarrow}\ then\ return(false) \\
\qquad if\ Q \xrightarrow{\alpha}\ and\ P \overset{\widehat{\alpha}}{\not\Longrightarrow}\ then\ return(false) \\
\qquad for\ each\ P \xrightarrow{\alpha} P_i, Q \overset{\widehat{\alpha}}{\Longrightarrow} Q_j \\
\qquad\qquad c_{i,j} := bisim(P_i, Q_j) \\
\qquad for\ each\ Q \xrightarrow{\alpha} Q_i, P \overset{\widehat{\alpha}}{\Longrightarrow} P_j \\
\qquad\qquad d_{i,j} := bisim(Q_i, P_j) \\
\qquad return((\bigwedge_i (\bigvee_j c_{i,j})) \wedge (\bigwedge_i (\bigvee_j d_{i,j}))). \\
match_{a?}(P,Q) = \\
\qquad m := nextSN(P,Q) \\
\qquad if\ P \xrightarrow{a\langle \overline{m}.0\rangle}\ and\ Q \overset{a\langle \overline{m}.0\rangle}{\not\Longrightarrow}\ then\ return(false) \\
\qquad if\ Q \xrightarrow{a\langle \overline{m}.0\rangle}\ and\ P \overset{a\langle \overline{m}.0\rangle}{\not\Longrightarrow}\ then\ return(false) \\
\qquad for\ each\ P \xrightarrow{a\langle \overline{m}.0\rangle} P_i, Q \overset{a\langle \overline{m}.0\rangle}{\Longrightarrow} Q_j \\
\qquad\qquad c_{i,j} := bisim(P_i, Q_j) \\
\qquad for\ each\ Q \xrightarrow{a\langle \overline{m}.0\rangle} Q_i, P \overset{a\langle \overline{m}.0\rangle}{\Longrightarrow} P_j \\
\qquad\qquad d_{i,j} := bisim(Q_i, P_j) \\
\qquad return((\bigwedge_i (\bigvee_j c_{i,j})) \wedge (\bigwedge_i (\bigvee_j d_{i,j}))). \\
match_{a!}(P,Q) = \\
\qquad m := nextSN(P,Q) \\
\qquad if\ P \xrightarrow{(\nu\widetilde{b})\overline{a}\langle E_i\rangle}\ and\ Q \overset{(\nu\widetilde{c})\overline{a}\langle F_j\rangle}{\not\Longrightarrow}\ then\ return(false) \\
\qquad if\ Q \xrightarrow{(\nu\widetilde{c})\overline{a}\langle F_i\rangle}\ and\ P \overset{(\nu\widetilde{b})\overline{a}\langle E_j\rangle}{\not\Longrightarrow}\ then\ return(false)
\end{array}
$$

$$
\begin{aligned}
&for\ each\ P \overset{(\nu\widetilde{b})\overline{a}\langle E_i\rangle}{\longrightarrow} P_i, Q \overset{(\nu\widetilde{c})\overline{a}\langle F_j\rangle}{\Longrightarrow} Q_j\\
&\qquad c_{i,j} := bisim((\nu\widetilde{b})(P_i|m.E_i),(\nu\widetilde{c})(Q_j|m.F_j))\\
&for\ each\ Q \overset{(\nu\widetilde{c})\overline{a}\langle F_i\rangle}{\longrightarrow} Q_i, P \overset{(\nu\widetilde{b})\overline{a}\langle E_j\rangle}{\Longrightarrow} P_j\\
&\qquad d_{i,j} := bisim((\nu\widetilde{c})(Q_i|m.F_i),(\nu\widetilde{b})(P_j|m.E_j))\\
&return((\bigwedge_i(\bigvee_j c_{i,j}))\wedge(\bigwedge_i(\bigvee_j d_{i,j}))).
\end{aligned}
$$

The algorithm is adapted from the algorithm for value-passing processes [1]. $NA(P) = \{\tau \mid \exists P'\ P \overset{\tau}{\longrightarrow} P'\} \cup \{l \mid \exists P'\ P \overset{l}{\longrightarrow} P'\} \cup \{\bar{l} \mid \exists P'\ P \overset{\bar{l}}{\longrightarrow} P'\} \cup \{a? \mid \exists P', m\ P \overset{a\langle\overline{m}.0\rangle}{\longrightarrow} P'\} \cup \{a! \mid \exists P', E\ P \overset{(\nu\widetilde{b})\overline{a}\langle E\rangle}{\longrightarrow} P'\}$. $NA(P) \cup NA(Q)$ is abbreviated as $NA(P,Q)$. It assumes a countably infinite subset $SN \subseteq N$ which is totally ordered. The function $nextSN(P,Q)$ returns the smallest name in SN that does not appear in the set of free names at states P and Q. We use $P \overset{\alpha}{\longrightarrow}$ to represent there exists P' such that $P \overset{\alpha}{\longrightarrow} P'$, and $Q \overset{\alpha}{\not\Longrightarrow}$ means there is no Q' such that $Q \overset{\alpha}{\Longrightarrow} Q'$.

The function $bisim(P,Q)$ starts with the initial pair (P,Q), trying to check the bisimilarity of P and Q by matching transitions from them. While travelling the normal transition graph, at each pair of nodes the algorithm produces the outgoing transitions and next states according to the operational semantics of linear processes. The transitions are then matched for bisimulation, and the algorithm goes on to the new state pairs if the matches are successful.

The function $match_\alpha$, performs a depth-first search on the product of the two normal transition graphs. If two states fail to match each other's transitions then they are not bisimilar and return $false$, otherwise return $true$.

4.3 The Correctness of *WBC*

The correctness of the algorithm for weak linear normal bisimulation is not difficult to justify. Each call of $match_\alpha(P,Q)$ performs a depth-first search in the product graph of the two normal transition graphs. $match_\alpha(P,Q)$ is recalled in the case of $d(P)+d(Q)$ has been decreased by at least one. This ensures that $match_\alpha(P,Q)$ can only be called for finitely many times. Therefore $bisim(P,Q)$ will always terminate. Furthermore we get the following proposition:

Proposition 4. *For any P, $Q \in Pr_L^c$, $bisim(P,Q)$ always terminates and $P \approx_{Ln} Q \Leftrightarrow P \approx_{Ct} Q \Leftrightarrow bisim(P,Q)$ returns true.*

Proof. By the above discussion and the definition of $\approx_{Ln}$, it is easy to see the correctness of WBC for $\approx_{Ln}$. Since by Proposition 2, $\approx_{Ln}$ and $\approx_{Ct}$ are coincident, the proposition holds. ∎

5 A Complete Inference System for Linear Higher Order π-Calculus

This section aims to provide a complete inference system, named WCE, for context bisimulation equivalence in the higher order π-calculus.

5.1 Context Congruence and Linear Normal Congruence

We know that $\approx_{Ct}$ is not fully substitutive: $P \approx_{Ct} Q$ does not imply $P+R \approx_{Ct} Q+R$. (For example, $b.0 \approx_{Ct} \tau.b.0$ while $a.0+b.0 \not\approx_{Ct} a.0+\tau.b.0$). So we cannot present a complete inference system for $\approx_{Ct}$. Hence similar to the case of CCS and π-calculus, we have to work with the modified relations: context congruence and linear normal congruence:

Definition 9. *We write $P \cong_{Ct} Q$, saying P and Q are weakly context congruent, if:*

(1) whenever $P \stackrel{\tau}{\longrightarrow} P'$, there exists Q' such that $Q \stackrel{\tau}{\Longrightarrow} Q'$ and $P' \approx_{Ct} Q'$;

(2) whenever $P \stackrel{\alpha}{\longrightarrow} P'$, there exists Q' such that $Q \stackrel{\alpha}{\Longrightarrow} Q'$, and $P' \approx_{Ct} Q'$, where α is in the form of l or $\bar{l}$;

(3) whenever $P \stackrel{a\langle E\rangle}{\longrightarrow} P'$, there exists Q' such that $Q \stackrel{a\langle E\rangle}{\Longrightarrow} Q'$ and $P' \approx_{Ct} Q'$;

(4) whenever $P \stackrel{(\nu\widetilde{b})\overline{a}\langle E\rangle}{\longrightarrow} P'$, there exist Q', F, $\widetilde{c}$ such that $Q \stackrel{(\nu\widetilde{c})\overline{a}\langle F\rangle}{\Longrightarrow} Q'$ and for all $C(U) \in Pr_L$ with $fn(C(U)) \cap \{\widetilde{b}, \widetilde{c}\} = \emptyset$, $(\nu\widetilde{b})(P'|C\langle E\rangle) \approx_{Ct} (\nu\widetilde{c})(Q'|C\langle F\rangle)$. Here $C(U)$ is a process containing a unique variable U.

Definition 10. *We write $P \cong_{Ln} Q$, saying P and Q are weakly linear normal congruent, if:*

(1) whenever $P \stackrel{\tau}{\longrightarrow} P'$, there exists Q' such that $Q \stackrel{\tau}{\Longrightarrow} Q'$ and $P' \approx_{Ln} Q'$;

(2) whenever $P \stackrel{\alpha}{\longrightarrow} P'$, there exists Q' such that $Q \stackrel{\alpha}{\Longrightarrow} Q'$, and $P' \approx_{Ln} Q'$, where α is in the form of l or $\bar{l}$;

(3) whenever $P \stackrel{a\langle\overline{m}.0\rangle}{\longrightarrow} P'$, there exists Q' such that $Q \stackrel{a\langle\overline{m}.0\rangle}{\Longrightarrow} Q'$ and $P' \approx_{Ln} Q'$, here m is a fresh name;

(4) whenever $P \stackrel{(\nu\widetilde{b})\overline{a}\langle E\rangle}{\longrightarrow} P'$, there exist Q', F, $\widetilde{c}$ such that $Q \stackrel{(\nu\widetilde{c})\overline{a}\langle F\rangle}{\Longrightarrow} Q'$, $(\nu\widetilde{b})(P'|m.E) \approx_{Ln} (\nu\widetilde{c})(Q'|m.F)$, here m is a fresh name.

5.2 The Equivalence between Weak Context Congruence and Weak Linear Normal Congruence for Pr_L^c

This section gives the equivalence between weak context congruence and weak linear normal congruence, which is used in the proof of soundness and completeness of the inference system.

Firstly, we show that $\cong_{Ct}$ is a congruence relation, i.e., preserved by all operators.

Lemma 9. *For all P, $Q \in Pr_L^c$, $P \cong_{Ct} Q$ implies*

(1) $\alpha.P \cong_{Ct} \alpha.Q$

(2) $P + R \cong_{Ct} Q + R$.

(3) $P|R \cong_{Ct} Q|R$.

(4) $(\nu a)P \cong_{Ct} (\nu a)Q$.

(5) $!P \cong_{Ct} !Q$.

(6) $\overline{a}\langle P\rangle.R \cong_{Ct} \overline{a}\langle Q\rangle.R$

Proof. Similar to Lemma 5. ∎

The following lemma is a higher order π-calculus version of Hennessy's Theorem.

Lemma 10. *For all* $P, Q \in Pr_L^c$, $P \approx_{Ct} Q$ *iff* ($P \cong_{Ct} Q$ *or* $P \cong_{Ct} \tau.Q$ *or* $\tau.P \cong_{Ct} Q$)

Now we can give the equivalence between $\cong_{Ln}$ and $\cong_{Ct}$.

Proposition 5. *For all* $P, Q \in Pr_L^c$, $P \cong_{Ln} Q$ *iff* $P \cong_{Ct} Q$.

Proof. Similar to Proposition 2. ∎

5.3 Inference System WCE for Pr_L^c

The following rules give an inference system of weak context congruence for Pr_L^c. We write this inference system as WCE.

1. $P = P$
2. $P = Q \Rightarrow Q = P$
3. $P = Q$ and $Q = R \Rightarrow P = R$
4. $P = Q \Rightarrow \bar{l}.P = \bar{l}.Q$
5. $P = Q \Rightarrow l.P = l.Q$
6. $P = Q \Rightarrow \tau.P = \tau.Q$
7. $P = Q \Rightarrow P + R = Q + R$
8. $P = Q \Rightarrow P|R = Q|R$
9. $P = Q \Rightarrow (\nu a)P = (\nu a)Q$
10. $P + 0 = P$
11. $P + P = P$
12. $P + Q = Q + P$
13. $P + (Q + R) = (P + Q) + R$
14. $P|0 = P$
15. $P|Q = \sum_{i\in I}(\nu\widetilde{b_i})(\alpha_i.(P_i|Q)) + \sum_{j\in J}(\nu\widetilde{c_j})(\beta_j.(P|Q_j)) + \sum_{\alpha_i\ opp\ \beta_j}\tau.R_{i,j}$, where $P = \sum_{i\in I}(\nu\widetilde{b_i})(\alpha_i.P_i)$ and $Q = \sum_{j\in J}(\nu\widetilde{c_j})(\beta_j.Q_j)$, α_i *opp* β_j and $R_{i,j}$ are defined as follows:
    (a) $\alpha_i \equiv a, \beta_j \equiv \bar{a}$; then $R_{i,j} \equiv (\nu\widetilde{b_i})P_i|(\nu\widetilde{c_j})Q_j$, where $a \notin \widetilde{b_i} \cup \widetilde{c_j}$;
    (b) $\alpha_i \equiv \bar{a}, \beta_j \equiv a$; then $R_{i,j} \equiv (\nu\widetilde{b_i})P_i|(\nu\widetilde{c_j})Q_j$, where $a \notin \widetilde{b_i} \cup \widetilde{c_j}$;
    (c) $\alpha_i \equiv a(U), \beta_j \equiv \bar{a}\langle E\rangle$; then $R_{i,j} \equiv (\nu\widetilde{c_j})((\nu\widetilde{b_i})P_i\{E/U\}|Q_j)$, where $a \notin \widetilde{b_i} \cup \widetilde{c_j}$;
    (d) $\alpha_i \equiv \bar{a}\langle E\rangle, \beta_j \equiv a(U)$; then $R_{i,j} \equiv (\nu\widetilde{b_i})(P_i|(\nu\widetilde{c_j})Q_j\{E/U\})$, where $a \notin \widetilde{b_i} \cup \widetilde{c_j}$.
16. $\alpha.\tau.P = \alpha.P$
17. $P + \tau.P = \tau.P$
18. $(\nu\widetilde{a})(\alpha.(P + \tau.Q)) + (\nu\widetilde{a})(\alpha.Q) = (\nu\widetilde{a})(\alpha.(P + \tau.Q))$
19. $(\nu a)0 = 0$
20. $(\nu a)(\nu b)P = (\nu b)(\nu a)P$
21. $(\nu a)(P + Q) = (\nu a)P + (\nu a)Q$
22. $(\nu a)(\alpha.P) = \alpha.(\nu a)P$ if $a \notin n(\alpha)$

23. $(\nu a)(\alpha.P) = 0$ if a is the port of α
24. $P\{\overline{m}.0/U\} = Q\{\overline{m}.0/U\}$ with a new name $m \Rightarrow a(U).P = a(U).Q$
25. $\tau.(\nu\widetilde{b})(P|m.E) = \tau.(\nu\widetilde{c})(Q|m.F)$ with a new name $m \Rightarrow (\nu\widetilde{b})(\overline{a}\langle E\rangle.P) = (\nu\widetilde{c})(\overline{a}\langle F\rangle.Q)$

This inference system includes two parts: One part consists of Rules 1-23, which is similar to the algebra theory of CCS. The other part consists of Rules 24 and 25, which mainly describes the algebra laws of higher order input and output actions. Rule 24 is the algebra description of higher order input action where universal quantification is eliminated. Rule 25 is the algebra description of higher order output action where universal quantification and replication operator do not appear. The soundness and completeness of the inference system can be derived from the coincidence between weak context congruence and weak linear normal congruence.

5.4 The Soundness and Completeness of the Inference System *WCE*

In this section, we will prove the soundness and completeness of WCE. Firstly we prove the soundness of WCE, whose proof relies on the equivalence between $\cong_{Ln}$ and $\cong_{Ct}$ for Pr^c_L. We write $WCE \vdash P = Q$ if there is a proof of $P = Q$ in the inference system WCE.

Proposition 6. *For any $P, Q \in Pr^c_L$, $WCE \vdash P = Q$ implies $P \cong_{Ct} Q$.*

Now we are ready to prove the completeness of WCE. The proof strategy is similar to the case of CCS. Firstly, we prove that for every process there is an equivalent normal form process (called full standard form process) which can be rewritten by WCE. Then by induction over the depth of processes, we prove that for any full standard form processes P and Q, $P \cong_{Ct} Q$ implies $WCE \vdash P = Q$. After that, the completeness of WCE is obvious.

Definition 11. *A process P is in standard form if $P \equiv \sum_{i=1}^{m}(\nu\widetilde{b})(\alpha_i.P_i)$, where P_i is also in standard form, $\widetilde{b} = \emptyset$ if α_i is not a higher order output action, and E_i is also in standard form if $\alpha_i = \overline{a}\langle E_i\rangle$.*

Lemma 11. *For any process P there is a standard form process Q of not greater depth such that $WCE \vdash P = Q$.*

Definition 12. *P is a full standard form if*

(1) $P \equiv \sum_{i=1}^{m}(\nu\widetilde{b})\alpha_i.P_i$, where each P_i is in full standard form, and E_i is also in full standard form if $\alpha_i = \overline{a}\langle E_i\rangle$;

(2) whenever $P \stackrel{(\nu\widetilde{b})\alpha}{\Longrightarrow} P'$ then $P \stackrel{(\nu\widetilde{b})\alpha}{\longrightarrow} P'$.

Lemma 12. *If $P \stackrel{(\nu\widetilde{b})\alpha}{\Longrightarrow} P'$ then $WCE \vdash P = P + (\nu\widetilde{b})(\alpha.P')$.*

Lemma 13. *For any standard form P there is a full standard form P' of equal depth, such that $WCE \vdash P = P'$.*

Proposition 7. *For any $P, Q \in Pr_L^c$, $P \cong_{Ct} Q$ implies $WCE \vdash P = Q$.*

By Propositions 6 and 7, the soundness and completeness of WCE is stated as follows:

Proposition 8. *The inference system WCE is sound and complete for $\cong_{Ct}$ over Pr_L^c.*

For Pr_L^c, we can similarly define weak normal congruence $\cong_{Nr}$, and prove that it coincides with $\cong_{Ct}$ and $\cong_{Ln}$. Since WCE is a sound and complete inference system for $\cong_{Ct}$, it is also sound and complete for $\cong_{Nr}$.

6 Conclusions

In this paper, we present an algorithm for checking weak context bisimulation over a linear higher order π-calculus. To achieve this aim, we present a new bisimulation, called linear normal bisimulation, and prove that it coincides with context bisimulation for our linear higher order π-calculus. Furthermore, we give an inference system for this linear higher order π-calculus.

One may have a question whether we can give a checking algorithm or an inference system for Pr_A^c. Unfortunately, the answer is negative. Parrow [11] has shown that the behavior of regular higher order π-calculus can be simulated by Pr_A^c under the sense of weak bisimulation. If there is a checking algorithm for Pr_A^c, then the bisimilarity of Pr_A^c is semi-decidable. Hence the bisimilarity of regular higher order π-calculus is also semi-decidable. But it is impossible since the expressive power of higher order π-calculus is very powerful. In CCS and π-calculus, there were some checking algorithms and some inference systems for the finite-control subclass which does not allow the | operator to occur in a recursively defined process [8,9]. But seeking checking algorithm or inference system for the finite-control higher order π-calculus seems a challenging problem.

References

1. Hennessy, M., Lin, H.: Symbolic bisimulations. Theoretical Computer Science 138, 353–389 (1995)
2. Hennessy, M., Lin, H.: Proof systems for message-passing process algebras. Formal Aspects of Computing 8, 379–407 (1996)
3. Jeffrey, A., Rathke, J.: Contextual equivalence for higher-order π-calculus revisited. In: Proceedings of Mathematical Foundations of Programming Semantics, Elsevier, Amsterdam (2003)
4. Jonsson, B., Parrow, J.: Deciding bisimulation equivalences for a class of non-finite-state program. Information and Computation 107, 272–302 (1993)
5. Larsen, K.G.: Efficient local correctness checking (extended abstract). In: Probst, D.K., von Bochmann, G. (eds.) CAV 1992. LNCS, vol. 663, pp. 30–43. Springer, Heidelberg (1993)
6. Li, Z., Chen, H.: Checking strong/weak bisimulation equivalences and observation congruence for the π-calculus. In: Larsen, K.G., Skyum, S., Winskel, G. (eds.) ICALP 1998. LNCS, vol. 1443, pp. 707–718. Springer, Heidelberg (1998)

7. Lin, H.: Complete proof systems for observation congruence in finite-control π-calculus. In: Larsen, K.G., Skyum, S., Winskel, G. (eds.) ICALP 1998. LNCS, vol. 1443, pp. 443–454. Springer, Heidelberg (1998)
8. Lin, H.: Computing bisimulations for finite-control π -calculus. Journal of Computer Science and Technology 15(1), 1–9 (2000)
9. Lin, H.: Complete inference systems for weak bisimulation equivalences in the π-calculus. Information and Computation 180(1), 1–29 (2003)
10. Milner, R.: Communication and Concurrency. Prentice-Hall, Englewood Cliffs (1989)
11. Parrow, J.: An introduction to the π-calculus. In: Bergstra, J., Ponse, A., Smolka, S. (eds.) Handbook of Process Algebra, North-Holland, Amsterdam (2001)
12. Parrow, J., Sangiorgi, D.: Algebraic theories for name-passing calculi. Information and Computation 120(2), 174–197 (1995)
13. Sangiorgi, D.: Expressing mobility in process algebras: first-order and higher-order paradigms. Ph.D thesis, Department of Computer Science, University of Einburgh (1992)
14. Sangiorgi, D.: Bisimulation in higher-order calculi. Information and Computation 131(2) (1996)
15. Thomsen, B.: Calculus for higher order communicating systems. Ph.D thesis, Department of Computer, Imperial College (1990)
16. Thomsen, B.: Plain *CHOCS*: A second generation calculus for higher order processes. Acta Informatica 30, 1–59 (1993)

Finding Counter Examples in Induction Proofs

Koen Claessen and Hans Svensson

Chalmers University of Technology, Gothenburg, Sweden
{koen,hanssv}@chalmers.se

Abstract. This paper addresses a problem arising in automated proof of invariants of transition systems, for example transition systems modelling distributed programs. Most of the time, the actual properties we want to prove are too weak to hold inductively, and auxiliary invariants need to be introduced. The problem is how to find these extra invariants. We propose a method where we find *minimal counter examples* to candidate invariants by means of *automated random testing* techniques. These counter examples can be inspected by a human user, and used to adapt the set of invariants at hand. We are able to find two different kinds of counter examples, either indicating (1) that the used invariants are too strong (a concrete trace of the system violates at least one of the invariants), or (2) that the used invariants are too weak (a concrete transition of the system does not maintain all invariants). We have developed and evaluated our method in the context of formally verifying an industrial-strength implementation of a fault-tolerant distributed leader election protocol.

1 Introduction

This paper gives a partial report on our experiences on using (semi-)automated theorem proving to formally verify safety properties of an industrial-strength implementation of a fault-tolerant leader election protocol in the programming language Erlang [19].

Leader election is a basic technique in distributed systems; a fixed set of processes has to determine a special process, the *leader*, among them. There is one basic safety property of such algorithms ("there should never be more than one leader"), and one basic liveness property ("eventually there should be one leader"). In *fault-tolerant* leader election, processes can die and be restarted at any point in time (during or after the election), making the problem immensely tricky.

Erlang is a language for distributed programming originally developed for implementing telecommunication systems at Ericson [3,2]. A key feature of the systems for which Erlang was primarily designed is fault-tolerance; Erlang has therefore built-in support for handling failing processes.

The implementation of the leader election algorithm we verified was developed by us, after we had uncovered some subtle bugs in an earlier existing implementation using testing techniques [4]. Our new implementation is based on an adaptation of a standard fault-tolerant leader election algorithm by Stoller [18] and is

B. Beckert and R. Hähnle (Eds.): TAP 2008, LNCS 4966, pp. 48–65, 2008.

now a standard library in Erlang. In our implementation, we had to make some changes to Stoller's original algorithm because of the way processes communicate in Erlang (via asynchronous message passing over unbounded channels) and the way fault-tolerance is handled in Erlang (a process can monitor another process, in which case it receives a special message when the other process dies).

From our previous experience, we knew that it is extremely hard to get these kinds of algorithms right. Indeed, we started by extensively testing the new implementation using our testing techniques [4], leading to our increased confidence in the correctness of the implementation. However, we had some reasons to be cautious. Firstly, our implementation was based on an adaptation of Stoller's original algorithm, so even if Stoller's algorithm were correct, our adaptation of it might not be. Secondly, Stoller never gives a formal proof of correctness in his paper [18]. His algorithm is in turn an adaptation of a classical leader election algorithm (called "The Bully Algorithm") by Garcia-Molina, which in turn only has been proven correct in the paper in a very informal way [12]. Stoller claims that his modifications are so minor that giving a new proof is not needed: *"The proofs that the Bully$_{FD}$ Algorithm satisfies SLE1 and SLE2 are very similar to the proofs of Theorems A1 and A2 in [GM82] and are therefore omitted."*

When we decided to formally verify our implementation, we first tried a number of different model checking methods (among others SPIN [13] and our own model checker McErlang [11]). Unfortunately, these could only be used for extremely small and unconvincing bounds on the number of processes, sizes of message queues, and number of times processes can die. This is partially due to the huge state space generated by the combination of asynchronous message passing and fault-tolerance.

The alternative we eventually settled on was to prove invariants of the system inductively by means of automated first-order logic theorem proving. Here, we model the implementation as an abstract transition system, and express the properties we want to prove as invariants on the states of the transition system. The reasons we chose this approach were (1) using first-order logic allowed us to prove the implementation correct for any number of processes, using unbounded message queues and an unbounded number of occurring faults, and (2) automated first-order theorem provers are relatively autonomous, in principle only requiring us to interact with the verification process at the level of choosing the invariants.

The main obstacle in this approach is that, most often, the (relatively small) set of invariants one is interested in establishing is not inductively provable. This means that the original set of invariants has to be strengthened by changing some of the invariants or by augmenting the set with new invariants, until the set is strong enough to be inductive. Very often, this is a non-trivial and labour-intensive task. In our case, we started with one invariant ("there should not be more than one leader") and we ended up with a set of 89 invariants. This is the sense in which we call our method *semi-automated*; if the right set of invariants is picked (manually), the proof is carried out automatically. Thus, the user of the method does not have to carry out proofs, but only has to formulate proof obligations.

The task of finding the right set of invariants is not only non-trivial, but can also be highly frustrating. The reason is that it is very easy for a user, in an attempt to make the set of invariants stronger, to add properties to the set which are in fact not invariants. When certain invariants can not be proven, the first-order theorem provers we use do not in general provide any reason as to why this is the case, leaving the user in the dark about what needs to be done in order to get the proof through.

We identified 4 different reasons for why a failed proof of a given invariant occurs: (1) the invariant is invalid, i.e. there exists a path from the initial state to a state where the invariant is falsified, (2) the invariant is valid, but too weak, i.e. it indeed holds in all reachable states, but it is not maintained by the transition relation, (3) the invariant is valid and is maintained by the transition relation, but the current axiomatization of the background theories is too weak, and (4) the invariant is valid and should be provable, but the theorem prover at hand does not have enough resources to do so.

The remedies for being in each of these cases are very different: For (1), one would have to weaken the invariant at hand; for (2) one would have to strengthen it; for (3) one would have to come up with extra axioms or induction principles; for (4) one would have to wait longer or break the problem up into smaller bits.

Having a concrete counter example to a proof attempt would show the difference between cases (1), (2) and (3). Thus, having a way of finding counter examples would greatly increase the productivity of the proposed verification method. Providing counter models to first-order formulas (or to formulas in more complex logics) is however an undecidable problem.

We have developed two novel methods, based on random property-based testing using the automated testing tool QuickCheck [9], that, by automatically re-using the invariants as test generators and test oracles, can automatically and effectively find counter examples of categories (1) and (2). Finding counter examples of category (3) remains future work.

Establishing inductive invariants is a very common method for verifying software (in particular in object-oriented programs, see for example [5,21]). We believe that the methods for finding counter examples in this paper can be adapted to other situations than verifying distributed algorithms.

The contributions of this paper are:

- A classification of different categories of counter examples in the process of establishing inductive invariants using a theorem prover
- Two methods for finding two of the most common categories of counter examples based on random testing
- An evaluation of the methods in the context of the verification of an industrial-strength implementation of a leader election protocol

The rest of the paper is organized as follows. The next section explains the method of verification we use in more detail. Section 3 explains the testing techniques we use. Section 4 reports on the results of our method in the verification of the leader election implementation. Section 5 concludes.

2 Verification Method

In this section, we describe the basic verification method we use to prove invariants. The method is quite standard; an earlier description of the method in the context of automated first-order logic reasoning tools can be found in [8]. The system under verification and the invariants are described using three components:

- A predicate *Init* describing the initial state,
- A predicate *Inv* describing the invariant,
- A predicate transformer [*Sys*] that abstractly describes one transition of the system.

For the predicate transformers, we borrow notation also used in dynamic logic [5] and the B-method [1,21]. For a program S and a post-condition Q, we write $[S]Q$ to be the weakest pre-condition for S that establishes Q as a post-condition. This in turn means that we can write

$$P \rightarrow [S]\, Q$$

which has the same meaning as the Hoare triple $\{P\}S\{Q\}$; in all states where P holds, making the transition described by S leads to states where Q holds.

The language we use to describe *Sys* is very simple. The three most important constructs are assignments, conditionals, and non-deterministic choice. The definition of predicate transformers we use is completely standard, and we will only briefly discuss the concepts here. For more details, the reader can consult [21]. Here are the definitions for the predicate transformers for assignments, conditionals, and non-deterministic choice, respectively.

$$\begin{aligned} [x := e]\, P &= P\{e/x\} \\ [\mathbf{if}\, Q\, \mathbf{then}\, S\, \mathbf{else}\, T]\, P &= (Q \rightarrow [S]P) \wedge (\neg Q \rightarrow [T]P) \\ [S \mid T]\, P &= [S]P \wedge [T]P \end{aligned}$$

Establishing *Inv* as an invariant amounts to proving the following two statements:

$$\begin{aligned} &\mathit{Init} \rightarrow \mathit{Inv} \\ &\mathit{Inv} \rightarrow [\mathit{Sys}]\, \mathit{Inv} \end{aligned}$$

In practice, *Inv* is really a conjunction of a number of smaller invariants:

$$\begin{aligned} \mathit{Init} &\rightarrow \mathit{Inv}_1 \wedge \mathit{Inv}_2 \wedge \cdots \wedge \mathit{Inv}_n \\ \mathit{Inv}_1 \wedge \mathit{Inv}_2 \wedge \cdots \wedge \mathit{Inv}_n &\rightarrow [\mathit{Sys}]\, (\mathit{Inv}_1 \wedge \mathit{Inv}_2 \wedge \cdots \wedge \mathit{Inv}_n) \end{aligned}$$

The above two proof obligations are split up into several sub-obligations; for the initial states, we prove, for all i, several obligations of the form:

$$Init \rightarrow Inv_i$$

For the transitions, we prove, for all i, several obligations of the form:

$$\left(\bigwedge_{j \in P_i} Inv_j\right) \rightarrow [Sys]\, Inv_i$$

So, for each invariant conjunct Inv_i, we have a subset of the invariants P_i that we use as a pre-condition for establishing Inv_i. Logically, we can use all invariants Inv_j as pre-condition, but in practice the resulting proof obligations would become too large to be manageable by the theorem provers we use. Also, from a proof engineering point of view, it is good to "localize" dependencies, so that when the set of invariants changes, we only have to redo the proofs for the obligations that were involved in the invariants we changed. (Note that the set P_i can actually include the invariant Inv_i itself.)

To simplify the problems as much possible, we also use an aggressive case splitting strategy, in the same way as described in [8]. Thus each of the above proof obligations is proved in many small steps.

In Fig. 1 we show an example of an invariant. The function `host`(p) returns the host for a given process p, the predicate **elem**(m, q) is true if a message m is present in a message queue q. In this example we have an incoming message queue `queue`(h) for each host h. (This simplification from having a message queue per process is possible since there is only one process alive per host.)

```
∀Pid, Pid2.(
  (elem(m_Halt(Pid),
              queue(host(Pid2)))
     → (host(Pid2) > host(Pid))
  )
)
```

The invariant states that `Halt`-messages are only sent to processes with lower priority: If there is a `Halt`-message from *Pid* in the queue of `host`(*Pid2*), then *host(Pid2)* is larger than *host(Pid)*. (Hosts with low numbers have high priority.)

Fig. 1. Example invariant

2.1 Failed Proof Attempts

This paper deals with the problem of what to do when a proof attempt of one of the proof obligations fails. Let us look at what can be the reason for a failed proof attempt when proving the proof obligations related to a particular candidate invariant Inv_i. We can identify 4 different reasons:

(1) The candidate invariant Inv_i is not an invariant of the system; there exists a reachable state of the system that falsifies Inv_i.

(2) The candidate invariant Inv_i actually is an invariant of the system, but it is not an inductive invariant. This means that there exists an (unreachable)

state where all invariants in the pre-condition set P_i of Inv_i are true, but after a transition, Inv_i is not true. This means that the proof obligation for the transition for Inv_i cannot be proven.

(3) The candidate invariant Inv_i actually is an invariant of the system, and it is an inductive invariant. However, our background theory is not strong enough to establish this fact. The background theory contains axioms about message queues, in what order messages arrive, what happens when processes die, etc. If these are not strong enough, the proof obligation for the transition for Inv_i cannot be proven.

(4) The proof obligations are provable, but the theorem prover we use does not have enough resources, and thus a correctness proof cannot be established.

When a proof attempt for a proof obligation fails, it is vital to be able to distinguish between these 4 cases. The remedies in each of these cases are different:

For (1), we have to *weaken* the invariant Inv_i, or perhaps remove it from the set of invariants altogether.

For (2), we have to *strengthen* the set of pre-conditions P_i. We can do this by strengthening some invariants in P_i (including Inv_i itself), or by adding a new invariant to the set of invariants and to P_i.

For (3), we have to *strengthen* the background theory by adding more axioms.

For (4), we have to *simplify* the problem by for example using explicit case-splitting, or perhaps to give the theorem prover more time.

2.2 Identifying the Categories

How can we identify which of the cases (1)-(4) we are in? A first-order logic theorem prover does not give any feedback in general when it does not find a proof. Some theorem provers, including the ones we used (Vampire [20], E-prover [16], SPASS [10], and Equinox [7]) do provide feedback in certain cases, for example in the form of a finite-domain counter model or a saturation, but this hardly ever happens in practice.

One observation that we can make is that for cases (1)-(3), there exist counter examples of different kinds to the proof obligations.

For (1), the counter example is a concrete trace from the initial state to the reachable state that falsifies the invariant Inv_i.

For (2), the counter example is a concrete state that makes the pre-conditions P_i true, but after one transition the invariant Inv_i does not hold anymore.

For (3), the counter example is a concrete counter model that makes the background theory true but falsifies the proof obligation. This counter model must be a *non-standard* model of the background theory, since the proof obligation is true for every standard model (which is implied by the fact that no concrete counter example of kind (2) exists).

We would like to argue that, if the user were given feedback consisting of (a) the category of counter example above, and (b) the concrete counter example, it would greatly improve productivity in invariant-based verification.

In the next section, we show how we can use techniques from random testing to find counter examples of type (1) and (2) above. We have not solved the problem of how to find counter examples of type (3), which remains future work. (This is an unsolvable problem in general because of the semi-decidability of first-order logic.) Luckily, cases (1) and (2) are most common in practice, because, in our experience, the background theory stabilizes quite quickly after the start of such a project.

We would like to point out a general note on the kind of counter examples we are looking for. Counter examples of type (1) are counter examples in a logic in which we can define transitive closure of the transition relation. This is necessarily a logic that goes beyond first-order logic. This logic for us exists only on the meta-level, since we are merely performing the induction base case and step case with theorem provers that can not reason about induction. Counter examples of type (2) are only counter examples of the induction step (and do not necessarily imply the existence of counter examples of the first kind). In some sense, these can be seen as non-standard counter examples of the logic used in type (1) counter examples. Counter examples of type (3) are also counter examples of the induction step, but they do not follow the intended behavior of our function and predicate symbols, and are therefore non-standard counter examples of the induction step.

3 Finding Counter Examples by Random Testing

This section describes the random testing techniques that we used to find concrete counter examples to the proof obligations.

3.1 QuickCheck

QuickCheck [9] is a tool for performing specification-based random testing, originally developed for the programming language Haskell. QuickCheck defines a simple executable specification logic, in which universal quantification over a set is implemented as performing random tests using a particular distribution. The distribution is specified by means of providing a test data generator. QuickCheck comes equipped with random generators for basic types (Integers, Booleans, Pairs, Lists, etc) and combinator functions, from which it is fairly easy to build generators for more complex data structures.

When QuickCheck finds a failing test case (a test case that falsifies a property), it tries to *shrink* this test case by successively checking if smaller variants of the original failing test case are still failing cases. When the shrinking process terminates, a (locally) minimal failing test case is presented to the user. The user can provide custom shrinking functions that specify what simplifications should be tried on the failing case. This is a method akin to *delta debugging* [22].

For example, if we find a randomly generated concrete trace which makes an invariant fail, the shrinking function says that we should try removing one step from the trace to see if it is still a counter example. When the shrinking process fails, the trace we produce is minimal in the sense that every step in the trace is needed to make the invariant fail. One should note that it is very valuable to have short counter examples; it drastically reduces the time spent on analyzing and fixing the errors found.

3.2 Trace Counter Examples

A *trace counter example* is a counter example of type (1) in the previous section. We decided to search for trace counter examples in the following manner (this is inspired by 'State Machine Specifications' in [14]). Given a set of participating processes, we can construct an exhaustive list of possible operations (examples of operations could be: process X receives a `Halt`-message, process Y crashes, process Z is started, etc). We constructed a QuickCheck generator that returns a random sequence of operations. To test the invariant we then create the initial state for the system (where all participants are dead and all message queues are empty) and apply the operation sequence. The result is a sequence of states, and in each state we check that the invariant holds.

If a counter example to the invariant is found, shrinking is performed by simply removing some operations. To further shrink a test case we also try to remove one of the participating processes (together with its operations). We illustrate how all of this works with the (trivially incorrect) invariant $\forall Pid. \neg isLeader(Pid)$ (i.e. there is never a leader elected). Formulated in QuickCheck, the property looks as follows:

```
prop_NeverALeader =
  \path -> checkPath leStoller (forAll pid (nott (isLeader pid))) path
```

We use the function `checkPath`, which takes three arguments: a model of an Erlang program (in this case `leStoller`), a first-order formula (the property) and a trace (called `path`), and checks that the given formula is true for all states encountered on the specified path. The QuickCheck property states that the result should be true for all paths. Running QuickCheck yields:

```
*QCTraceCE> quickCheck prop_NeverALeader
*** Failed! Falsifiable (after 3 tests and 3 shrinks):
Path 1 [AcStart 1]
```

The counter example is a path involving one process (indicated by "`Path 1`", and one step where we start that process (indicated by "`AcStart 1`"), and clearly falsifies the property. (The leader election algorithm is such that if there is only a single participant, it is elected immediately when it is started.) This counter example has been shrunk, in 3 shrinking steps, from an initial, much larger, counter example. The steps it went through, removing unnecessary events, in this case were:

```
Path 1 [AcOnMsg 1 AcLdr,AcOnMsg 1 AcDown,AcOnMsg 1 AcAck,AcOnMsg 1 AcHalt,
        AcStart 1,AcStart 1,AcOnMsg 1 AcNormQ,AcPer 1]
Path 1 [AcStart 1,AcStart 1,AcOnMsg 1 AcNormQ,AcPer 1]
Path 1 [AcStart 1,AcStart 1]
Path 1 [AcStart 1]
```

Here, "`AcOnMsg` p m" indicates that process p receives a message of type m. The different message types ("`AcLdr`", "`AcDown`", "`AcAck`", etc.) are part of the internal details of Stoller's leader election protocol [18] and are not explained here.

Being able to quickly generate locally minimal counter examples to candidate invariants greatly improved our productivity in constructing a correct set of invariants.

3.3 Induction Step Counter Examples

Step counter examples are counter examples of type (2). To find step counter examples is more challenging. Step counter examples can be expected when the stated invariant holds, but its pre-conditions are too *weak* to be proved. The proof fails in the step case, that is there exists a (**non**-reachable) state s such that the invariant is true in s, but false in some state s', such that $s' \in next(s)$. The difference from trace counter examples is that we are now looking for non-reachable states, which are significantly harder to generate in a good way.

Our first, very naive, try was to simply generate completely random states, and check if the proof obligation can be falsified by these. We implemented this strategy by constructing a random generator for states and tried to use QuickCheck in the straightforward way. However, not surprisingly, this fails miserably. The reason is that it is very unlikely for a randomly generated state to fulfill all pre-conditions of the proof obligation for the transition. Other naive approaches, such as enumerating states in some way, do not work either, since the number of different states are unfeasibly large, even with very small bounds on the number of processes and number of messages in message queues.

The usual way to solve this in QuickCheck testing is to make a *custom generator* whose results are very likely to fulfill a certain condition. However, this is completely unpractical to do by hand for an evolving set of about 90 invariants.

Instead, we implemented a *test data generator generator*. Given a first-order formula ϕ, our generator-generator automatically constructs a random test data generator which generates states that are very likely to fulfill ϕ. So, instead of manually writing a generator for each invariant Inv_i, we use the generator-generator to generate one. We then use the resulting generator in QuickCheck to check that the property holds.

Our generator-generator, given a formula ϕ, works as follows. Below, we define a process, called `adapt` that, given a formula ϕ and a state s, modifies s so that it is more likely to make ϕ true. The generator first generates a completely random state s, and then successively *adapts* s to ϕ a number of times. The exact number of times can be given as a parameter.

The `adapt` process works as follows. Given a formula ϕ and a state s, we do the following:

1 Check if s fulfills ϕ. If so, then we return s.
2 Otherwise, look at the structure of ϕ.
   - If ϕ is a conjunction $\phi_1 \wedge \phi_2$, recursively adapt s to the left-hand conjunct ϕ_1, and then adapt the result to the right-hand conjunct ϕ_2.

- If ϕ is a disjunction $\phi_1 \vee \phi_2$, randomly pick a disjunct ϕ_i, and adapt s to it.
- If ϕ starts with a universal quantifier $\forall x \in S.\psi(x)$, S will be concretely specified by the state s. We construct a big explicit conjunction $\bigwedge_{x \in S} \psi(x)$, and adapt s to it.
- If ϕ starts with an existential quantifier $\exists x \in S.\psi(x)$, construct a big explicit disjunction $\bigvee_{x \in S} \psi(x)$, and adapt s to it.
- If ϕ is a negated formula, push the negations inwards and adapt s to the non-negated formula.
- If ϕ is a (possibly negated) atomic formula, change s so that the atomic formula is true, if we know how to (see below). Otherwise, just return s.

Quantifiers in ϕ always quantify over things occurring in the state s, for example the set of all processes, or the set of all processes currently alive, etc. When adapting s to ϕ, these sets are known, so we can create explicit conjunctions or disjunctions instead of quantifiers.

When randomly picking a disjunct, we let the distribution be dependent on the size of the disjuncts; it is more likely here to pick a large disjunct than a small disjunct. This was added to make the process more fair when dealing with a disjunction of many things (represented as a number of binary disjunctions).

Finally, we have to add cases that adapt a given state s to the atomic formulae. The more cases we add here, the better our adapt function becomes. Here are some examples of atomic formulae occurring in ϕ, and how we adapt s to them:

- "message queue $q1$ is empty", in this case we change the state s such that $q1$ becomes empty;
- "process $p1$ is not alive", in this case we remove $p1$ from the set of alive processes in s;
- "queue $q1$ starts with the message $Halt$", in this case we simply add the message $Halt$ to the queue $q1$.

Note that there is no guarantee that an adapted state satisfies the formula. For example, when adapting to a conjunction, the adaption process of the right-hand conjunct might very well undo the adaption of the left-hand conjunct. It turns out that successively adapting a state to a formula several times increase the likelihood of fulfilling the formula. There is a general trade-off between adapting a few states many times or adapting many states fewer times. The results of our experiments suggest that adapting the same state 4-8 times is preferable (Sect. 4).

The final property we give to QuickCheck looks as follows; remember the problem

$$\left(\bigwedge_{j \in P_i} Inv_j \right) \rightarrow [Sys]\, Inv_i$$

and let `invs` be the left hand side of the implication, `inv` is Inv_i and `applySys` corresponds to the []-operation:

```
prop_StepProofObligation invs inv sys =
  \state ->
    forAll (adapt formula state) $ \state' ->
      checkProperty formula state'
  where formula = and (nott inv' : invs)
        inv'    = applySys sys inv
```

This can be read as: For all states s, and for all adaptions s' of that state s to the proof obligation, the proof obligation should hold. The function `adapt` is our implementation of the adapt generator-generator, and `checkProperty` checks if a given formula is true in a given state. Remember that we want to find a counter example state, that is why we try to adapt the state so that the pre-conditions (`invs`) are fulfilled but `inv'` is not.

The experimental results are discussed in the next section.

4 Results

In this section we present some results from the usage of search for counter examples in the verification of the leader election algorithm. Since the data comes from only one verification project it might not be statistically convincing, but it should be enough to give some idea of how well the search for counter examples works in practice.

4.1 Trace Counter Examples

To illustrate the effectiveness of trace counter examples we first show one particular example. In Fig. 2 we see an invariant A that was added to the set of pre-conditions in order to be able to prove another invariant B (i.e. this was the action taken after a failed proof attempt in category 2, as described in Sect. 2.1). The original invariant B was easily proved after this addition, however we could not prove the new invariant A. After several days of failed proof attempts, we managed to (manually) find a counter example. The counter example was really intricate, involving four different nodes and a non-trivial sequence of events.

With this unsatisfying experience in fresh memory, we were eager to try the trace counter example finder on this particular example. The result was very positive, the counter example was quickly found (in the presented run after 170 tests), and we could quickly verify that it was equivalent to the counter example that we found manually. The result of the QuickCheck run on this example is presented in Fig. 3.

The counter example consists of a `Path` value. From this value we can conclude that the counter example involves four processes. We can also see the sequence of operations leading to a state where the invariant is falsified. This sequence contains five process starts (`AcStart`), three process crashes (`AcCrash`) and two receives of `Down`-messages by process number 3 (`AcOnMsg`). It is interesting to see that the fourth process is never started, and never actually does anything, nevertheless it must be present in order to falsify the invariant (or else the shrinking would have removed it).

$$
\begin{array}{l}
\forall Pid, Pid2, Pid3.((\\
\quad ((Pid \in \texttt{alive}) \\
\quad\; \wedge\ \mathbf{elem}(\texttt{m\_Down}(Pid2), \\
\qquad\qquad \texttt{queue}(\texttt{host}(Pid))) \\
\quad\; \wedge\ (\texttt{lesser}(\texttt{host}(Pid)) \subseteq \\
\qquad\quad (\texttt{down}[\texttt{host}(Pid)] \cup \{\texttt{host}(Pid2)\})) \\
\quad\; \wedge\ (\texttt{status}[\texttt{host}(Pid)] = \texttt{elec\_1})) \\
\quad\; \rightarrow \neg((\texttt{pendack}[\texttt{host}(Pid3)] > \texttt{host}(Pid)) \\
\qquad\quad \wedge\ (Pid3 \in \texttt{alive}) \\
\qquad\quad \wedge\ (\texttt{status}[\texttt{host}(Pid3)] = \texttt{elec\_2})) \\
\quad) \\
)
\end{array}
$$

Whenever a process (Pid) is alive, in the first election phase (`elec_1`) and it receives a `Down`-message such that Pid has received `Down`-messages from everyone with higher priority (that is the hosts in the set `lesser(host(`Pid`)))`. Then no other process (here $Pid3$) is alive, in the second election phase and having communicated with Pid (i.e. having a `pendack` value larger than `host(`Pid`))`.

Fig. 2. A broken invariant

```
*** Failed! Falsifiable (after 170 tests and 30 shrinks):
Path 4 [AcStart 2,AcStart 3,AcCrash 2,AcStart 1,AcCrash 1,
        AcOnMsg 3 AcDown,AcStart 2,AcOnMsg 3 AcDown,AcStart 1,AcCrash 1]
```

Fig. 3. Trace counter example

Evaluation of Trace Counter Examples. Although the verification process was complicated, we did not have very many badly specified invariants around to test with. The presented example was the most complicated and in total we had some five or six *real* 'broken' invariants to test with. (All of them produced a counter example.) To further evaluate the trace counter example search in a more structural way, we used a simplistic kind of *mutation testing*. We took each invariant and negated (or if it was already negated, removed the negation) all sub-expressions occurring on the left hand side of an implication. Thereafter we tried the trace counter example search for each of the mutated invariants.

In total we generated 272 mutated invariants. We tried to find a trace counter example for each, and succeeded in 187 cases (where we randomly generated 300 test cases for each invariant). However, we should not expect to find a trace counter example in all cases, since some of the mutated invariants are still true invariants. Manual inspection of 10 of the 85 ($272 - 187 = 85$) failed cases revealed only two cases where we should expect to find a counter example. (A re-run of the two examples with a limit of 1000 generated tests was run, and a counter example was found in both cases.)

4.2 Induction Step Counter Examples

To illustrate how the inductive step counter examples could be used we use the invariant presented below as an example. This invariant was actually the last invariant that was added in order to complete the proof of the leader election algorithm. The invariant specifies a characteristic of the acknowledgement messages sent during election.

$$
\begin{array}{l}
\forall \mathit{Pid}, \mathit{Pid2}, \mathit{Pid3}.(\\
\quad (((\mathit{Pid2} \neq \mathit{Pid3}) \\
\qquad \wedge\ \mathbf{elem}(\texttt{m\_Ack}(\mathit{Pid}, \mathit{Pid2}), \\
\qquad\qquad \texttt{queue}(\texttt{host}(\mathit{Pid}))) \\
\qquad \wedge\ (\texttt{host}(\mathit{Pid2}) = \texttt{host}(\mathit{Pid3}))) \\
\qquad \rightarrow \neg\mathbf{elem}(\texttt{m\_Ack}(\mathit{Pid}, \mathit{Pid3}), \\
\qquad\qquad \texttt{queue}(\texttt{host}(\mathit{Pid}))) \\
\quad) \\
)
\end{array}
$$

If *Pid2* and *Pid3* are two different processes at the same host, and an Ack-message from *Pid2* to *Pid* is in *Pid*'s queue, then there can not also be an Ack-message in the queue of *Pid* sent by *Pid3* to *Pid*.

Fig. 4. Invariant for step counter example example

The first proof attempt included invariants 3, 14 and 15 (which are also invariants that specify properties about Ack-messages), i.e. we tried to prove $(Inv_3 \wedge Inv_{14} \wedge Inv_{15} \wedge Inv_{89}) \rightarrow [Sys]\, Inv_{89}$. This proof attempt fails, and if we search for an induction step counter example we get the following state:

```
State with 2 processes:
* Alive: {(2,3),(2,5)}
* Pids:  {(2,3)}
[ Process: (1,2)
  Status: norm   Elid: (2,3)  Ldr: 1  Pendack: 2
  Queue: [Ack (1,2) (2,3)]
  Acks: {}   Down: {},

  Process: (2,3)
  Status: wait   Elid: (1,2)  Ldr: 2  Pendack: 2
  Queue: [Halt (1,2)]
  Acks: {}   Down: {}]
```

The system state consists of two sets `alive` (that contains the process identifiers of all processes currently alive) and `pids` (that contains all process identifiers ever used). A process identifier is implemented as a pair of integers. Furthermore, the individual state of each process is also part of the system state. Each process state has a number of algorithm-specific variables (`Status`, `Elid`, etc.), and an incoming message queue.

In the counter example we see that the second process has a Halt-message from the first process in its queue at the same time as there is an Ack-message in the queue of the first process. That means that in the next step the second process could acknowledge the Halt-message, and thus create a state in which the invariant is falsified. Indeed such a situation can not occur, and we actually already had an invariant (with number 84) which stated exactly this. Therefore, if we instead try to prove: $(Inv_3 \wedge Inv_{14} \wedge Inv_{15} \wedge Inv_{84} \wedge Inv_{89}) \longrightarrow [Sys]\, Inv_{89}$ we are successful.

Evaluation of Step Counter Examples. In the verification of the leader election algorithm we used 89 sub-invariants which were proved according to the scheme

$$(Inv_1 \wedge Inv_2 \wedge \cdots \wedge Inv_k) \longrightarrow [Sys]\, Inv_1.$$

Since the automated theorem provers are rather sensitive to the problem size, we put some effort into creating *minimal* left hand sides of the implication. That is, we removed the sub-invariants that were not needed to prove a particular sub-invariant.

Therefore, a simple way to generate evaluation tests for the step counter example search is to remove yet another sub invariant from the left hand side and thus get a problem which in most cases (the minimization was not totally accurate) is too weak to be proved in the step case. Thus, we generate a set of problems like

$$(Inv_1 \wedge Inv_2 \wedge \cdots Inv_{k-1} \wedge Inv_{k+1} \wedge \cdots \wedge Inv_n) \longrightarrow [Sys]\, Inv_1$$

and evaluate the step counter example search on this set of problems.

In this way, the 89 proof obligations were turned into 351 problems to test the step counter example search with. More careful analysis revealed that 30 of the problems were actually still provable, thus leaving 321 test cases. The result of running the step counter example search in QuickCheck with 500 test cases for each problem, and a varying number of adapt rounds, is presented in Fig. 5.

In the figure we see that with only one iteration of adapt we find a counter example for around 75% of the tested problems. By increasing the number adapt rounds, we find a counter example for 97% of the tested problems within 500 test cases.

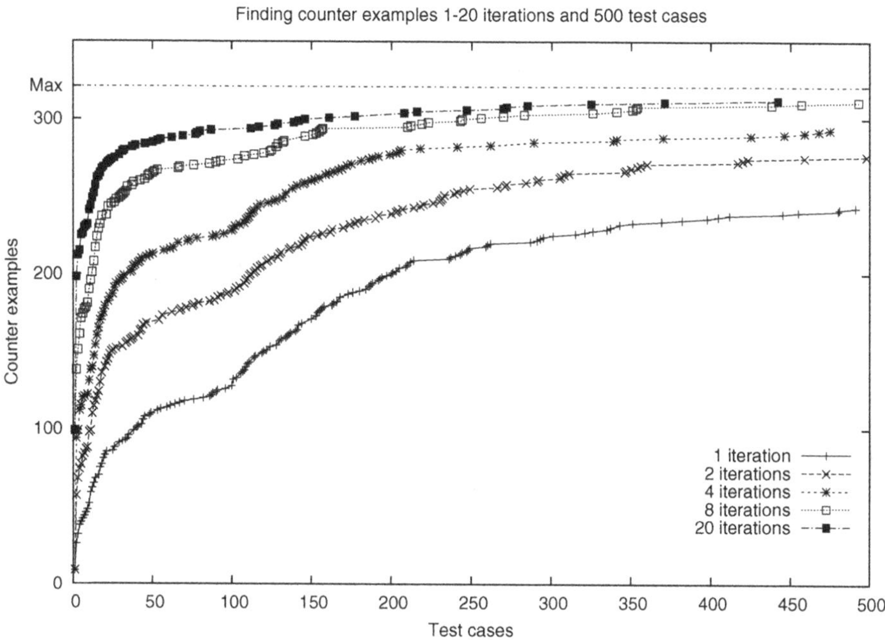

Fig. 5. Step counter example results

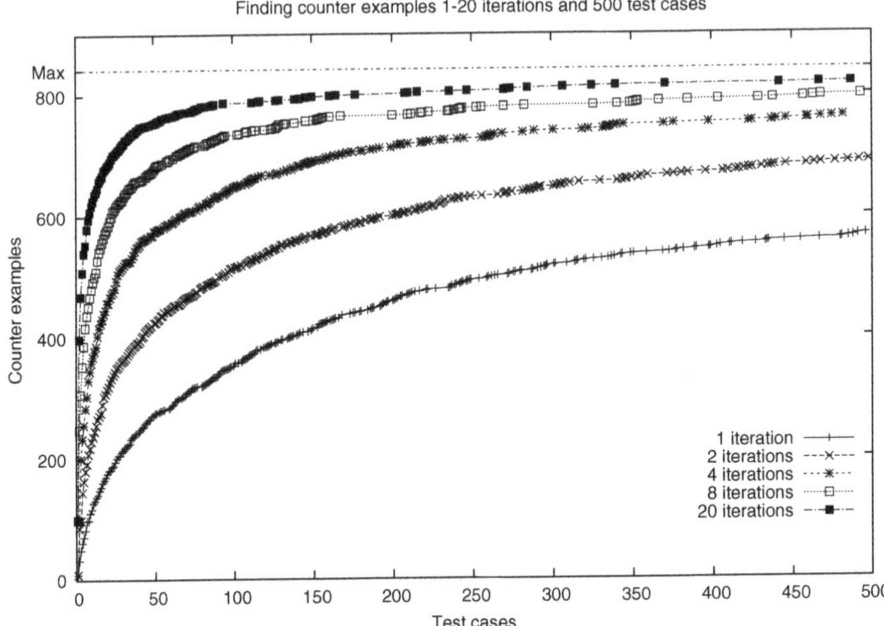

Fig. 6. Step counter example results

In reality, case-splitting [8] turned these 321 into 1362 smaller problems of which 524 are provable. The results of running the step counter example search in QuickCheck for each of these smaller problems are presented in Fig. 6. The results are quite similar to the results in the earlier figure.

Our conclusion is that this way of finding counter examples is remarkably effective, especially keeping in mind that the counter example search we presented is a fully automatic and a very cheap method. Running QuickCheck for a failed proof attempt takes only from a few seconds, sometimes up to a few minutes.

Another important aspect is the quality of the counter examples; i.e. given an induction step counter example, how hard is it to figure out how to strengthen the invariant to make it provable. Of course this is hard to measure, and any judgement here is highly subjective. We randomly selected some of the found counter examples and inspected them more carefully. In most cases it was easy to find out which sub-invariant to add, which was the original purpose of the method.

Interestingly, in some examples, the counter example indicated that a certain sub-invariant was missing, which was different from the sub-invariant we had removed. (Remember, we generated the tests by removing one sub-invariant from already proved examples.) It turned out that we could actually prove the problem by either using the removed sub-invariant *or* the sub-invariant suggested by the counter example. For example: from the (already proved) problem $(Inv_4 \wedge Inv_7 \wedge Inv_8) \longrightarrow [Sys]Inv_8$ we removed Inv_4. This resulted in a counter example, which indicated that adding Inv_2 would probably make it possible to prove the sub-invariant. Indeed the problem $(Inv_2 \wedge Inv_7 \wedge Inv_8) \longrightarrow [Sys]\, Inv_8$ could be proved. The reason for this is that Inv_2 and Inv_4 were partially overlapping. The conclusion must nevertheless be that an induction step counter example is most often very useful.

5 Discussion and Conclusion

We have identified different categories of reasons why proof attempts that establish inductive invariants may fail, and developed a method that can identify 2 of these categories by giving feedback in terms of a concrete counter example.

We would like to argue that the results show that this is a useful method; very often counter examples are found when they should be found, and they are easy to understand because of the (local) minimality. The method is also very cheap, once the system is set up, it does not take much time or resources to run 300 random tests. Every time we make changes to the set of invariants, a quick check can be done to make sure no obvious mistakes have been made.

For related work, just like pure first-order logic theorem provers, interactive theorem proving systems usually do not provide feedback in terms of a counter example either. ACL2 [15] provides feedback by producing a log of the failed proof attempt. While sometimes useful, we would like to argue that feedback in terms of counter examples (and in terms of different kinds of counter examples) is more directly useful for a user. In some work in the context of rippling [17], a failed proof attempt is structurally used to come up with an invariant for while-loops in imperative programs.

The interactive higher-order logic reasoning system Isabelle comes with a version of QuickCheck [6]. However, there is no control over generators or shrinking present in this version. The work presented here can possibly be integrated with Isabelle by extending their QuickCheck with the necessary features.

Some might argue that the main problems presented in the paper disappear when moving to a reasoning system that supports induction, for example ACL2 or a higher-order theorem prover. However, in such systems it is still useful to have a notion of different reasons why inductive proofs fail, and the three types of counter examples (1), (2) and (3) are just as useful in such systems.

For future work, we are looking to further reduce the gap between problems where proofs are found and problems where counter examples are found. We are currently working to augment a theorem prover to also give us feedback that can be used to identify categories (3) and (4). For category (3), an approximation of a non-standard counter model is produced, for category (4), the theorem prover can tell why it has not found a proof yet.

Moreover, we want to study liveness more closely, and integrate liveness checking (and finding counter examples) in the overall verification method.

Finally, to increase the applicability of our work, we would like to separate out the different parts of our current system; the counter example finding from the Erlang-specific things, and the leader-election-specific axioms and invariants from the general Erlang axioms.

References

1. Abrial, J.-R.: The B-Book: Assigning Programs to Meanings. Cambridge University Press, Cambridge (1996)
2. Armstrong, J.: Programming Erlang – Software for a Concurrent World. The Pragmatic Programmers (2007), `http://books.pragprog.com/titles/jaerlang`
3. Armstrong, J., Virding, R., Wikström, C., Williams, M.: Concurrent Programming in Erlang. Prentice-Hall, Englewood Cliffs (1996)
4. Arts, T., Claessen, K., Svensson, H.: Semi-formal development of a fault-tolerant leader election protocol in Erlang. In: Grabowski, J., Nielsen, B. (eds.) FATES 2004. LNCS, vol. 3395, pp. 140–154. Springer, Heidelberg (2005)
5. Beckert, B., Hähnle, R., Schmitt, P.H. (eds.): Verification of Object-Oriented Software. LNCS (LNAI), vol. 4334. Springer, Heidelberg (2007)
6. Berghofer, T., Nipkow, S.: Random testing in isabelle/hol. In: Software Engineering and Formal Methods. SEFM 2004. Proceedings of the Second International Conference, September 28-30, 2004, pp. 230–239 (2004)
7. Claessen, K.: Equinox, a new theorem prover for full first-order logic with equality. Presentation at Dagstuhl Seminar 05431 on Deduction and Applications (October 2005)
8. Claessen, K., Hähnle, R., Mårtensson, J.: Verification of hardware systems with first-order logic. In: Proc. of Problems and Problem Sets Workshop (PaPS) (2002)
9. Claessen, K., Hughes, J.: QuickCheck: a lightweight tool for random testing of haskell programs. In: ICFP 2000: Proceedings of the fifth ACM SIGPLAN international conference on Functional programming, pp. 268–279. ACM, New York (2000)
10. Weidenbach, C., et al.: SPASS: An automated theorem prover for first-order logic with equality, `http://spass.mpi-sb.mpg.de`
11. Fredlund, L.-Å., Svensson, H.: McErlang: A model checker for a distributed functional programming language. In: Proc. of International Conference on Functional Programming (ICFP), ACM SIGPLAN, New York (2007)
12. Garcia-Molina, H.: Elections in a distributed computing system. IEEE Transactions on Computers C-31(1), 48–59 (1982)
13. Holzmann, G.J.: The Spin Model Checker: Primer and Reference Manual. Addison-Wesley, Reading (2003)
14. Hughes, J.: QuickCheck testing for fun and profit. In: Hanus, M. (ed.) PADL 2007. LNCS, vol. 4354, pp. 1–32. Springer, Heidelberg (2006)
15. Kaufmann, M., Moore, J.S.: ACL2 - A Computational Logic / Applicative Common Lisp, `http://www.cs.utexas.edu/users/moore/acl2/`
16. Schulz, S.: The e equational theorem prover, `http://eprover.org`
17. Stark, J., Ireland, A.: Invariant discovery via failed proof attempts. In: Proceedings, 8th International Workshop on Logic Based Program Synthesis and Transformation (1998)
18. Stoller, S.D.: Leader election in distributed systems with crash failures. Technical Report 481, Computer Science Dept., Indiana University, May 1997. Revised (July 1997)
19. Svensson, H., Arts, T.: A new leader election implementation. In: ERLANG 2005: Proceedings of the 2005 ACM SIGPLAN workshop on Erlang, pp. 35–39. ACM Press, New York (2005)

20. Voronkov, A.: Vampire, `http://www.vampire.fm`
21. Wordsworth, J.B.: Software Engineering with B. Addison-Wesley, Reading (1996)
22. Zeller, A.: Isolating cause-effect chains from computer programs. In: SIGSOFT 2002/FSE-10: Proceedings of the 10th ACM SIGSOFT symposium on Foundations of software engineering, pp. 1–10. ACM, New York (2002)

A Logic-Based Approach to Combinatorial Testing with Constraints

Andrea Calvagna[1] and Angelo Gargantini[2]

[1] University of Catania - Italy
andrea.calvagna@unict.it
[2] University of Bergamo - Italy
angelo.gargantini@unibg.it

Abstract. Usage of combinatorial testing is wide spreading as an effective technique to reveal unintended feature interaction inside a given system. To this aim, test cases are constructed by combining *tuples* of assignments of the different input parameters, based on some effective combinatorial strategy. The most commonly used strategy is two-way (*pairwise*) coverage, requiring all combinations of valid assignments for all possible pairs of input parameters to be covered by at least one test case. In this paper a new heuristic strategy developed for the construction of pairwise covering test suites is presented, featuring a new approach to support expressive constraining over the input domain. Moreover, it allows the inclusion or exclusion of ad-hoc combinations of parameter bindings to let the user customize the test suite outcome. Our approach is tightly integrated with formal logic, since it uses test predicates to formalize combinatorial testing as a logic problem, and applies an external model checker tool to solve it. The proposed approach is supported by a prototype tool implementation, and early results of experimental assessment are also presented.

1 Introduction

Verification of highly-configurable software systems, such as those supporting many optional or customizable features, is a challenging activity. In fact, due to its intrinsic complexity, formal specification of the whole system may require a great effort. Modeling activities may become extremely expensive and time consuming, and the tester may decide to model only the inputs and require they are sufficiently covered by tests. On the other hand, unintended interaction between optional features can lead to incorrect behaviors which may not be detected by traditional testing [22,33].

A combinatorial testing approach is a particular kind of functional testing technique consisting in exhaustively validating all combinations of size t of a system's inputs values. This is equivalent to exhaustively testing t-strength interaction between its input parameters, and requires a formal modeling of just the system features as input variables. In particular, pairwise interaction testing aims at generating a reduced-size test suite which covers all *pairs* of input values.

B. Beckert and R. Hähnle (Eds.): TAP 2008, LNCS 4966, pp. 66–83, 2008.

Significant time savings can be achieved by implementing this kind of approach, as well as in general with t-wise interaction testing, which has been experimentally shown to be really effective in revealing software defects [21]. A test set that covers all possible pairs of variable values can typically detect 50% to 75% of the faults in a program [27,9]. Other experimental work shown that 100% of faults are usually triggered by a relatively low degree of features interaction, typically 4-way to 6-way combinations [22]. For this reason combinatorial testing is used in practice and supported by many tools [26].

From a mathematical point of view, the problem of generating a minimal set of test cases covering all pairs of input values is equivalent to finding a *covering array* (CA) of *strength* 2 over a heterogeneous alphabet [18]. Covering arrays are combinatorial structures which extend the notion of *orthogonal arrays* [2]. A covering array $CA_\lambda(N; t, k, \boldsymbol{g})$ is an N x k array with the property that in every N x t sub -array, each t-tuple occurs at least λ times, where t is the strength of the coverage of interactions, k is the number of components (degree), and $\boldsymbol{g} = (g_1, g_2, ...g_k)$ is a vector of positive integers defining the number of symbols for each component. When applied to combinatorial system testing only the case when $\lambda = 1$ is of interest, that is, where every t-tuple is covered at least once.

In this paper we present our approach to combinatorial testing, which is tightly integrated with formal logic, since it uses test predicates to formalize combinatorial testing as a logic problem. The paper is organized as follows: section 2 gives some insight on the topic and recently published related works. Section 3 presents our approach and an overview of the tool we implemented, while section 4 explains how we deal with constraints over the inputs. Section 5 presents some early results of experiments carried out in order to assess the validity of the proposed approach. Finally, section 6 draws our conclusions and points out some ideas for future extension of this work.

2 Combinatorial Coverage Strategies

Many algorithms and tools for combinatorial interaction testing already exist in the literature. Grindal et al. count more than 40 papers and 10 strategies in their recent survey [15]. There is also a web site [26] devoted to this subject. We would like to classify them according to Cohen et al. [7], as:

a) *algebraic* when the CA is given by mathematical construction as in [20]. These theoretic based approaches generally leads to optimal results, that is minimal sized CA. Unfortunately, no mathematical solution to the covering array generation problem exists which is generally applicable. Williams and Probert [31] showed that the general problem of finding a minimal set of test cases that satisfy $t-$wise coverage can be NP-complete. Thus, heuristic approaches, producing a sub-optimal result are widely used in practice.
b) *greedy* when some search heuristic is used to incrementally build up the CA, as done by AETG [5] or by the In Parameter Order (IPO)[27]. This approach is always applicable but leads to sub-optimal results. Typically, only an upper bound on the size of constructed CA may be guaranteed. The majority of

existing solutions falls in this category, including the one we are proposing here.

c) *meta-heuristic* when genetic-algorithms or other less traditional, bio-inspired search techniques are used to converge to a near-optimal solution after an acceptable number of iterations. Only few examples of this applications are available, to the best of our knowledge [6,25].

Besides this classifications, it must be observed that most of the currently available methods and tools are strictly focused on providing an algorithmic solution to the mathematical problem of covering array generation only, while very few of them account also for other complementary features, which are rather important in order to make these tools really useful in practice, like i.e. the ability to handle constraints on the input domains. We have identified the following requirements for an effective combinatorial testing tool, extending the previous work on this topic by Lott et al. [23]:

Ability to state complex constraints. This issue has been recently investigated by Cohen et al. [7] and recognized as a highly desirable feature of a testing method. Still according to Cohen et al., just one tool, PICT [8], was currently found able to handle *full* constraints specification, that is, without requiring remodeling of inputs or explicit expansion of each forbidden test cases. However, there is no detail on how the constraints are actually implemented in PICT, limiting the reuse of its technique. Most tools require the user to re-write the specification in a way that the inputs are separated and unconstrained, but when combined the satisfy the constraints. AETG [5] and the TestCover [28] service follow this approach. Other tools, like the IBM Whitch [16], require the user to explicitly list all the forbidden combinations. Note that if constraints on the input domain are to be taken into account then finding a valid test case becomes an NP-hard problem [3]. In our work, not only we address the use of full constraints as suggested in [7] but we feature the use of generic predicates to express constraints over the inputs (see section 4 for details). Furthermore, while Cohen's general constraints representation strategy has to be integrated with an external tool for combinatorial testing, our approach tackles every aspect of the test suite generation process.

Ability to deal with user specific requirements on the test suite. The user may require the explicit exclusion or inclusion of specific test cases, e.g. those generated by previous executions of the used tool or by any other means, in order to customize the resulting test suite. The tool could also let the user interactively guide the on-going test case selection process, step by step. Moreover the user may require the inclusion or exclusion of *sets of* test cases which refer to a particular critical scenario or combination of inputs. In this case the set is better described symbolically, for example by a predicate expression over the inputs. Note that *instant* [15] strategies, like algebraic constructions of orthogonal arrays and/or covering arrays, and *parameter-based*, iterative strategies, like IPO, do not allow this kind of interaction.

Integration with other testing techniques. Combinatorial testing is just *one* testing technique. The user may be interest to integrate results from many testing techniques, including those requiring very complex formalisms (as in [14,12,11,13]). This shall not be limited to having a common user-interface for many tools. Instead, it should go in the direction of generating a unique test-suite which simultaneously accounts for multiple kinds of coverages (e.g., combinatorial, state, branch, faults, and so on). Our method, supported by a prototype tool, aims at bridging the gap between the need to formally prove any specific properties of a system, relying on a formal model for its description, and the need to also perform functional testing of its usage configurations, with a more accessible *black-box* approach based on efficient combinatorial test design. Integrating the use of a convenient model checker within a framework for pairwise interaction testing, our approach gives to the user the easy of having just one convenient and powerful formal approach for both uses.

Recently, several papers investigated the use of verification methods for combinatorial testing. Hnich et al. [19] translates the problem of building covering arrays to a Boolean satisfiability problem and then they use a SAT solver to generate their solution. In their paper, they leave the treatment of auxiliary constraints over the inputs as future work. Conversely, Cohen et al. [7] exclusively focuses on handling of with constraints and present a SAT-based constraint solving technique that has to be integrated with external algorithms for combinatorial testing like IPO. Kuhn and Okun [21] try to integrate combinatorial testing with model checking (SMV) to provide automated specification based testing, with no support for constraints. In this work we investigate the integration of model checkers with combinatorial testing in the presence of constraints while supporting all of the additional features listed above.

3 A Logic Approach to Pairwise Coverage

We now describe our approach to combinatorial testing which we can classify as *logic-based* and which is supported by the *ASM Test Generation Tool* (ATGT)[1]. ATGT was originally developed to support structural [14] and fault based testing [13] of *Abstract State Machines* (ASMs), and it has been extended to support also combinatorial testing. Since pairwise testing aims at validating each possible pair of input values for a given system under test, we then formally express each pair as a corresponding logical expression, a *test predicate* (or test goal), e.g.:

$$p_1 = v_1 \wedge p_2 = v_2$$

where p_1 and p_2 are two inputs or monitored variables of enumerative or boolean domain and v_1 and v_2 are two possible values of $p1$ and $p2$ respectively. The easiest way to generate test predicates for the pairwise coverage of an ASM model is to employ a combinatorial enumeration algorithm, which simply loops over

[1] A preview release of the tool is available at the following URL: http://cs.unibg.it/gargantini/projects/atgt/.

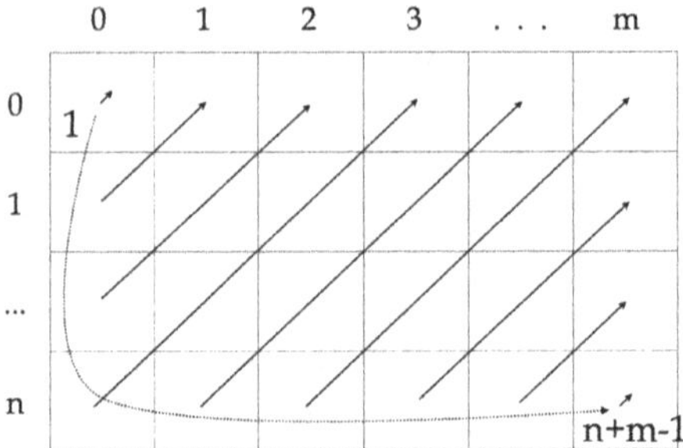

Fig. 1. Antidiagonal order in combinatorial indexing of the values pairs, n and m being the ranges of two input parameters

the variables and their values to build all the possible test predicates. Another variation of the test predicate generation algorithm we support is the *antidiagonal* algorithm, which instead has been specially devised to output an ordered set of logic test predicates (tp) such that no two consecutive $tp \equiv p_1 = v_1 \wedge p_2 = v_2$ and $tp' \equiv p'_1 = v'_1 \wedge p'_2 = v'_2$ where $p_1 = p'_1$ and $p_2 = p'_2$ will have $v_1 = v'_1$ or $v_2 = v'_2$. Simply put, for each pair of input variables, the algorithm indexes through the matrix of their possible values in *antidiagonal* order, see Fig.1. Thus, generating their sequence of pair assignments such that both values always differ from previous ones. [2] This alternative way of ordering of the pairs combinations to be covered is motivated by a performance improvement it produces on the execution of our covering array generation algorithm, as will be explained later in Sect. 3.3.

In order to correctly derive assignment pairs required by the coverage we assume the availability of a formal description of the system under test. This description includes at least the listing of input parameters and respective domains (finite and discrete). The description has to be entered in the ATGT tool as an ASM specification in the AsmetaL language [29]. The description is then parsed and analyzed by our tool in order instantiate a convenient corresponding data structure. As an example, consider the following, which declares two parameters both with domain size three, without constraints:

```
asm simpleexample signature :
   enum domain D = {V1 | V2 | V3 }
   dynamic monitored p1 : D
   dynamic monitored p2 : D
```

The ASM model has to declare the domains, which currently must be either boolean or an enumeration of constants, like in the given example. The keyword *monitored* alerts the tool that the following parameter is in the set of input variables under test. Non monitored variables and variables of other types are ignored.

[2] Apart from the set's first and last pairs special cases.

3.1 Tests Generation

A *test case* is a set of assignments, binding each monitored (input) variable to a value in its proper domain. It is easy to see that a test case implicitly covers as many *t-wise* test predicates as $\binom{n}{t}$, where n is the number of system's input parameters and $t = 2$ (for pairwise interaction testing) is the *strength* of the covering array. A given test suite satisfies the *pairwise* coverage iff *all* test predicates are satisfied by at least one of its test cases. Note that the smallest test suite is that in which each test predicate is covered by *exactly* one test case. Note that a test predicate in pairwise coverage binds only two variables to their values, while a test case assigns values to all the monitored variables.

By formalizing the pairwise testing by means of logical predicates, finding a test case that satisfy a given predicate reduces to a logical problem of satisfiability. To this aim, many logical solvers, like e.g. constraint solvers, SAT algorithms, SMT (Satisfiability Modulo Theories) solver, or model checkers can be applied. Our approach exploits a well known model checker tool, namely the bounded and symbolic model checker tool SAL [10]. Given a test predicate *tp*, SAL is asked to verify a *trap property* [11] which is the logical negation of *tp*: $\mathsf{G}(\mathsf{NOT}(tp))$. The *trap property* is not a real system property, but enforces the generation of a counter example, that is a set of assignments falsifying the trap property and satisfying our test predicate. The counter example will contain bindings for all monitored inputs, including those parameters missing (free) in the predicate, thus defining the test case we were looking for.

A first basic way to generate a suitable test suite consists in collecting all the test predicates in a set of *candidates*, extracting from the set one test predicate at the time, generating the test case for it by executing SAL, removing it from the candidates set, and repeating until the candidates set is empty. This approach, which according to [15] can be classified as iterative, is very inefficient but it can be improved as follows.

Skip already covered test predicates. Every time a new test case s is added to the test suite, s always covers $\binom{n}{t}$ test predicates, so the tool detects if any additional test predicate *tp* in the candidates is covered by s by checking whether s is a model of *tp* (i.e. it satisfies *tp*) or not, and in the positive case it removes *tp* from the candidates.

Randomly process the test predicates. Randomly choosing the next predicate for which the tool generates a test case makes our method *non deterministic*, as the generated test suite may differer in size and composition at each execution of the algorithm. Nevertheless, it is important to understand the key role played on the final test suite outcome by just the order in which the candidate test predicates are choose for processing. In fact, each time a *tp* is *turned* into a corresponding test case it will dramatically impact on the set of remaining solutions which are still possible for the next test cases. This is clear if we consider the following: the ability to reduce the final test suite size depends on the ability to *group* in each test case the highest possible number of uncovered tps.

The *grouping* possibilities available in order to build a test case starting from the tp currently selected for processing are directly proportional to the number and ranges of involved input variables, and limited by input constraint relations. Thus, for a given example, they can vary from *tp* to *tp*, and since each processing step will actually subtract to the next grouping possibilities, eventually the first step, that is the choice of first tp to process, will be the most influent, as it will indirectly impact on the whole test suite composition process.

Ordered processing of test predicates. A different policy is to order the *tps* in the candidates pool according to a well defined ordering criterion, and then process them sequentially. At each iteration, the pool is again sorted against this criterion and the first test predicate is selected for processing. In order to do this we define a *novelty* comparison criteria as follows.

Definition 1. *Let* t_1 *and* t_2 *bet two test predicates, and* T *a test suite. We say that* t_1 *is more novel than* t_2 *if the variables assignments of* t_1 *have been already tested in* T *less times than the assignments of* t_2.

Ordering by novelty and taking the most novel one helps ensuring that during the test suite construction process, for each parameter, all of its values will be evenly used, which is also a general requirement of CAs. To this purpose, usage counting of all values of all parameters in current test suite is performed and continuously updated by the algorithm, when this optional strategy is enabled.

Despite deterministic processing of the *tps* has the advantage of producing repeatable results, and we also included this option in our tool, it requires additional computational effort in order to guess the correct processing order of the test predicates, that is, that producing the best *groupings*. On the other hand, random processing strategy accounts for average performance in all suite of practical applications, and the rather small computation times easily allows for several trials to be shoot, and the best result to be statistically improved without significant additional effort.

3.2 Reduction

Even if one skips the test predicates already covered, the final test suite may still contain some test cases which are redundant. We say that a test case is *required* if contains at least a test predicate not already covered by other test cases in the test suite. We then try to reduce the test suite by deleting all the test cases which are not required in order to obtain a final test suite with fewer test cases. Note, however, that an unnecessary test case may become necessary after deleting another test case from the test suite, hence we cannot simply remove all the unnecessary test predicates at once. We have implemented a greedy algorithm, reported in Alg. 1, which finds a test suite with the minimum number of required test cases.

Algorithm 1. Test suite reduction

T = test suite to be optimized
Op = optimized test suite
Tp = set of test predicates which are not covered by tests in Op

0. set Op to the empty set and add to Tp all the test predicates
1. take the test t in T which covers most test predicates in Tp and add t to Op
2. remove all the test predicates covered by t from Tp
3. if Tp is empty then return Op else goto 1

3.3 Composing Test Predicates

Since a test predicate binds only the values of a pair of variables, all the other variables in the input set are still free to be bound by the model checker. Besides guiding the choice of the selected test predicate in some effective way, we can only hope that the model checker will choose the values of unconstrained variables in order to avoid unnecessary repetitions, such that the total number of test cases will be low. It is apparent that a guide in the choice of the values for all the variables not specified by the chosen test predicate is necessary to improve the effectiveness of test case construction, even if this may require a greater computational effort. To this aim, our proposed strategy consist in *composing* more test predicates into an *extended*, or *composed* test predicate,which specifies the values for as many variables as possible. We define a *composed* test predicate the conjoint of one or more test predicates. When creating a composed test predicate, we must ensure that we will be still able to find a test case that covers it. In case we try to compose too many test predicates which contradict each other, there is no test case for it. We borrow some definitions from the propositional logic: since a sentence is *consistent* if it has a model, we can define consistency among test predicates as follows.

Definition 2. ***Consistency*** *A test predicate tp_1 is consistent with a test predicate tp_2 if there exists a test case which satisfies both tp_1 and tp_2.*

Let us assume now, for simplicity, that there are no constraints over the variables values so that the composition will take into account just the variables values of the test predicates we compose. The case where constraints over the model are defined will be considered in Sect. 4.

Theorem 1. *Let $tp_1 : v_1 = a_1 \wedge v_2 = a_2$ and $tp_2 : v_3 = a_3 \wedge v_4 = a_4$ be two pairwise test predicates. They are consistent if and only if $\forall i \in \{1, 2\} \forall j \in \{3, 4\} v_i = v_j \rightarrow a_i = a_j$.*

We can add a test predicate tp to a composed test predicate TP, only if tp is consistent with TP. This keeps the composed test predicate consistent.

Algorithm 2. Pseudo code for the main algorithm

```
C = the set of logical test predicates of the form (p1=v1 AND p2=v2), to be covered
T = the Test Suite initially empty
0. reset usage counts for bindings of all parameters.
1. if C is empty then return T and stop
2. (optional) sort the tps in C according to their novelty or shuffle C
3. pick up the first tp, P, from C
4. try composing P' by joining P with other consistent test predicates in C
5. run SAL trying to prove the trap property G(not(P'))
6. convert resulting counter example into the test case tc, and add tc to T
7. remove from C all tps in P' and all additional tps covered by tc
8. update usage frequencies for all covered tps.
9. goto step 1
```

Theorem 2. *A conjoint TP of test predicates is consistent with a test predicate tp if and only if every t in TP is consistent with tp.*

Now the test suite is built up by iteratively adding new test cases until no more tps are left uncovered, but each test predicate is *composed* from scratch as a logical conjunction of as many still uncovered tps as possible. The heuristic stage of this approach is in the process of extracting from the pool of *candidate* tps the best sub-set of consistent tps to be joined together into TP. Than, the resulting composed test predicate is in turn is used to derive a new test case by means of a SAL counterexample.

3.4 Composing and Ordering

The initial ordering of the predicates in the candidate pool may influence the later process of merging many pairwise predicates into an extended one. In fact, the candidates tps for merging are searched sequentially in the candidates pool. The more diversity there will be among subsequent elements of the pool and the higher will be the probability that a neighboring predicate will be found compatible for merging. This will in turn impact on the ability to produce a smaller test suite, faster, given that the more pairwise predicates have been successfully compacted into the same test case and the less number of test cases will be needed to have a complete pairwise coverage.

There are more than one strategy we tested in order to produce a effective ordering of the predicates, to easy the merging process. In the implemented tool one can choose the test predicate at step 2 by the following several *pluggable* policies which impact on the efficiency of method. By adopting the *random* policy, the method randomly chooses at step 2 the next test predicate and check if it is consistent. By *novelty* policy the method chooses the most novel test predicate and try to combine it with the others already chosen. The resulting whole process is described in Alg. 2.

4 Adding Constraints

We now introduce the constraints over the inputs which we assume are given in the specification as axioms in the form of boolean predicates. For example for the well known asm specification example Basic Billing System (BBS) [23], we introduce an axiom as follows:

axiom inv_calltype **over** billing, calltype :
  billing = COLLECT implies calltype != INTERNATIONAL

To express constraints we adopt the language of propositional logic with equality (and inequality)[3]. Note that most methods and tools admit only few templates for constraints: the translation of those templates in equality logic is straightforward. For example the **require** constraint is translated to an *implication*; the **not supported** to a *not*, and so on. Even the method proposed in [7] which adopt a similar approach to ours prefer to allow constraints only in a form of forbidden configurations [17], since it relies for the actual tests generation on existing algorithms like IPO. A forbidden combination would be translated in our model as *not* statement. Our approach allows the designer to state the constraints in the form he/she prefers. For example, the model of mobile phones presented in [7] has 7 constraints. The constraint number 5 states that *"Video camera requires a camera and a color display"*. In [7], this constraint must be translated into two forbidden tuples, while we allow the user simply to write the following axiom, which is very similar to the informal requirement.

axiom inv_5 **over** videoCamera, camera, display :
videoCamera implies (camera!= NO_CAMERA and display != BLACK_WHITE)

A constraint may not only relate two variable values (to exclude a pair), but it can contain generic bindings among variables. Any constraint models an explicit binding, but their combination may give rise to complex implicit constraints. In our approach, the axioms must be satisfied by any test case we obtain from the specification, i.e. a test case is *valid* only if it does not contradict any axiom in our specification. While others [4] distinguish between forbidden combinations and combinations to be avoided, we consider only forbidden combinations, i.e. combinations which do satisfy the axioms. Finding a valid test case becomes with the constraints a challenge similar to finding a counter example for a theorem or proving it. For this reason verification techniques are particularly useful in this case and we have investigated the use of the bounded and symbolic model checkers in SAL.

To support the use of constraints, they must be translated in SAL and this requires to embed the axioms directly in the trap property, since SAL does not support assumptions directly. The trap property must be modified to take into account the axioms. The general schema for it becomes:

---

[3] SAL, as other SMT solvers, has decision theories for linear arithmetic, uninterpreted functions, etc.. However, since we consider only inputs with enumerative domains, users can only write constraints as logic propositions with equality at most.

```
G(<AND axioms>) => G(NOT(<test predicate>))                (1)
```

A counter example of the trap property (1) is still a valid test case. In fact, if the model checker finds an assignment to the variables that makes the trap property false, it finds a case in which both the axioms are true and the implied part of the trap property is false. This test case covers the test predicate and satisfies the constraints.

Without constraints, we were sure that a trap property derived from a consistent test predicate had always a counter example. Now, due to the constraints, the trap property (1) may not have a counter example, i.e. it could be true and hence provable by the model checker. We can distinguish two cases. The simplest case is when the axioms are inconsistent, i.e. there is no assignment that can satisfy all the constraints. In this case each trap property is trivially true since the first part of the implication (1) is always false. The inconsistency may be not easily discovered by hand, since the axioms give rise to some implicit constraints, whose consequences are not immediately detected by human inspection. For example a constraint may require $a \neq x$, another $b \neq y$ while another requires $a \neq x \rightarrow b = y$; these constraints are inconsistent since there is no test case that can satisfy them. Inconsistent axioms must be considered as a fault in the specification and this must be detected and eliminated. For this reason when we start the generation of tests, if the specifications has axioms, we check that the axioms are consistent by trying to prove:

```
G(NOT <AND axioms>)
```

If this is proved by the model checker, then we warn the user, who can ignore this warning and proceed to generate tests, but no test will be generated, since no valid test case can be found. We assume now that the axioms are consistent. Even with consistent axioms, some (but not all) trap properties can be true: there is no test case that can satisfy the test predicate and the constraints. In this case we define the test predicate as *unfeasible.*

Definition 3. *Let tp a test predicate, M the specification, and C the conjunction of all the axioms. If the axioms are consistent and the trap property for tp is true, i.e.* $M \wedge C \models \neg tp$*, then we say that tp is unfeasible. Let tp be the pair of assignments* $v_1 = a_1 \wedge v_2 = a_2$*, we say that this pair is unfeasible.*

An unfeasible pair of assignments represents a set of invalid test cases: all the test cases which contain this pair are invalid. Our method is able to detect infeasible pairs, since it can actually prove the trap property derived from it. The tool finds and marks the infeasible pairs, and the user may derive from them invalid test cases to test the fault tolerance of the system.

For example, the following test predicate results infeasible for the BBS example:

calltype = INTERNATIONAL and billing = COLLECT −−−> unfeasible

Note that since the BMC is in general not able to prove a theorem, but only to find counter examples, it would be not suitable to prove unfeasibility of test predicates. However, since we know that if the counter example exists then it has length 1, if the BMC does not find it we can infer that the test predicate is unfeasible.

4.1 Composition and Constraints

By introducing constraints, Theorems 1 and 2 are no longer valid and the composition method presented in Sect. 3.3 must be modified. Every time we want to add a test predicate to a conjoint of test predicates we have to check its consistency by considering the constraints too. We can exploit again the model checker SAL. Given a test predicate *tp*, the axioms *Axs* and the conjoint *TPs*, we can try to prove by using SAL:

```
G(<TPs>) AND G(<Axs>) => G(NOT(tp))
```

If this is proved, we skip *tp* since it is inconsistent with *TPs*, otherwise we can add *tp* to *TPs* and proceed.

4.2 User Defined Test Goals and Tests

Our framework is suitable to deal with user defined test goals. In fact, the user may be interested to test some particular critical situations or input combinations and these combinations are not simple pairwise assignments. Sometimes these combinations are n assignments to n variables (for example with $n=3$ one could specify a 3-wise coverage) but this is not the most general case. We assume that the user defined test goals are given as generic logical predicates, allowing the same syntax as for the constraints. The user wants to obtain a test case which covers these test goals. For example, we allow the user to write the following test goal:

```
testgoal loop:
    access = LOOP and billing != CALLER
        and calltype != LOCALCALL;
```

which requires to test a combination of inputs such that access is LOOP but the billing is not the CALLER and the calltype is not LOCALCALL. A counter example for the trap property derived from the test goal loop is again a test case that covers the test goal.

Besides user defined test goals, we allow also user defined test cases (sometimes called *seeds*) The user may have already some tests cases to be considered, which have already been generated (by any other means). For example, the user may add the following test:

```
test basic_call:
      access = LOOP, billing = CALLER,
      calltype = LOCALCALL, status = SUCCESS;
```

Table 1. Test suite size and time (in sec.) using several options

		one tp at the time								collect + reduction		
spec	mc	no opt	*time*	skip	+rnd	+antDg	+nov	**red**	*time*	no rnd	rnd	*time*
TCAS	SMC	837	*310*	352	113	300	280	241	*113*	107	100	*45*
TCAS	BMC	837	*352*	452	120	452	420	419	*200*	110	101	*48*
three_four	SMC	48	*22*	37	20	37	30	10	*15*	19	10	*10*
three_four	BMC	48	*16*	37	23	37	28	10	*18*	20	10	*10*

Note that a test case specifies the exact value of all the input variables, while a test predicate specifies a generic scenario. ATGT allows the tester to load an external file containing user defined tests and test goals. When an external file is loaded, ATGT adds the user defined test in the set of test predicates to be covered. Than it adds the user defined tests and it checks which test predicates are satisfied by these tests. In this way the tester can decide to skip the test predicates covered by tests he/she has written ad hoc.

5 Early Evaluation

We have experimented our method in three different ways. First we explored the impact of the run-time configuration options on the tool itself. The second set of experiments aimed at exploring the tool's combinatorial algorithm performance. And the last set of experiment assessed the validity of our approach in the presence of constrained models. Experiments were executed on a PPC G4 1,5Mhz processor, equipped with 1Gbyte of physical memory.

We report in Tab. 1 the results of the experiments regarding the use of all the options presented in this paper applied to the case study *TCAS*, which models a Traffic Collision Avoidance System described in [21] and to the benchmark model *three_four* which contains three variables with four possible values each. If no optional features are selected (no opt column) the test suite will contain as many tests as the test predicates. Still covering one test predicate at the time, if one applies the skip policy and either the random, or the anti diagonal or the novelty technique, the size of the test suite and the time taken is reduced. However, if one applies the reduction algorithm (**red** column) we found no difference among which other technique is applied before the reduction. The best results are obtained applying the collect and the reduction. In this case we found the best results when applying the random strategy (rnd column). While it is widely recognized that the Bound Model Checker (BMC) performs better then the Symbolic Model Checker (SMC) when searching for counter example, we found the opposite: the SMC generally performed better than BMC.

In Table 2 we compared the size of the test suites obtained applying our best method with results from several tools available in the literature [8][18]. This new set of experiments was designed in order assess the scalability of the combinatorial algorithm we implemented. Note that we adopt below the exponential symbolic notation used in [18] to represent the problem domain size. Reported

Table 2. Combinatorial performance comparison

Task	ATGT	AETG [5]	PairTest [27]	TConfig [32]	CTS [16]	Jenny [30]	AllPairs [24]	PICT [8]
3^4	11	9	9	9	9	11	9	9
3^{13}	23	15	17	15	15	18	17	18
$4^{15}3^{17}2^{29}$	62	41	34	40	39	38	34	37
$4^1 3^{39} 2^{35}$	65	28	26	30	29	28	26	27
2^{100}	25	10	15	14	10	16	14	15
4^{10}	37		31	28	28	30		
4^{20}	54		34	28	28	37		
4^{30}	68		41	40	40	41		
4^{40}	88		42	40	40	43		
4^{50}	104		47	40	40	46		
4^{60}	114		47	40	40	49		
4^{70}	127		49	40	40	50		
4^{80}	136		49	40	40	52		
4^{90}	143		52	43	43	53		
4^{100}	151		52	43	43	53		
10^{20}	367	180	212	231	210	193	197	210

results clearly show that our algorithm performed worse than the others for every benchmark. Despite the performance is still reasonable for simpler tasks, it decays rapidly with the increase of the task size. Also, the time to generate the tests (which are not reported but are in the order of few tens to many hundreds of seconds) are significantly greater than the average time taken by other tools, mainly due to the fact that we iteratively call an external program (SAL) by exchanging files. However, this problem could be alleviated easily with an hardware upgrade. As far as the time taken by the generation of tests is kept within minutes, we believe that it is not an issue, since this test suite generation is done only once. Note that the pure numeric performance of the combinatorial algorithm was never meant to be an objective of primary importance in our intentions, being it really to explore the viability of using model checkers for testing purposes. The current ATGT combinatorial test generation algorithm has been devised purposely to support us to this aim only, that is, being more flexible and integrated with other testing techniques, as explained earlier in this paper. We are very confident that its combinatorial efficiency could still be improved significantly if desired, although we intentionally left this issue outside the scope of this paper.

In Table 3 results for constrained asm specifications are reported. All the example's domains used in this case were subject to a number of restrictions in the form of asm axioms, quantitatively reported in the third column. Computed test suite sizes with and without constraints are reported. In this set of experiments we considered three example specifications taken from the literature. BBS is a basic billing system presented in [23] that processes telephone call data with four call properties, and in which every property has three possible values.

Cruise Control models a simple cruise control system originally presented in [1], while the Mobile Phone example models the optional features of a real-world mobile phone product line, and has been recently presented in [7]. In all the computed test suites the tool was able to correctly handle the axioms restrictions in order ensure complete coverage of all non-forbidden pairs, without the need to enumerate those pairs explicitly. This has been particularly helpful in the last example, involving many explicit and also a few implicit (to be derived) constraints. Size of computed test suite is also the least possible in the presence of the constraints, and equals the size of the test suite computed in [7]. Note that in two of the considered cases the test suite size increased with respect to their unconstrained equivalent, while it decreased in the last one, where constraints where more pervasive. Figure 2 reports all the AsmetaL axioms translating the constraints for this model.

Table 3. Test suite sizes for constrained models

Name	Task size	# of constraints	constrained size	unconstrained size
BBS	3^4	1	13	11
Cruise Control	$4^1 3^1 2^4$	2	8	6
Mobile Phone	$3^3 2^2$	7	9	11

```
axiom inv_1 over display, email : display=BW implies email!=GV
axiom inv_2 over display, camera : display=BW implies camera!=MP2
axiom inv_3 over camera, email : camera=MP2 implies email!=GV
axiom inv_4 over display, camera : display=MC8 implies camera!=MP2
axiom inv_5 over videoCamera, camera, display :
                    videoCamera implies (camera!=NOC and display!=BW)
axiom inv_6 over camera, videoRingtones : camera=NOC implies !videoRingtones
axiom inv_7 over display, email, camera :
                    !(display=MC16 and email=TV and camera=MP2)
```

Fig. 2. Constraints for mobile phone example

6 Conclusions and Future Work

In this paper we presented a logic based approach to combinatorial testing, supporting a number of original features, to the best of our knowledge, which have been also implemented in the software tool ATGT. These contributions include: support for Asm specifications, support for expressing constraints on the input domain as formal predicate expression on the input variables, integrated support for multiple types of coverages evaluation over the same system specification, support for combinatorial test case generation through selectable random or deterministic strategies, and support for user-level customization of the derived combinatorial test suite by import or banning of specific set of test cases. This work is currently on going and early evaluation results have been presented in this paper. We believe that our approach satisfies, even though not completely, the three goals stated in the introduction: ability to state complex constraints, ability to deal with user specific requirements on the test suite, and integration with other testing technique.

We plan to improve our technique along these directions. We already support enumerations and boolean, but we plan to extend also to: domain products (e.g. records), functions (arrays), derived functions, and discrete, finite sub-domains of integer. Converting integers to enumerations by considering each number one enumeration constant, is unfeasible unless for very small domains. We plan to investigate the partition of integer domains in sub-partitions of interest. We plan to extend the language of the constraints by allowing generic temporal logic expressions, which may specify how the inputs evolve. For this reason, we chose the model checker SAL instead of a simple SMT solver in the first place: it is able to deal with temporal constraints and transition systems. Moreover, further improvements can include taking into account the output and state variables, assuming that a complete behavioral model for the given system is available, and the binding of monitored input variables to some initial value at the system start state. We plan to apply combinatorial testing to complete specifications and compare it with other types of testing like structural testing [12] and fault based testing [13], which, however, require a specification complete of outputs, controlled variables, and transition rules.

References

1. Atlee, J.M., Buckley, M.A.: A logic-model semantics for SCR software requirements. In: International Symposium on Software Testing and Analysis, ACM, New York (1996)
2. Bose, R.C., Bush, K.A.: Orthogonal arrays of strength two and three. The Annals of Mathematical Statistics 23(4), 508–524 (1952)
3. Bryce, R.C., Colbourn, C.J.: Prioritized interaction testing for pair-wise coverage with seeding and constraints. Information & Software Technology 48(10), 960–970 (2006)
4. Bryce, R.C., Colbourn, C.J., Cohen, M.B.: A framework of greedy methods for constructing interaction test suites. In: ICSE 2005, pp. 146–155. ACM, New York (2005)
5. Cohen, D.M., Dalal, S.R., Fredman, M.L., Patton, G.C.: The AETG system: An approach to testing based on combinatorial design. IEEE Transactions On Software Engineering 23(7) (1997)
6. Cohen, M.B., Colbourn, C.J., Gibbons, P.B., Mugridge, W.B.: Constructing test suites for interaction testing. In: ICSE 2003, pp. 38–48 (2003)
7. Cohen, M.B., Dwyer, M.B., Shi, J.: Interaction testing of highly-configurable systems in the presence of constraints. In: ISSTA International symposium on Software testing and analysis, pp. 129–139. ACM Press, New York (2007)
8. Czerwonka, J.: Pairwise testing in real world. In: 24th Pacific Northwest Software Quality Conference (2006)

9. Dalal, S.R., Jain, A., Karunanithi, N., Leaton, J.M., Lott, C.M., Patton, G.C., Horowitz, B.M.: Model-based testing in practice. In: International Conference on Software Engineering ICSE, May 1999, pp. 285–295. Association for Computing Machinery, New York (1999)
10. de Moura, L., Owre, S., Rueß, H., Shankar, J.R.N., Sorea, M., Tiwari, A.: SAL 2. In: Alur, R., Peled, D.A. (eds.) CAV 2004. LNCS, vol. 3114, pp. 496–500. Springer, Heidelberg (2004)
11. Gargantini, A., Heitmeyer, C.: Using model checking to generate tests from requirements specifications. In: Nierstrasz, O., Lemoine, M. (eds.) ESEC 1999 and ESEC-FSE 1999. LNCS, vol. 1687, Springer, Heidelberg (1999)
12. Gargantini, A., Riccobene, E.: Asm-based testing: Coverage criteria and automatic test sequence generation. JUCS 10(8) (November 2001)
13. Gargantini, A.: Using model checking to generate fault detecting tests. In: Gurevich, Y., Meyer, B. (eds.) TAP 2007. LNCS, vol. 4454, pp. 189–206. Springer, Heidelberg (2007)
14. Gargantini, A., Riccobene, E., Rinzivillo, S.: Using spin to generate tests from ASM specifications. In: Börger, E., Gargantini, A., Riccobene, E. (eds.) ASM 2003. LNCS, vol. 2589, Springer, Heidelberg (2003)
15. Grindal, M., Offutt, J., Andler, S.F.: Combination testing strategies: a survey. Softw. Test, Verif. Reliab 15(3), 167–199 (2005)
16. Hartman, A.: Ibm intelligent test case handler: Whitch, `http://www.alphaworks.ibm.com/tech/whitch`
17. Hartman, A.: Graph Theory, Combinatorics and Algorithms Interdisciplinary Applications, Chapter Software and Hardware Testing Using Combinatorial Covering Suites, pp. 237–266. Springer, Heidelberg (2005)
18. Hartman, A., Raskin, L.: Problems and algorithms for covering arrays. DMATH: Discrete Mathematics 284(1-3), 149–156 (2004)
19. Hnich, B., Prestwich, S.D., Selensky, E., Smith, B.M.: Constraint models for the covering test problem. Constraints 11(2-3), 199–219 (2006)
20. Kobayashi, N., Tsuchiya, T., Kikuno, T.: Non-specification-based approaches to logic testing for software. Journal of Information and Software Technology 44(2), 113–121 (2002)
21. Kuhn, D.R., Okum, V.: Pseudo-exhaustive testing for software. In: SEW 2006: IEEE/NASA Software Engineering Workshop, pp. 153–158. IEEE Computer Society, Los Alamitos (2006)
22. Kuhn, D.R., Wallace, D.R., Gallo, A.M.: Software fault interactions and implications for software testing. IEEE Trans. Software Eng. 30(6), 418–421 (2004)
23. Lott, C., Jain, A., Dalal, S.: Modeling requirements for combinatorial software testing. In: A-MOST 2005: Proceedings of the 1st international workshop on Advances in model-based testing, pp. 1–7. ACM Press, New York (2005)
24. McDowell, A.: All-pairs testing, `http://www.mcdowella.demon.co.uk/allpairs.html`
25. Nurmela, K.: Upper bounds for covering arrays by tabu. Discrete Applied Mathematics 138(1-2), 143–152 (2004)
26. Pairwise web site, `http://www.pairwise.org/`
27. Tai, K.C., Lie, Y.: A test generation strategy for pairwise testing. IEEE Trans. Softw. Eng. 28(1), 109–111 (2002)
28. TestCover tool, `http://www.testcover.com/`
29. The asmeta project, `http://asmeta.sourceforge.net`
30. Jenny Combinatorial Tool, `http://www.burtleburtle.net/bob/math/jenny.html`

31. Williams, A.W., Probert, R.L.: A measure for component interaction test coverage. In: AICCSA, pp. 304–312. IEEE Computer Society, Los Alamitos (2001)
32. Williams, A.W.: Determination of test configurations for pair-wise interaction coverage. In: Proceedings of the 13th International Conference on the Testing of Communicating Systems (TestCom 2000), August 2000, pp. 59–74 (2000)
33. Yilmaz, C., Cohen, M.B., Porter, A.A.: Covering arrays for efficient fault characterization in complex configuration spaces. IEEE Trans. Software Eng. 32(1), 20–34 (2006)

Functional Testing in the Focal Environment

Matthieu Carlier and Catherine Dubois

CÉDRIC-ENSIIE,
1 square de la résistance, 91025 Évry Cedex, France
{carlier,dubois}@ensiie.fr

Abstract. This article presents the generation and test case execution under the framework Focal. In the programming language Focal, all properties of the program are written within the source code. These properties are considered, here, as the program specification. We are interested in testing the code against these properties. Testing a property is split in two stages. First, the property is cut out in several elementary properties. An elementary property is a tuple composed of some pre-conditions and a conclusion. Lastly, each elementary property is tested separately. The pre-conditions are used to generate and select the test cases randomly. The conclusion allows us to compute the verdict. All the testing process is done automatically.

1 Introduction

The Focal environment [9], developed by the Focal project[1] (initiated by T. Hardin and R. Rioboo and further developed by researchers coming from laboratories LIP6, CÉDRIC and INRIA), allows one to incrementally build library components and to formally prove their correctness. A component of a Focal library can contain specifications, implementations of operations and proofs that the implementations satisfy their specifications. In the early development stages, components contain only specifications, then step by step components are refined and completed with implementations by a refinement mechanism based on inheritance. Proofs may be done at any time. The Focal environment incorporates a prover called Zenon [4] which can automatically discharge proof obligations, with the help of intermediate lemmas given by the user. Focal components are translated into OCaml executable code and are verified by the Coq proof assistant [12].

Even if the Focal environment ensures a high level of confidence because of its methodology based on specification and proof, we cannot do without testing. Here are some reasons:

– The user, based on the informal specification from the user or the domain expert, writes the formal system specification. In Focal, it consists in formal properties maybe distributed in different components. For some of them the developer will provide a proof that the code is correct with respect to this

[1] `http://focal.inria.fr`

B. Beckert and R. Hähnle (Eds.): TAP 2008, LNCS 4966, pp. 84–98, 2008.

formal specification. But some of the properties may not be proven, for example low level properties about the addition of machine integers (we trust them because of external formal formalizations) or very general mathematical properties. In the latter case, these properties are assumed to be true (the keyword **assumed** is used instead of giving a sketch of proof). These properties may become test objectives.

- In the context of a functional validation process, when it is independent from the validation done by the development team, engineers often verify by testing the correctness of the final software with respect to their own specification. Let us call this specification the external one. So thanks to the inheritance mechanism of Focal, these external properties can be encoded in Focal in a component, from which the implementation will inherit. Then as previously it becomes possible to verify by testing if the code satisfies these new properties.
- There exist some basic types in Focal, e.g. `int`. This type is translated into the Ocaml type `int` and the Coq type `Z`. So in the executable code, machine integers are used but proofs are done with inductively defined integers. So we have *some* confidence in the code but we must test code to verify if the properties are verified, in particular around the bounds.
- Some OCaml untrusted code may be imported in a Focal certified code. No proof is done on this imported code.
- When Zenon, the prover integrated with Focal, does not succeed in proving a property automatically, two issues are possible: either it is not true or Zenon needs to be helped by giving some intermediate lemmas the user has to find. So before beginning the latter expensive task, we can test a not yet proven property in order to discover a counter-example or to have more confidence in the property. It can also be used to have confidence in the lemmas we need to introduce while proving a property (e.g. invariants, technical intermediate lemmas, supplementary assertions). In this context, testing is used for debugging specifications and programs before a proof is attempted or while it is being attempted. Such testing facilities have been integrated into the Isabelle [2] or Agda/Alfa [10] proof assistants.

In this paper we propose to test the code with respect to the expected properties written by the specifier or expressly introduced by the tester as for instance metamorphic relations (as introduced by Chen, Tse and Zhou [6]). We describe the testing framework and the corresponding tool FocalTest. More precisely a property, considered as an executable predicate, is exercised with some randomly generated inputs. Experience shows this style of testing is a useful method for debugging programs and specifications as exemplified by the tool Quickcheck developed for Haskell by Claessen and Hugues [8].

The tool FocalTest automatically produces the test environment and the drivers to conduct the tests. We benefit from the inheritance mechanism to isolate this testing code, called the testing harness in the paper, from the components written by the programmer.

The paper is organized as follows. First we briefly present the environment Focal and its large-spectrum language also called Focal. Then in Section 3, we define the syntax of the properties allowed for testing and overviews the testing procedure. The generation of the testing harness is detailed in Section 4. We illustrate our purpose with the triangle example in Section 5. Section 6 proposes a coverage analysis. Lastly we mention some related work before some concluding remarks and perspectives.

2 The Focal Environment and Its Language

The program development environment Focal is a framework dedicated to the complete development of certified components —in the sense of piece of specification/code proved correct with respect to the specifications— from the specification stage to the implementation one. In this section we give a brief overview of the underlying language, also called Focal. For further explanations please consult the documentation at `http://focal.inria.fr` and [9].

The language Focal is a functional language whose syntax is close to OCaml. It also incorporates some object oriented features such as inheritance, abstraction, late binding and redefinition. It allows us to define two kinds of structures, *species* and *collections*.

Roughly speaking a species defines a set of values that can be manipulated through functions called *methods*. At early stages in the development, those values and methods are abstract. For methods it means the user only writes their type, i.e. the types of the parameters and the result. He/she can also write specifications as properties involving the methods. As an example let us consider the species `Setoid` that specifies the notion of a set equipped with an equivalence relation `equal`:

```
species setoid  =
  rep;
  sig equal in self -> self -> bool;
  property equal_refl: all x in self, equal(x,x)
  property equal_sym: all x, y in self, equal(x,y) -> equal(y,x);
  property equal_trans: all x, y, z in self,
    equal(x,y) -> equal(y,z) -> equal(x,z);
end
```

This small example deserves some explanations about syntax: `self` is put for the type of the elements defined in the current species. The keyword `rep` introduces the type of the elements manipulated by the methods of the species. In the early development phases, it is usually abstract as in the example, it is later refined and defined as a concrete type *à la ML* called the *carrier type*.

Let us complete this species with a binary method `different` which returns `true` if its arguments are different and `false` otherwise. We can define this function although `equal` is not already defined (`#not_b` is the predefined operation on booleans) thanks to the mechanism of *late binding*. Furthermore we can demonstrate a property, that is `different` and `equal` are dual from each other. The proof is not detailed here —no proof will be shown in the paper— because its form does no matter in this paper.

```
let different(x,y)= #not_b(equal(x,y));
theorem different_not_equal: all x, y in self,
   different(x,y) <-> (not equal(x,y))
   proof:
   ...
```

Species may be defined from scratch but they are usually defined by using inheritance, more precisely multiple inheritance. Thus a Focal development forms a hierarchy whose nodes are species. Nodes close to a root correspond to pieces of specifications whereas deep nodes are made more and more precise, and then are close to implementations. Along inheritance paths, methods, carriers, properties can be refined (defined or redefined, proved in the case of properties). When a carrier type is defined in an inherited species, it cannot be redefined.

A species is said *complete* when every declared method (inherited or not) is defined and every stated property (inherited or not) has been proved or admitted (in such a case the proof is replaced by the special keyword `assumed`).

Collections are the implementations of species. A collection derives from a complete species. Collections are the leaves of the inheritance graph, cannot be refined by inheritance (like a *final* Java class for example). A collection is close to an abstract data type: it defines a type whose representation is abstracted and elements of the collection can only be manipulated with the help of the collection (those of the generating species, inherited or not).

The type of a collection is its interface obtained from the complete species the collection derives from: by removing definitions and proofs and abstracting the `rep` type in all the method types. The interface of a collection is named as the complete generative species it comes from. Interfaces can be ordered by inclusion, which gives a very simple notion of sub-typing.

Species can be parameterized by collections. The formal parameter is introduced by a name c and an interface I. Any collection CC having an interface including I can be used as an actual parameter for c. In the species body, the methods and properties of the parameter are denoted by `c!m`. The fact that CC has been created upon a complete species ensures that no link error can arrive at runtime and that proofs of CC can be used as lemmas. Species can also be parameterized by elements of collections, themselves introduced as parameters, thus introducing a dependence between parameters. Type-checking forbids dependence cycles between parameters.

3 Testing Properties

3.1 Overview

Usually, software testing requires the definition of an oracle that will determine whether or not an input/output pair satisfies a given predicate. The oracle is traditionally the tester itself, another existing program or an executable specification. In this case, during the execution of a test case, the tester or the testing tool will compare the actual output with the expected output computed by the oracle in order to establish the verdict. Our motivation is to verify the code by testing some properties extracted from the specifications or expressly written from test purpose. Since a property defines an executable predicate, we just need to know if the target property holds or not for some valuations of its bounded variables. Thus properties serve as oracles in their general acception.

The only information required in the test of a property are the test set and the verdict of the calculus. We can consider the property under test as a tuple composed of some *pre-conditions* and a *conclusion* that will help us to decide if test data are relevant or not and to compute the test verdict.

Testing a property of a species S requires to execute the methods involved in the statement. Thus those methods need to be defined in S or inherited. Furthermore the carrier type must be defined at this stage in order to be able to design test cases. For simplicity we impose that S is a complete species (no matter whether the proofs are done or not, we do not care about them). This hypothesis can be relaxed without any difficulty. In fact, a dependency analysis, already implemented in the Focal compiler, is enough to verify if the property to be tested can be executed.

The property under test is either defined in the species or inherited. Thus it can have been written at any development stage and can be a very abstract one.

3.2 Testable Properties

Focal allows us to express a large class of properties. Because efficiently testing any property is not possible at first glance[2], we restrict ourselves to the class of *testable* properties which take the following form:

$$\forall X_1 : \tau_1 \ldots X_n : \tau_n.\alpha_1 \Rightarrow \ldots \Rightarrow \alpha_n \Rightarrow (A_1^1 \vee \ldots \vee A_{n_1}^1) \wedge \ldots \wedge (A_1^m \vee \ldots \vee A_{n_m}^m)$$

where the α_i are produced by the grammar

$$\alpha ::= \alpha \vee \alpha | \alpha \wedge \alpha | A$$

The atomic formulas A and A_i^j are calls to Focal boolean methods, with an optional negation, and $\tau_1 \ldots \tau_n$ denote Focal types.So, testable properties are some first order formulas in prenex form without any existential quantifier. These formulas may contain free variables, the Focal compiler ensures that these variables are well defined somewhere in the species or the inheritance path.

We distinguish two parts in these properties: the pre-condition and the conclusion.

Definition 1. *Let* $P \equiv \forall X_1 : \tau_1 \ldots X_n : \tau_n.\alpha_1 \Rightarrow \ldots \alpha_n \Rightarrow \beta$*. We call the* pre-condition *(resp. the* conclusion*) of the property* P*, the predicate* $Pre(P) = \alpha_1 \wedge \ldots \wedge \alpha_n$ *(resp.* $Con(P) = \beta$*).*

[2] The $\exists$ quantifier is known to be a difficult problem.

3.3 Elementary Properties

In order to test a property, we first transform it into a set of simpler properties called *elementary properties* by applying the rewriting rules detailed in Figure 1. All the properties issued from the transformation will be tested separately. They are all together logically equivalent to the initial property (see Theorem 1). The reason why we transform a property into a set of elementary ones is that the property may specify a large variety of behaviors. Intuitively, an elementary property specifies a more restricted effect.

$$\alpha_1 \Rightarrow \ldots \Rightarrow (\beta_1 \vee \ldots \vee \beta_m) \Rightarrow \ldots \Rightarrow \alpha_n \longmapsto \begin{cases} \alpha_1 \Rightarrow \ldots \Rightarrow \beta_1 \Rightarrow \ldots \Rightarrow \alpha_n \\ \alpha_1 \Rightarrow \ldots \Rightarrow \beta_2 \Rightarrow \ldots \Rightarrow \alpha_n \\ \vdots \\ \alpha_1 \Rightarrow \ldots \Rightarrow \beta_m \Rightarrow \ldots \Rightarrow \alpha_n \end{cases}$$

$$\alpha_1 \Rightarrow \ldots \Rightarrow (\beta_1 \wedge \ldots \wedge \beta_m) \Rightarrow \ldots \Rightarrow \alpha_n \longmapsto \alpha_1 \Rightarrow \ldots \Rightarrow \beta_1 \Rightarrow \ldots \Rightarrow \beta_m \Rightarrow \ldots \Rightarrow \alpha_n$$

$$\alpha_1 \Rightarrow \ldots \Rightarrow \alpha_n \Rightarrow (\beta_1 \wedge \ldots \wedge \beta_m) \longmapsto \begin{cases} \alpha_1 \Rightarrow \ldots \Rightarrow \alpha_n \Rightarrow \beta_1 \\ \vdots \\ \alpha_1 \Rightarrow \ldots \Rightarrow \alpha_n \Rightarrow \beta_m \end{cases}$$

Fig. 1. Rewriting system

In the rewriting rules (Figure 1), quantifiers are omitted. The first rule consists in eliminating a disjunction appearing in the left hand side of a property, it creates a set (more precisely a multi-set) of properties. Intuitively, it corresponds to a case analysis. The second rule transforms a conjunction in the left hand side by its equivalent form with implications. The third rule splits the conjunction in the right hand side of the last implication. Like the first rule, it creates as many properties as sub-formulas in the initial right hand side conjunction.

These transformation rules constitute a rewriting system. It terminates (trivial by considering the number of $\Rightarrow$ and $\Leftrightarrow$ occurrences and the number of $\vee$ and $\wedge$ occurrences) and is confluent (all critical pairs can be joined). So every testable property P can be rewritten in a normal form (each formula of the set obtained from a rewriting step is again rewritten until convergence), which is a multi-set of formulas written $P_\downarrow^*$. The elements of $P_\downarrow^*$ are called the *elementary properties* of the original property. They have the following form:

$$\forall X_1 : \tau_1 \ldots X_n : \tau_n.\ A_1 \Rightarrow \ldots A_n \Rightarrow B_1 \vee \ldots \vee B_m$$

where A_i and B_i are atomic formulas.

Theorem 1. *Let P the property $\forall X_1 : \tau_1 \ldots X_n : \tau_n . A_1 \Rightarrow \ldots A_n \Rightarrow B_1 \vee \ldots \vee B_m$. So P is equivalent to $\bigwedge_{f \in P_\downarrow^*} \forall X_1 : \tau_1 \ldots X_n : \tau_n . f$*

3.4 Test Procedure

The original property is not considered in the test procedure. It is replaced in this process by its elementary properties. Each elementary property is considered and tested separately. Thus each elementary property has its own test set (composed of independent test cases).

A test case is a valuation σ which maps each quantified variable X_i to a value. It is randomly generated; we detail the generation in a next section. The elementary property $\forall X_1 : \tau_1 \ldots X_n : \tau_n . A_1 \Rightarrow \ldots A_n \Rightarrow B_1 \vee \ldots \vee B_m$ is then checked by considering its pre-condition and its conclusion in two steps:

- firstly, the pre-condition is evaluated with respect to σ. This is the validation part of the test case. If the pre-condition reduces to *false* or *fails*, the test case is rejected as being irrelevant. If it evaluates to *true*, go on with the next step;
- lastly, if the test case passes the pre-condition, we can compute the verdict. For that purpose, we evaluate the conclusion with respect to σ. If the result is *true*, then the verdict is OK. If it is *false*, the verdict is KO and we have found a counter-example that exemplifies the property is not satisfied for that test set. Anf if an exception is raised, the tester should decide himself if the exception is expected or not.

4 Test Harness

In this section we describe the test environment and the drivers we automatically produce to conduct the tests.

4.1 Structure

Our tool does not modify the species S that contains the property to be tested, FocalTest automatically derives a species $SHarness$ from S, called here the *test harness* of S. This species principally contains a method `random` of type `int -> self` which generates random values of the carrier type, a method `test_prop` which implements the test loop and a method `gen_report` which produces the testing report (e.g. in XML format).

For the synthesis and execution of test cases, we need to create and manipulate some data of the types given for the quantified variables of the property under test.

The type of a quantified variable in a property can be `self`, a basic Focal type `int`, `bool` ..., a concrete ML like type, a cartesian product or one of the abstract types described by the collections which may parameterize the species under test. In the latter case the type receives the name of the parameter. For example, in a species S parameterized by a collection C we can use the type C in particular to describe the carrier type of S (e.g. `rep = int * C` means an element of the species S is represented by a pair composed of an integer and an element of C).

We suppose the methods which generate values for the basic Focal types are known. In the case of the `self` type, we need the associated concrete representation. It is available since we have assumed the species is complete. So, FocalTest will produce the data generator by following the structure of the type (see next section for more details). In the case where S is parameterized by a collection C of interface $S1$ and when the carrier type refers to a parameter of the species (e.g. `rep = int * C`), the generator of *rep* values will call the generator for values of type C. So, in this case the harness of S is a species parameterized by a collection C' whose interface is $S1Harness$ that is the harness derived from $S1$.

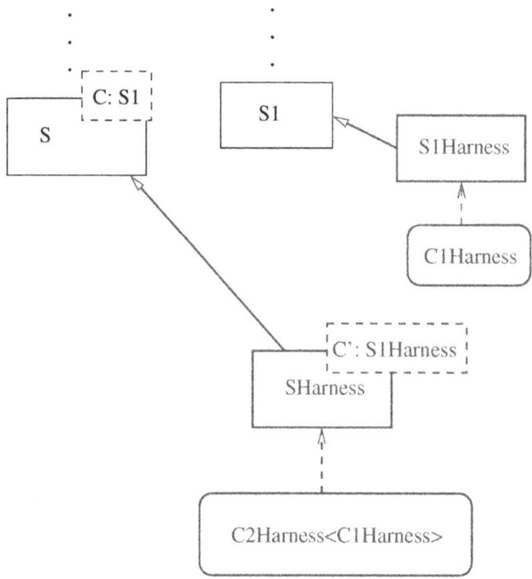

Fig. 2. The test hierarchy: target and harness

By extension, we call harness the set of species which add the random generators and the testing loop.

Figure 2 shows an example of a Focal hierarchy equipped with harness. Square boxes represent species (complete species in our context) whereas rounded boxes represent collections. Dotted arrows represent abstraction links between a collection and the species it is built from (e.g. `C1` and `S1`). Plain arrows represent inheritance dependencies (e.g. `S2Harness` inherits from `S2`). The parameter of a species is represented by a small dotted rectangle in the right upper corner (e.g. `S2` is parameterized by `C` of interface `S1`). When an instance is created, the effective parameter is indicated between `<` and `>` (e.g. the collection `C2` is the result of the application of `S2` on the parameter `C1`). In this example `S1` is complete. Finally FocalTest creates the collection `C2Harness` by applying `SHarness` to `C1Harness`, a collection built from `S1Harness`.

4.2 Test Data Generation

The FocalTest tool automatically creates the methods which pseudo-randomly generate values for the quantified variables of the test target. For each type τ appearing in the target property, FocalTest automatically defines a generator which can produce values of this type. its body is created by following the structure of τ. For a product type $\tau_1 * \tau_2$, it means FocalTest generates firstly the method for the type τ_1, secondly the method for the type τ_2 and lastly the methods for the product by combining the two previous generators. Focal allows to define concrete types that are defined by enumerating the values constructors. In the case of a concrete type, FocalTest generates for each constructor the generators for the constructor parameters and then combines them into the method generating values for the full type. In the case of the special imported OCaml types like *int*, FocalTest relies on the existing methods and imports them. In case of recursive data-types, we first choose the nature of the constructor, recursive/non-recursive with probability 1/2. Then we take uniformly a constructor in the chosen family.

Our approach to generate random values is a naive one. The distribution is not uniform and the generators tend to generate small sized values. However, they do not exclude any value, in other words, the functions are surjective. This can be improved, taking benefit from work as for instance [11].

5 FocalTest Experimentation

This section illustrates the usage of FocalTest on a classical example in testing literature, the triangle type program. The program takes the three lengths of the sides of a triangle and returns the nature of the triangle formed by input lengths: `Equilateral`, `Isosceles`, `Scalene` or `Error` if the three lengths do not define a triangle. So, the output of the program is the next Focal type:

```
type triangle_type =
  Equilateral in triangle_type;  Isosceles   in triangle_type;
  Scalene     in triangle_type;  Error       in triangle_type;
```

The length of a triangle edge is represented by an integer considered as an element from a commutative monoid. Thus, triangles are entities of a collection whose carrier type is a 3-tuple of lengths. The method implementing the specification given upper is named `type_triangle`, it has type `self` → `triangle_type`.

Two kinds of properties, soundness and correctness properties, are defined to specify the link between the arguments and the returned value of `type_triangle`. The soundness properties specify which constraints on lengths hold when the method `type_triangle` returns a specific value. The completeness properties specify which value can be returned by `triangle_type`.

The properties are shown in Figure 3. We have only detailed some of them because lack of space. The property `triangle_type_correct_equiv` states that if the method `triangle_type` returns the value `Equilateral` for the triangle `t`, then its three lengths are equal and greater than zero. The other correctness properties are similar.

```
property triangle_type_complete: all t in self,
  triangle_type(t) = Equilateral or triangle_type(t) = Isosceles or
  triangle_type(t) = Scalene or triangle_type(t) = Error;

property triangle_type_correct_equiv: all t in self,
  triangle_type(t) = Equilateral ->
  (edge!equal(fst(t), snd(t)) and edge!equal(fst(t), thrd(t)) and
  edge!equal(snd (t), thrd(t)) and edge!gt(fst(t), edge!zero))
```

Fig. 3. Some properties about *type_triangle*

This Focal development has been tested under FocalTest. The integers implementing lengths were constrained to be chosen in the interval 0–10. We tested 14 properties among those that were specified. These ones led to 40 elementary properties and asked FocalTest to generate 10 test cases for each property. This experiment detected no bugs. The test generation and execution were immediate. A potential overhead can be observed because of the harness compilation. For a large majority of the properties, less than 100 irrelevant test cases were required before obtaining the 10 valid required test cases. Some properties asked for about 1 000 irrelevant test cases.

For evaluating the quality of our testing tool, we created 10 mutants of the triangle program. We used mutation operations such as the replacement of an operator or a connector by another one (e.g. $\leq$ by $\geq$, $\wedge$ by $\vee$), the replacement of a variable by another one in a property, the replacement of a constant by another constant. We have evaluated the capacity of FocalTest to kill mutants. For this purpose, FocalTest has been run on each mutant several times, each time with new randomly generated test data, with the same parameters as previously. We can notice three behaviours among the 10 mutants. 2 mutants led to properties with unsatisfiable preconditions, a timeout was raised after 100 000 invalid test cases for each execution of FocalTest. Another mutant was never killed, indeed the domain (1–10) we chose was too restrictive and negative values should have killed the mutant (an experimentation with such a domain for lengths allowed us to confirm it). The 7 remaining mutants were killed every time FocalTest was run.

6 Coverage Analysis

Before defining some coverage criteria, we formalize the notion of pre domain and establish the basis of our testing method.

6.1 Pre-conditions and Pre-domains

The pre-condition and the conclusion of a testable property play a fundamental role. Intuitively, the pre-condition defines a set of values.

Theorem 2. *Let P_1 and P_2 such that $P_1 \longmapsto P_2$, then $Pre(P_2)$ implies $Pre(P_1)$.*

Proof. All rules but the first leaves the pre-condition unchanged. So we have to prove the fact for the first rule only. In that case, the pre-condition changes from $\alpha_1 \wedge \ldots \wedge (\beta_1 \vee \ldots \vee \beta_m) \wedge \ldots \wedge \alpha_n$ to the pre-conditions $\alpha_1 \wedge \ldots \wedge \beta_i \wedge \ldots \wedge \alpha_n$ for some $i \in [1, m]$. The conclusion is then obvious.

The next theorem allows us to extend the previous property to an elementary property of P.

Theorem 3. *Let P by a testable property and P' an elementary form of P. Then $Pre(P')$ implies $Pre(P)$.*

So any elementary property of a testable property P has a pre-condition weaker than the pre-condition of P. So any valid test case for an elementary property of P is a valid test case for P.

Definition 2. *Let $P \equiv \forall X_1 : \tau_1 \ldots X_n : \tau_n.\alpha_1 \Rightarrow \ldots \alpha_n \Rightarrow \beta$ be a testable property. We call* pre-domain of P, *the set $PrD(P)$ where $(v_1, \ldots, v_n) \in PrD(P)$ if and only if $Pre(P)$ holds for $X_1 = v_1, \ldots, X_n = v_n$.*

Intuitively, for a property P, $PrD(P)$ defines the set of all valuations σ which validate the pre-condition of P. The following theorem shows us the link between a property and its elementary forms according to the notion of pre-domain.

Theorem 4. *If a property P' is an elementary form of a property P then $PrD(P') \subseteq PrD(P)$*

Proof. Since, $Pre(P')$ implies $Pre(P)$, $PrD(P') \subseteq PrD(P)$ follows.

Hence, the pre-condition of each elementary form can be considered as the definition of a domain, identifying a kind of equivalence class of the pre-domain of the initial property. Because the pre-domain of an elementary form is a subset of the pre-domain of the original property, we can consider an elementary property as a sub-property. The original property is the combination of these sub-properties. So testing these properties separately is a gain since we have a finer granularity.

By the last theorem, all elementary forms of a property define a domain of test cases which is a subset of the original property's domain. But we should prove we do not loose any element of the pre-domain of P by considering only the elementary properties. Any test case in the pre-domain of P should be in the pre-domain of, at least, one elementary property of P.

Theorem 5. *Let P be a property. Let $P'_1, \ldots, P'_n$ the properties resulting from the application of a rewriting rule on P. Then, $PrD(P) = \cup_{i=1}^{n} PrD(P'_i)$.*

Proof. All rules but the first one leave the pre-condition unchanged. So the property is immediately true for these rules. For the first rule, if $Pre(P) = \alpha_1 \wedge \ldots \wedge (\beta_1 \vee \ldots \vee \beta_m) \wedge \ldots \wedge \alpha_n$ then $Pre(P'_i) = \alpha_1 \wedge \ldots \wedge \beta_i \wedge \ldots \wedge \alpha_n$. So, $\cup_{i=1}^{n} PrD(P'_i) = \{v_1, \ldots v_m | (v_1, \ldots, v_m) \in \cup_{i=1}^{n} PrD(P'_i)\}$. Also, by definition of PrD, $(v_1, \ldots, v_m) \in \cup_{i=1}^{n} PrD(P'_i) \leftrightarrow Pre(P'_1) \vee \ldots \vee Pre(P'_n)$ holds for $X_1 = v_1, \ldots, X_m = v_m$. We prove by definition of Pre that $Pre(P'_1) \vee \ldots \vee Pre(P'_n) \Leftrightarrow Pre(P)$. And so $\cup_{i=1}^{n} PrD(P'_i) = \{v_1, \ldots, v_m | (v_1, \ldots, v_m) \in PrD(P)\} = PrD(P)$.

Theorem 6. *Let P be a testable property. Then* $PrD(P) = \bigcup_{P' \in P_{\downarrow}^{*}} PrD(P')$.

The last theorem (following from Theorem 5 and associativity of $\cup$) tells us that the rewriting system preserves pre-domains. Testing the elementary properties separately is complete; any test case relevant for the original property is a possibly test case for at least one elementary property. Two pre-domains may overlap or even be equal (for example the third rule creates many properties all sharing the same pre-domain). It would be interesting to detect that two non equal pre-domains overlap. It probably means that the original property contains some redundant parts.

An elementary form coverage criteria consists in considering all the elementary properties obtained by the rewriting rules except the third one (to avoid pre-condition duplication). Then for each elementary property P'_1, select a test case in $PrD(P'_1)$ which is not a member of $PrD(P'_2)$ for some other elementary form P'_2. When a test case belonging to the pre-domains of two different elementary properties is discovered, it is worth reporting it.

6.2 A MC/DC Like Criteria

In the last section, we have proposed a first coverage criteria. Since a pre-condition can be considered as a decision, we explore some decision coverage. More precisely we are interested in the MC/DC coverage.

In the MC/DC criteria we have to demonstrate that every condition in a decision changes the outcome of the decision independently of the other conditions. For this purpose, for each condition there should be two test cases where the condition evaluates differently while the other conditions evaluate to the same value while the outcome of the decision is modified for both test cases. In a property (or an elementary form), the pre-condition and the conclusion are both decisions. A MC/DC style criteria for a set of elementary forms consist in applying for each elementary form the following scenario:

- select a test set satisfying the MD/DC criteria on the pre-condition. Because the pre-condition is a conjunction of a number of conditions, only one test set can be applied. It requires one test case where all decisions are evaluated to *false* (so the outcome of the pre-condition is *false* also). And for each decision, one test case where this decision evaluates to *false* while the other ones evaluate to true. It requires $n + 1$ test cases where n is the number of decisions;
- select a test set satisfying the MC/DC criteria on the conclusion: i) a set of test cases where all conditions but one evaluate to *false*. Each test case should evaluate the pre-condition to true; ii) a test set where all conditions evaluate to *false*.

For the first requirement, we ensure that the pre-condition can be evaluated to *false*. If the pre-condition cannot be evaluated to *false*, it means the pre-condition plays no role in the elementary form. This would emphasize that in the property (before rewriting) there is a part of the pre-condition without any effect. It also ensures each element of the pre-condition has an effect. A condition of the pre-condition which cannot be set to *false* means the pre-condition of the original property contains some useless parts.

With the second requirement, we ensure first, in the case the pre-condition is true, all conditions in the conclusion are independent from each other and they can all together set the conclusion to true. Like for the pre-condition, if a condition of the conclusion is not independent from the others, it means the conclusion of the original property contains useless parts. The second requirement ensures also that the conclusion can be evaluated to *false*.

Presently FocalTest is able to calculate the coverage of such a criterion by the generated test sets, but only for the conclusion of each elementary property. Pre-conditions are not yet taken into account because as soon as a test case valuates a precondition to *false*, FocalTest rejects it. We have run FocalTest 10 times on the triangle example (10 test cases per property). We have obtained a rate of 76% in the coverage of the conclusions, as defined previously.

7 Related Work

A lot of works have been done in the area of testing, especially for imperative languages and more recently for object oriented languages. For functional languages, the interest is more recent. One of the most advanced tools for testing functional programs is probably QuickCheck a tool for testing Haskell programs [8]. It provides a powerful specification language based on the first order logic and offers some combinators to write specification. The user has to type a correctness property and sends it to QuickCheck. The property could be a simple predicate or a more complex one with a pre-condition part. The tool analyses the type of the proposition and generates randomly test data, submits them and calculates the verdict for an arbitrary number of test cases. For a more effective use of QuickCheck, the user may define his own data generator. For example, if a property deals with a sorted list of integers, the user can provide a generator which only returns sorted lists. The Quickcheck approach and its good evaluation by users have inspired our own approach. Gast [13] is similar to Quickcheck for the language Clean. The user does not have to supply test data generators, they are automatically generated for arbitrary data types. On this point, we share the same particularity. But for recursive types, Gast does not randomly select the size of the values, it performs a breadth-first enumeration. And so, it is usually limited to small sized values, e.g. lists. On the contrary FocalTest tries to generate random values by distinguishing recursive constructors and non-recursive constructors and chooses one of them with a uniform distribution.

Other tools integrated in proof assistants have been inspired by the previous approach. For example, in Isabelle [2] by Berghofer and Nipkow or in Agda [10] by Dybjer, Haiyan and Takeyama. They allow the user to test some theorems before attempting a proof. and thus to debug specifications and proofs.

Another initiative has been proposed and implemented in Isabelle/HOL. The testing tool HOL-Testgen [5] on top of Isabelle-HOL aims to add some unit testing features. It allows the user to write test specifications. The tool partitions the input space of the specification and generates automatically the test script in SML. The implementation is then tested. HOL-Testgen exploits the common testing hypothesis formalized in [3], e.g. the regularity hypothesis. A regularity level k hypothesis means that if an implementation satisfies the requirements for test data of size less or equal than k then the implementation is correct for all data.

Our approach considers a formal specification as a test oracle. A decision procedure for the test oracle is automatically derived from the specification. Many researchers have proposed such an approach, e.g. [1,7]. We do not use a runtime assertion checker directly on the assertions written by the user but on an equivalent set of more tractable and traceable properties (for coverage computations for example).

8 Conclusion and Future Work

In this paper we have presented the FocalTest tool that permits to validate one or several components with respect to the specifications written in them. It can be used *a posteriori* or during the development process to debug specifications and implementations or also to have some confidence in a property before proving it. Although the case study presented in the paper is a small one, it demonstrates that our approach and its associated tool, FocalTest, are useful to find bugs. Furthermore, FocalTest has been used on the Focal standard library itself. It has permitted to reveal an error in a component: a comparison operator was wrong in a property which was not proven. In that case, the code was correctly written but the specification was not.

We rely on randomly selected test cases. A first requirement is put on these test cases: they must satisfy the pre-condition of the property under test. We can repeat the random draw until convenient values are produced but it can be an expensive process for some kind of pre-condition. To overcome this drawback, several solutions can be proposed. A first one is to provide the user with the possibility to define a specific purpose data generator tuned to generate valid test cases. Another method consists in exploring very carefully the pre-condition and more precisely the definition of the involved methods in order to produce constraints upon the values of the variables. Then it would remain to instantiate the constraints in order to generate test cases ready to be submitted. This method is a *white box* method testing whereas the currently implemented method is a *black box* testing method. This direction is one of our perspectives to improve our testing method and is currently under study.

References

1. Antoy, S., Hamlet, D.: Automatically checking an implementation against its formal specification. IEEE Trans. Softw. Eng. 26(1), 55–69 (2000)
2. Berghofer, S., Nipkow, T.: Random testing in Isabelle/HOL. In: Cuellar, J., Liu, Z. (eds.) Software Engineering and Formal Methods (SEFM 2004), pp. 230–239. IEEE Computer Society, Los Alamitos (2004)
3. Bernot, G., Gaudel, M.-C., Marre, B.: Software testing based on formal specifications: a theory and a tool. Software Engineering Journal 6(6) (1991)
4. Bonichon, R., Delahaye, D., Doligez, D.: Zenon: An extensible automated theorem prover producing checkable proofs. In: Dershowitz, N., Voronkov, A. (eds.) LPAR 2007. LNCS (LNAI), vol. 4790, pp. 151–165. Springer, Heidelberg (2007)
5. Brucker, A.D., Wolff, B.: Test-Sequence Generation with HOL-TestGen – With an Application to Firewall Testing. In: Gurevich, Y., Meyer, B. (eds.) TAP 2007. LNCS, vol. 4454, Springer, Heidelberg (2007)
6. Chen, T.Y., Tse, T.H., Zhou, Z.: Fault-based testing without the need of oracles. Information & Software Technology 45(1), 1–9 (2003)
7. Cheon, Y., Leavens, G.T.: A simple and practical approach to unit testing: The jml and junit way. In: Magnusson, B. (ed.) ECOOP 2002. LNCS, vol. 2374, pp. 231–255. Springer, Heidelberg (2002)
8. Claessen, K., Hughes, J.: QuickCheck: a lightweight tool for random testing of Haskell programs. ACM SIGPLAN Notices 35(9), 268–279 (2000)
9. Dubois, C., Hardin, T., Viguié Donzeau-Gouge, V.: Building certified components within focal. In: Loidl, H.-W. (ed.) Revised Selected Papers from the Fifth Symposium on Trends in Functional Programming, TFP 2004. Trends in Functional Programming, München, Germany, vol. 5, pp. 33–48. Intellect (2006)
10. Dybjer, P., Haiyan, Q., Takeyama, M.: Combining testing and proving in dependent type theory. In: Basin, D., Wolff, B. (eds.) TPHOLs 2003. LNCS, vol. 2758, pp. 188–203. Springer, Heidelberg (2003)
11. Flajolet, P., Sedgewick, R.: Analytic Combinatorics, ch. I-IX. In: Draft available electronically from P. Flajolet's home page (2007)
12. INRIA. Coq, version 8.1 (November 2006), `http://coq.inria.fr/`
13. Koopman, P.W.M., Alimarine, A., Tretmans, J., Plasmeijer, M.J.: Gast: Generic automated software testing. In: Peña, R., Arts, T. (eds.) IFL 2002. LNCS, vol. 2670, pp. 84–100. Springer, Heidelberg (2003)

Bounded Relational Analysis of Free Data Types

Andriy Dunets, Gerhard Schellhorn, and Wolfgang Reif

Lehrstuhl für Softwaretechnik und Programmiersprachen,
Institut für Informatik,
Universität Augsburg,
86135 Augsburg Germany
{dunets,schellhorn,reif}@informatik.uni-augsburg.de
http://www.informatik.uni-augsburg.de/swt

Abstract. In this paper we report on our first experiences using the relational analysis provided by the Alloy tool with the theorem prover KIV in the context of specifications of freely generated data types. The presented approach aims at improving KIV's performance on first-order theories. In theorem proving practice a significant amount of time is spent on unsuccessful proof attempts. An automatic method that exhibits counter examples for unprovable theorems would offer an extremely valuable support for a proof engineer by saving his time and effort. In practice, such counterexamples tend to be small, so usually there is no need to search for big instances. The paper defines a translation from KIV's recursive definitions to Alloy, discusses its correctness and gives some examples.

Keywords: First-order logic, theorem proving, SAT checking, abstract data types, model checking, verification, formal methods.

1 Introduction

In our work we present an integration of an automatic procedure for finding finite counter examples or witnesses for first-order theories in the theorem prover KIV [4]. KIV supports both functional and state-based approaches to model systems. In this paper, we concern ourselves with the functional approach, which uses hierarchically structured higher-order algebraic specifications. More precisely, we are interested in the automation of its first-order part.

As first-order logic is undecidable we can construct either a decision procedure for decidable fragments or use an automated prover for full logic. Both approaches are useful for provable goals.

Since most of the time in interactive theorem proving is spent to find out why certain goals are not provable, an alternative approach is to try to disprove conjectures and to generate counter examples. Therefore, we were inspired by the automatic analysis method for first-order *relational* logic with *transitive closure* implemented in the Alloy Analyzer [10] and its successful application in the Mondex challenge by Ramananandro [15]. Alloy's algorithm handles the full first-order relational logic with quantifiers and transitive closure [11].

B. Beckert and R. Hähnle (Eds.): TAP 2008, LNCS 4966, pp. 99–115, 2008.

Because formal theories in KIV are constructed using structured algebraic specifications, the sought-after automatic procedure involving Alloy Analyzer would represent a relational analysis of algebraic data types. A fundamental work on this topic was done by Kuncak and Jackson [12]. They present a method for the satisfiability checking of first-order formulas which is based on finite model finding, formulate essential properties which should be satisfied by an analyzed data structure and identify a class of the amenable formulas. A reduction from reasoning about infinite structures to reasoning about finite structures was achieved for a minimal theory consisting of selectors only.

In this paper we elaborate the results in [12] by extending the considered language from just selector functions to constructors and recursive functions as they usually occur in first-order theories. We apply these results to universally closed formulas in the KIV theorem prover. As a first step in this direction, the approach presented in this paper is confined to the analysis of recursive definitions over free data types[1], e.g. lists, stacks, binary trees. In our experiments we used Alloy Analyzer version 4.0 [10].

1.1 Related Work

There are different approaches of combining interactive methods with automated ones, which have in common the aim to strengthen interactive proving tools by adding automatic methods. One approach is to use automated theorem provers based on resolution or other calculi as a *tactic* in KIV to prove first-order theorems. A fundamental investigation of a conceptual integration that goes beyond a loose coupling of two proof systems was performed in [1] and some improvements on exploiting the structure of algebraic theories were presented in [16]. In [13] an automation procedure for a theorem prover is described which bridges numerous differences between Isabelle with its higher-order logic and resolution provers Vampire and SPASS (restricted first-order, untyped, clause form). In [7] a proof certification using theorem prover Isabelle/HOL for a decision procedure for the quantifier-free first-order logic in SMT-solver haRVey is described. The theorem prover is used to guarantee soundness of automatically produced proofs, while the automated tool is used as an *oracle*.

Nevertheless automated theorem provers are of limited use, since they do not support induction necessary to reason about algebraic types and recursive definitions. They are also applicable only for provable theorems, while most of the time in interactive theorem proving is spent on unsuccessful proof attempts.

For many applications knowing a counter model to a wrong assumption is as useful as knowing that a conjecture is true itself. This idea is realized in [6], where a proof procedure based on finite model finding techniques is designed for first-order logic. Reversely, [14] presents a so-called small model theorem, which calculates a threshold size for data types. If no counter examples are found at the threshold, the theorem guarantees that increasing the scope still produces no counter examples.

[1] Syntactically different terms built up from the constructors denote different values.

1.2 Outline

We provide some background on the theorem prover KIV and the specification of algebraic data types in Section 2. Section 3 gives a short overview of the Alloy Analyzer tool, the logic it uses and the analysis. Section 4 introduces in generating models for free data types in Alloy. Section 5, which is the central one, provides a detailed insight into an axiomatization of recursive functions for finite models in Alloy. In Section 6 we report on our first experiences from an application in KIV for an example, that has been analyzed earlier using KIV's own counter example generation. This is followed by conclusions and an outlook in Section 7. Throughout this work we use lists as a representative example of free algebraic data types.

2 Theorem Prover KIV

KIV is a tool for formal system development. It provides a strong proof support for all validation and verification tasks and is capable of handling large-scale theories by efficient proof techniques and an ergonomic user interface. Details on KIV can be found in [4,5].

2.1 Specification of Algebraic Data Types

The basic logic underlying the KIV system combines *Higher-Order Logic* (HOL) and *Dynamic Logic* (DL) [8], which allows to reason over imperative programs (partial and total correctness as well as program equivalence are expressible).

In this work we are particularly interested in the FOL part of the KIV system. The reason is, that in almost all proof tasks carried out interactively in KIV, whether in the basic logic or in extensions for temporal logic proofs [2], ASM specifications [19], statecharts [21,3] or Java program proofs [20], eventually a lot of first-order proof obligations arise. These are typically discharged using *simplifier rules.* Most simplifier rules are first-order lemmas which are automatically used for rewriting and other simplifications. In large case studies the number of used rewrite rules is often several thousands, many of them imported from the KIV library of data types.

Defining and proving such simplifier rules is therefore a regular task in interactive verification. Usually, some of these theorems are wrong on the first attempt, so a quick check that identifies unprovable ones is very helpful.

A theory in KIV describes data types, e.g. naturals, lists, arrays or records, which afterwards are used in DL programs. Theories are specified using *structured algebraic specifications.* To specify data structures adequately, in addition to first-order axioms we also need axioms for induction. Unfortunately an induction scheme cannot be specified by a finite set of first-order formulas. As a replacement *generation clauses* are used: s **generated by** $c_1, \ldots, c_n$, where s is a

```
generic data specification
   parameter elem
   list = [] |  . + . ( . .first : elem;  . .rest : list);
   variables
      x, y, z : list;
   order predicates  . < . : list x list;
end generic data specification

enrich list with
   functions
       . + . : list x list -> list;
       rev   : list -> list;
   axioms
      app-nil  : [] + x = x;
      app-cons : (a + x) + y = a + (x + y);
      rev-nil  : rev([]) = [];
      rev-cons : rev(a + x) = rev(x) + (a + []);
end enrich
```

Fig. 1. KIV specification of lists

sort, and $c_1, \ldots, c_n$ are its constructors. The simplest example of a generated sort are natural numbers: *nat* **generated by** $0, +1$.

A basic specification consists of three parts: a description of the signature, the axioms and the principles of induction. Figure 1 shows the specification of lists in KIV. It contains a *basic specification* of the sort *elem* (not shown), a *generic data specification* of lists and finally an *enrichment* of the list data specification by recursive functions *app* and *rev*. Line `list = [] | ...` generates four axioms specifying the free data type *list*. The first axiom is **generated by** clause which declares that the sort is generated by its constructors: `list` **generated by** `[],+`. From freeness the following axioms are generated. *selector* axioms: $(a+x).first = a$, $(a+x).rest = x$, *uniqueness* of constructors: $a+x \neq []$ and *injectivity* of constructors: $a + x = b + x \leftrightarrow a = b \wedge x = y$.

For free data types, axioms for the order predicate $<$, which corresponds to the subterm relation, are automatically included in the theory. In the enrichment we specify two recursive functions *rev* and *app* (overloaded $+$ for *append*). These are defined by *structural recursion* over the first argument of a function.

3 Alloy Analyzer

In this section we introduce a logic which underlies this work. This logic is also used as an intermediate language to which Alloy input is translated and which is also handled by the Alloy algorithm. Although the logic is multi-sorted, for the sake of a better illustration we consider only two sorts: *elem* and *list*. In the

$$
\begin{aligned}
\textbf{sort} &::= list \mid elem \\
F &::= A \mid \forall x \in sort.\ F \mid \exists x \in sort.\ F \mid F_1 \wedge F_2 \mid \neg F_1 \\
A &::= (x_1, \ldots, x_n) \in R^n \mid x_1 = x_2 \\
R^n &::= r^n, n \neq 2 \\
R^2 &::= \ {}^\wedge R_1^2 \mid r^2
\end{aligned}
$$

$$M = (L, E, \gamma), \qquad \alpha : Vars \to L \cup E$$

$$
\begin{aligned}
[\![\forall\ \text{x}\in\text{list. F}]\!]^{M,\alpha} &\equiv \forall\, l \in L.\ [\![\text{F}]\!]^{M,\alpha'},\ \ \alpha' = \alpha[x := l] \\
[\![\exists\ \text{x}\in\text{list. F}]\!]^{M,\alpha} &\equiv \exists\, l \in L.\ [\![\text{F}]\!]^{M,\alpha'},\ \ \alpha' = \alpha[x := l] \\
[\![\forall\ \text{x}\in\text{elem. F}]\!]^{M,\alpha} &\equiv \forall\, e \in E.\ [\![\text{F}]\!]^{M,\alpha'},\ \ \alpha' = \alpha[x := o] \\
[\![\exists\ \text{x}\in\text{elem. F}]\!]^{M,\alpha} &\equiv \exists\, e \in E.\ [\![\text{F}]\!]^{M,\alpha'},\ \ \alpha' = \alpha[x := o] \\
[\![F_1 \wedge F_2]\!]^{M,\alpha} &\equiv [\![F_1]\!]^{M,\alpha} \wedge [\![F_2]\!]^{M,\alpha} \\
[\![\neg F_1]\!]^{M,\alpha} &\equiv \neg[\![F_1]\!]^{M,\alpha}
\end{aligned}
$$

$$
\begin{aligned}
[\![(x_1, \ldots, x_n) \in R^n]\!]^{M,\alpha} &\equiv (\alpha(x_1), \ldots, \alpha(x_n)) \in [\![R^n]\!]^{M,\alpha} \\
[\![{}^\wedge R^2]\!]^{M,\alpha} &\equiv \{(x_1, x_2) \mid \exists n \geq 1.\ \exists l_1, \ldots, l_n \in L.\ \bigwedge_{i=1}^{n} (l_{i-1}, l_i) \in [\![R^2]\!]^{M,\alpha}\} \\
[\![r^n]\!]^{M,\alpha} &\equiv \gamma(r^n)
\end{aligned}
$$

Fig. 2. Syntax and Semantics for Relational Logic with Transitive Closure [11]

next section we will discuss an axiomatization of free data types in this logic, where we will use the specification of lists as a generic example.

3.1 Logic

The logic used by the Alloy analyzer is a first-order relational logic with transitive closure [11]. Figure 2 shows its syntax and semantics. The input language of Alloy has a very rich syntax, but here we stick only to the most essential part.

We consider two sorts: lists and elements. Formulas F can be constructed using universal as well as existential quantifiers. Atomic formulas A are defined using $\in$ operator on variables $x_1, \ldots, x_n$ for a n-ary relation R^n and using equality operator. Relation-valued expressions R^n are introduced using terminal symbols r^n. In case of binary relations R^2 a transitive closure operator can be applied: ${}^\wedge R^2$.

Other types of atomic formulas like $R_1^n \subseteq R_2^n$ or $R_1^n = R_2^n$ are provided by the Alloy's syntax which can be derived from the basic ones:

$$
\begin{aligned}
\textbf{setOp} &::= \cup \mid \cap \mid \setminus \\
A &::= R_1^n \subseteq R_2^n \mid R_1^n = R_2^n \\
R^n &::= R_1^n\ \textbf{setOp}\ R_2^n \mid R_1^k.R_2^{k'},\ \ where\ k + k' - 1 = n
\end{aligned}
$$

where

$$
\begin{aligned}
R_1^n \subseteq R_2^n &\equiv \forall \bar{x}.\, \bar{x} \in R_1^n \rightarrow \bar{x} \in R_2^n \\
R_1^n = R_2^n &\equiv R_1^n \subseteq R_2^n \;\wedge\; R_2^n \subseteq R_1^n \\
(x_1, \ldots, x_{k+k'-1}) \in R_1^k.R_2^{k'} &\equiv \exists y.\, (x_1, \ldots, x_{k-1}, y) \in R_1^k \\
&\qquad \wedge\, (y, x_k, \ldots, x_{k+k'-1}) \in R_2^{k'}
\end{aligned}
$$

This logic has a standard semantics of multisorted logic. Formulas of the logic are interpreted over structures $M = (L, E, \gamma)$, where L and E represent disjoint domains of both sorts *list* and *elem*. Function γ interprets relational symbols r^n by mapping them on the relations between individual atoms of M, e.g. for a binary relational symbol $first \subseteq list \times elem$ the corresponding mapping would be $\gamma(first) \subseteq L \times E$. Further, a valuation function $\alpha : Vars \rightarrow L \cup E$ assigns values from M to free variables x_i of an evaluated formula. A generic definition of $[\![\varphi]\!]^{M,\alpha}$ for a given structure M and a valuation α is shown in Figure 2. For a given structure M and a formula φ we call M *model* of φ *iff* $[\![\varphi]\!]^{M,\alpha}$ is *true* for *any* valuation α, i.e. $M \models \varphi$. Similarly, we define $M \models \{\varphi_1, \ldots, \varphi_n\}$ *iff* $M \models \varphi_i$ holds for each φ_i.

3.2 Model Finding

Alloy implements a fully automatic analysis for a relational logic and is an efficient model finder. By defining a signature and a set of axioms Φ_{ax} we specify the analyzed system. For a formula φ and a given scope r (upper bound on the size of the domains) Alloy searches for models M satisfying axioms Φ_{ax} but violating the property φ, i.e. $M \models \Phi_{ax} \cup \{\neg\varphi\}$.

We utilize this capability to search for structures $M = (E, L, \gamma)$ which represent finite cutouts from infinite term algebras. We recall, that analyzed formulas are normalized to $Q_1 v_1 :: s_1. \ldots Q_n v_n :: s_n.\ \psi$ where ψ is a quantifier-free formula with free variables $v_1, \ldots, v_n$. In the case of a successful search, Alloy identifies a finite structure M and a valuation α_0 for the specified scope r such that $\neg[\![\psi]\!]^{M,\alpha_0}$. For example, for a universal formula $\forall x, y :: list.\ x = y$ and the scope $r \geq 2$ Alloy would identify M with L containing at least two different atoms l_0, l_1 such that $\neg[\![x = y]\!]^{M,\alpha[x:=l_0,y:=l_1]}$. A detailed demonstration using a more sophisticated example is given in Section 6, where an implementation of interval lists does not satisfy an invariant.

3.3 Translation of KIV Formulas to Relational Form

Since Alloy is based on relational logic, KIV specifications involving functions have to be translated to specifications using relations. Therefore, as a first step we map each function symbol f to the corresponding relation (predicate) F:

$$
f : \underline{s} \rightarrow s' \qquad \rightsquigarrow \qquad F : \underline{s} \times s'
$$

The basic idea is that the relation F encodes the graph of the function f:

$$[\![f]\!](a_1,\ldots,a_n) = b \Leftrightarrow [\![F]\!](a_1,\ldots,a_1,b) \tag{1}$$

where $[\![\mathrm{f}]\!]$ is the semantics of f in a model of the KIV specification and $[\![\mathrm{F}]\!]$ is the semantics of F in the corresponding model of the translated specification.

To achieve this we need two axioms for every function, that state that F is the translation result of a total function, namely the `uniqueness` axiom:

$$\forall x_1,\ldots,x_n,y,z.\ F(x_1,\ldots,x_n,y) \wedge F(x_1,\ldots,x_n,z) \rightarrow y = z \tag{2}$$

and the `totality` axiom:

$$\forall x_1,\ldots,x_n.\ \exists y.\ F(x_1,\ldots,x_n,y) \tag{3}$$

We also need to translate the axioms of KIV to axioms over relations. This can be done schematically, the main idea is to introduce auxiliary variables for all intermediate results and to finally replace $f(x_1,\ldots,x_n) = y$ by $F(x_1,\ldots,x_n,y)$. We give a formal definition which assumes that each axiom φ has been normalized to have all quantifiers in front of the formula (prenex normal form):

$$\varphi \equiv Q_1 v_1 :: s_1 \ldots . Q_n v_n :: s_n.\ \psi, \tag{4}$$

where ψ is a quantifier-free formula with free variables $v_1,\ldots,v_n$.

The restriction to prenex normal form is not really necessary, but avoids a discussion about a suitable renaming of bound variables and occurrences of terms. As an example, consider a formula φ from the specification of lists in KIV:

$$\varphi \ \equiv\ \forall x,y :: list.\ rev(x+y) = rev(y) + rev(x) \tag{5}$$

Its quantifier-free subformula ψ contains the function symbols *rev* and $+$ (for the *append* function). Therefore the translated axiom will use predicates REV : $list \times list$ for *rev* and APP : $list \times list \times list$ for $+$.

To define the translation, we need two sets of terms: the set of "top-level" terms $\mathfrak{T}_{top}$, which consist of all terms t_i that occur in equations $t_i = t_j$ or predicates $P(t_1,\ldots t_n)$ of ψ and which are not just variables. In our example $\mathfrak{T}_{top} \equiv \{rev(x+y), rev(y)+rev(x)\}$. Second we need the set $\mathfrak{T}_{all}$ of all non-variable subterms of terms in $\mathfrak{T}_{top}$. For our example $\mathfrak{T}_{all} \equiv \mathfrak{T}_{top} \cup \{x+y, rev(y), rev(x)\}$.

Based on these two sets the translated formula $\tau(\varphi)$ of an axiom φ is then defined as follows:

Definition 1 (Relational form)
Given a mapping $\vartheta : \mathfrak{T}_{all} \rightarrow Vars$ that generates fresh variables for terms in $\mathfrak{T}_{all}$ and a functional formula φ in KIV of the form given in (4). We construct its relational counterpart $\tau(\varphi)$ for Alloy:

$$\begin{aligned}\tau(\varphi) \ &\equiv Q_1 v_1 :: s_1 \ldots . Q_n v_n :: s_n.\ \forall\ \vartheta(\mathfrak{T}_{all}).\\ &\bigwedge_{f(t_1,\ldots,t_k)\in\mathfrak{T}_{all}} (\vartheta(t_1),\ldots,\vartheta(t_k),\vartheta(f(t_1,\ldots,t_k))) \in F \rightarrow\ \psi[\mathfrak{T}_{top} \backslash \vartheta(\mathfrak{T}_{top})]\end{aligned}$$

where $\psi[\mathfrak{T}_{top}\backslash\vartheta(\mathfrak{T}_{top})]$ *is* ψ *with terms from* $\mathfrak{T}_{top}$ *substituted by corresponding fresh variables* $\vartheta(\mathfrak{T}_{top})$.

To continue with our example above, we compute $\tau(\varphi)$ for (5):

$$\tau(\varphi) \equiv$$
$$\forall x, y :: list.\ \forall z_1, z_2, z_3, z_4, z_5 :: list.\ (z_3, z_1) \in REV \ \wedge\ (z_4, z_5, z_2) \in APP$$
$$\wedge\ (x, y, z_3) \in APP \ \wedge\ (y, z_4) \in REV \ \wedge\ (x, z_5) \in REV \ \rightarrow\ z_1 = z_2$$

It is easy to prove (by induction on the complexity of terms and formulas) that the syntactical transformation τ preserves the meaning of formulas in the following sense: for each model of the original formula φ, the corresponding relational model (where the semantics of F is defined via (1)) satisfies $\tau(\varphi)$. Similarly, for each model of $\tau(\varphi)$, that also satisfies the axioms *Totality* and *Uniqueness*, a model of the original signature can be constructed such that φ and (1) hold. The transformation has linear complexity with respect to the size of a formula.

4 Generating Models of Free Data Types in Alloy

The semantics of free data types is defined on algebraic structures called *term algebras* which represent concrete models of specifications. In term algebras carrier sets are composed of inductively generated terms. Terms are generated using *constructor* operations (functions), e.g. the constant *nil* and the function *cons* : *elem* × *list* → *list* for lists.

Here we refer to the work of Kuncak and Jackson [12]. We adopt their ideas to generate term algebras in Alloy. We have to specify corresponding structures $M = (E, L, \gamma)$, where E and L represent domains and γ interprets relational symbols r^n over E and L. Again we are using *lists* as a generic example of a free data type.

In Alloy new sorts (types of atoms) are introduced by the keyword **sig**. We specify two new sorts: *elem* and *list*, see Figure 3. Using the keyword **extends** we split the set of atoms of type *list* in two disjunctive subsets: the singleton set *nil* (defined to have exactly one atom, keyword **one**) and the set *cons* which can have an arbitrary number of atoms within specified bounds. Atoms of type *cons* represent results of the constructor function *cons* : *elem* × *list* → *list* and are always connected over selector relations *first* and *rest* with atoms from which they are constructed. On the right side in Figure 3 the generated metamodel of the signature is shown.

In the next step we specify axioms in Alloy which restrict relations *first* and *rest* to behave properly in M. The following four axioms (SUGA) are necessary, see Figure 4. SUGA axioms generate infinite structures M which contain an isomorphic copy of the term model $M_\infty = (E, L, \gamma)$. Here the language is restricted only to selector functions *first* and *rest*.

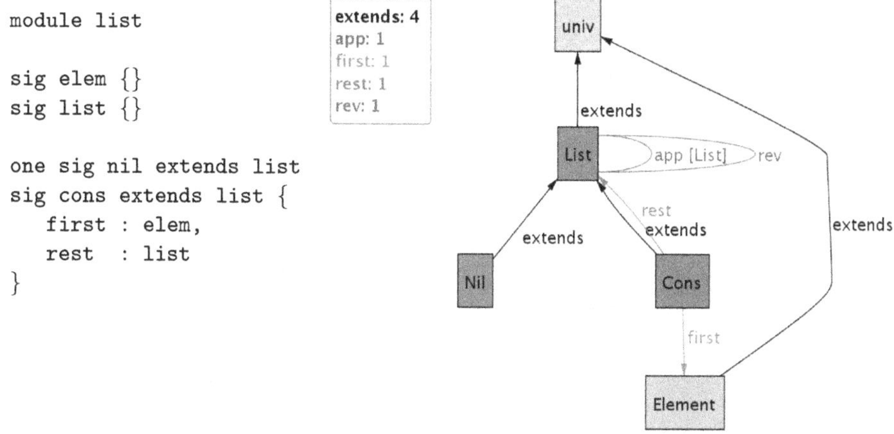

Fig. 3. Metamodel of lists in Alloy

$$
\begin{array}{rl}
\textit{selectors:} & \forall l : list.\ l \neq nil \rightarrow \exists!\ l' : list,\ e : elem.\ l.rest = l' \ \wedge\ l.first = e \\
 & \forall l : list,\ e : elem.\ (nil, e) \notin rest\ \wedge (nil, l) \notin first \\
\textit{uniqueness:} & \forall l, l' : list.\ l.first = l'.first\ \wedge\ l.rest = l'.rest\ \rightarrow\ l = l' \\
\textit{generator:} & \forall l' : list,\ e : elem.\ \exists l : list.\ l.first = e\ \wedge\ l.rest = l' \\
\textit{acyclicity:} & \forall l : list.\ (l, l) \notin \hat{}rest
\end{array}
$$

Fig. 4. SUGA axioms

The infiniteness of M_∞ prevents it to be constructed by Alloy. A possible solution to this problem is to omit the *generator* axiom (SUA axioms). This results in producing finite models M_0 which represent specific parts of original infinite structure M_∞, so-called *subterm-closed* models, i.e. models closed under transitive closure of selector relation *rest*, see Figure 5.

[12] establishes a finite satisfiability result by proving that for a specific class of formulas[2] (existential - bounded universal, EBU) satisfiability can be checked on finite models of SUA axioms (axioms without generator). For this purpose a notion of bounded quantification is introduced, see [12]. Roughly, if a witness for an EBU formula is found in a finite model M_0, we can pick the same witness in the infinite model M_∞. So a semi-decision procedure involving Alloy can be constructed that checks satisfiability of these formulas.

Unfortunately, we found that these encouraging results apply to theories only, where just selector functions are present in formulas. In order to use it in practice we have to cope with several difficulties. In the next section we will discuss what we have done to incorporate recursively defined functions in the method and what implications can possibly emerge.

[2] e.g., formula $\forall x :: list.\ \exists y :: list.\ (x, x, y) \in APP$ contains unbounded quantification and has no finite models.

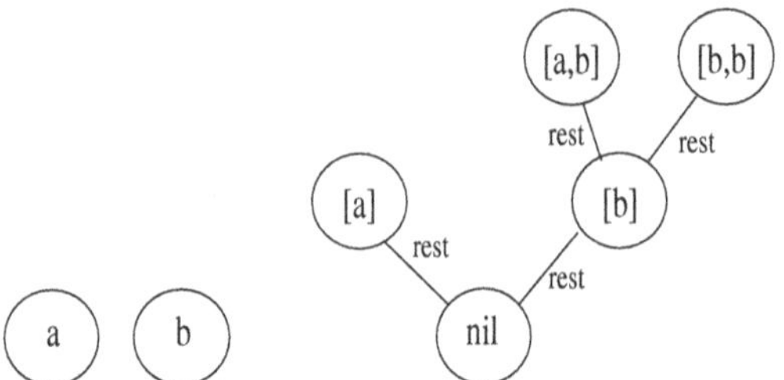

Fig. 5. Finite subterm-closed substructure M_0 of infinite structure M_∞ (2 *elem* and 5 *list* atoms). Relation *first* is omitted for reasons of clearness.

5 Axiomatization of Recursive Functions

We would like to extend our language containing just selector relational symbols {*first,rest*} to the complete language with recursive functions that we use in KIV. Such recursive definitions have the following form:

Definition 2 (KIV axioms for recursion). *To define a function* $f : s_1 \times \cdots \times s_k \to s_1$ *by structural recursion over the first argument, axioms of the following form are used:*

$$\forall u, \underline{v}.\ \ \psi_i \to f(c_i(u), \underline{v}) = \Psi_i(f, u, \underline{v})$$

where each c_i *is one of the constructors for the sort* s_1*, each* Ψ_i *is a term that contains invocations of* f *with the first argument* u*. The cases* ψ_i *for one of the constructors* c *form a complete case distinction, i.e. the disjunction of all* ψ_i*, where* $c_i = c$ *is true.*

As a first step we translate the signature. Both the constructors and the recursive definitions have to be defined. For the constructor function *cons* we add a predicate definition in Alloy:

```
pred cons [e: elem, l: list, c: list] { c.first = e and c.rest = l }
```

Recursive functions like *APP* and *REV* are added to the list signature and thus declared as relations between the corresponding sorts:

```
sig list {
   app: list -> lone list,
   rev: lone list
}
```

By the keyword **lone** we tell Alloy that a relation satisfies the uniqueness axiom (2) of the relational translation, i.e. that there is at most one result for append and reverse. The totality axiom (3) would be satisfied too by using the keyword **one** instead of **lone**, but assuming totality of reverse or append prevents finite models. Therefore we drop this axiom, just like the generator axiom for constructors.

As a second step we have to add appropriate axioms as facts to the Alloy specification that are translated from the axioms of the KIV specification from Figure 1. A simple idea would be to translate axioms directly (using τ) but this yields too weak axioms. Therefore we first combine the axioms for each function into one axiom. The resulting axioms for reverse and append are

$$\begin{aligned} &app(x, y) = z \leftrightarrow x = [] \land z = y \lor \exists\, a_0, x_0.\ x = a_0 + x_0 \land z = a_0 + app(x_0, y) \\ &rev(x) = y \leftrightarrow x = [] \land y = [] \lor \exists\, a_0, x_0.\ x = a_0 + x_0 \land y = rev(x_0) + a_0 \end{aligned}$$

Although the translation is schematic, it exploits uniqueness and totality. We then translate the resulting axioms to relations. For reverse we get:

$$\begin{aligned} \forall x, y :: list.\ (x, y) \in REV \leftrightarrow\ & (x \in NIL\ \land\ y = x\ \lor \\ & \exists a :: elem,\ z, z_1, z_2, z_3 :: list.\ (a, z_1, x) \in CONS \\ & \quad \land\ (z_1, z) \in REV\ \land\ z_2 \in NIL\ \land\ (a, z_2, z_3) \in CONS \\ & \quad \land\ (z, z_3, y) \in APP) \end{aligned} \tag{6}$$

The translated formula is stronger than what we would get by translating the original axioms: these only would give the implication from right to left of (6). The other direction would have to be inferred using the uniqueness and totality axioms. For the equivalence we do not need uniqueness and totality any more, since it is an instance of the well-founded recursion theorem:

Theorem 1 (Well-founded recursion). *Given a specification that is enriched with a new function g defined by the single axiom*

$$g(\underline{v}) = \Psi(g, \underline{v})$$

where all arguments of recursive calls to g in Ψ are smaller than $\underline{v}$ with respect to a well-founded order $<$. Then for each model M of the original specification the enrichment defines exactly one function g.

A formal proof of this theorem, which views Ψ as a higher-order function, can be found in [9]. For our case g is the relation (= boolean function) F. The theorem implies that just translating the equivalence already fixes exactly one relation F. Since the relational translation, when adding uniqueness and totality gives the relation F that is equal to the graph of f, the translated axiom *alone* must already specify the correct F.

The well-founded recursion theorem is applicable not only for the term models but also for the finite models that Alloy constructs, since the restriction of the well-founded subterm relation to finite models is obviously well-founded again. It is also applicable for the original recursive definitions in KIV.

Together we have: the recursive definitions of KIV extend the term model by a unique function f. The relational transformation also gives a unique extension of the term model M_∞ by a relation F, which is the graph of f. For a finite subterm-closed model M_0 we get a unique function F_0 using the translated axiom for f too.

The critical question now is: does F_0 in M_0 satisfy the same theorems as F in M_∞? We will give a positive answer below for a class of formulas with universal and bounded existential quantification similar to [12]. The answer has the precondition, that function F, when restricted to the model M_0 (written $F \mid M_0$ in the following) is equal to F_0. In all the examples that we have checked we found that $F \mid M_0 \subseteq F_0$, and it remains as an open question whether this holds in general. In most examples even $F \mid M_0 = F_0$ holds, APP being one positive example. Nevertheless, we found examples, where $F \mid M_0$ is a proper subset of F_0. REV is one instance of the problem:

Example 1. Consider the subterm-closed model M_0 with $L_0 = \{[], [a], [c], [b,c], [b,a], [a,b,c], [c,b,a]\}$. In this model the atoms $[a,b,c]$ and $[c,b,a]$ are not connected by the relation REV_0, even though in the infinite model $REV([a,b,c], [c,b,a])$ holds. The reason is that the intermediate result of reversing $[b,c]$, the list $[c,b]$ (stored as z in axiom (6)) is not in L_0.

The general problem is that subterm-closedness does not guarantee, that the model is closed against chains of results computed by recursive invocations of the defined function. In the example, this chain of results for $[a,b,c]$ is: $rev([])$, $rev([c])$, $rev([b,c])$, $rev([a,b,c])$, since $rev([a,b,c])$ calls $rev([b,c])$ etc.. There is no problem if all results of this chain beyond a certain point are not in the finite model, the problem appears only, if the result of one call (here: $rev([b,c])$ is not in the model, but the result of the next (here: $rev([a,b,c])$) is again in the model. Therefore we have to find a constraint, that rules out such models. We must make sure that with the result of $rev([a,b,c]) = [c,b,a]$ being in the model, the previous result $rev([b,c]) = [c,b]$ is in the model too.

A constraint that guarantees this, is that the model is prefix-closed:

$$\begin{aligned} \forall y :: list.\ y \in NIL \ \vee\ \exists z_3, z_4, z_5 :: list.\ z_4 \in NIL \wedge (a, z_4, z_5) \in CONS \\ \wedge\ (z_3, z_5, y) \in APP \end{aligned}$$

It seems that this constraint can be derived for surjective functions in general, where we know that any element of the model is a result of the function. The constraint then says that each y (a result of f) must be computable from the results $z_1, \ldots z_n$ of recursive calls. For a recursive definition of F of the form

$$F(\underline{x}, y) \ \leftrightarrow\ \Psi(F(\underline{t_1}, u_1), F(\underline{t_2}, u_2), \ldots, F(\underline{t_n}, u_n), \underline{x}, y)$$

the constraint for constructing a result from the previous call therefore is

$$\forall y, \underline{x}.\ \exists z_1, \ldots z_n.\ \Psi(u_1 = z_1, u_2 = z_2, \ldots, u_n = z_n, \underline{x})$$

The constraint works for reverse and gives the constraint (7) after simplification. The definition of *append* function gives the trivial constraint of subterm-closedness which is fortunately already satisfied by SUA models. For functions which are not surjective, the constraint would have to quantify *only* over all y in the image of f, but this is not possible, since the only way to characterize the image is again via the recursion. An example which shows the problem is

Example 2. Consider the non-surjective function *palindrome* with axioms

$$pal([\,]) = [\,], \quad pal(a + x) = a + (pal(x) + (a + [\,]))$$

Obviously not all atoms are results of *pal*. The solution above states that any atom being the result of f can be deconstructed according to the axiomatization of f. But in case of *pal* function for some atoms there are no such deconstruction, Alloy would not be able generate any model. The fundamental problem about this is that we don't know (cannot formulate in the "deconstruction"-axiom) ahead whether some atom is an image of f or not.

Assuming that for all F the equation $F|_{M_0} = F_0$ holds, we can get a similar result as in [12], using the following class of formulas:

Definition 3 (Bounded quantifiers and UBE formulas). *A bounded existential quantifier is of the form $\exists v :: s.\ v < t \rightarrow \psi$, where t is an arbitrary term and $<$ is a subterm order*[3]. *An UBE formula uses universal and bounded existential quantifiers.*

[12] defines EBU formulas, since they are interested in satisfiability, while we define their negation, since we are interested in counterexamples. Their bounded quantification allows $v \in S$ with an arbitrary set S instead of $v < t$, which at first glance looks much more liberal. In fact it is not, since the symbols available to describe a set S are selectors and nothing else. Since selectors can describe subterms of existing terms only, subterm-closedness is then enough to ensure the existence of witnesses. As soon as we allow other functions, the more general form fails to work in the following theorem.

Theorem 2 (Finite refutation). *Let φ be an UBE formula in KIV, $\tau(\varphi)$ its transformation to Alloy and M_∞ the term algebra for the KIV theory translated to use relations. Let M_0 be a finite subterm-closed substructure of M_∞, which also preserves all relations F from M_∞ i.e. $F|_{M_0} = F_0$. Further, let $M_0 \not\models \tau(\varphi)$. Then $M_\infty \not\models \tau(\varphi)$.*

The proof of this theorem is exactly like Kuncak's proof by induction over the structure of a formula. It allows to find counter examples for UBE formulas, by incrementally constructing finite models. To be complete, we would have to increase the bound indefinitely, but for practical purposes the search can be stopped as soon as it either finds a counter example or takes too long.

6 Experimental Results

We applied our technique to most representative examples in KIV. As an automatic translator to Alloy input language is not yet implemented, we used manually compiled Alloy models.

[3] Always provided for free data types in KIV.

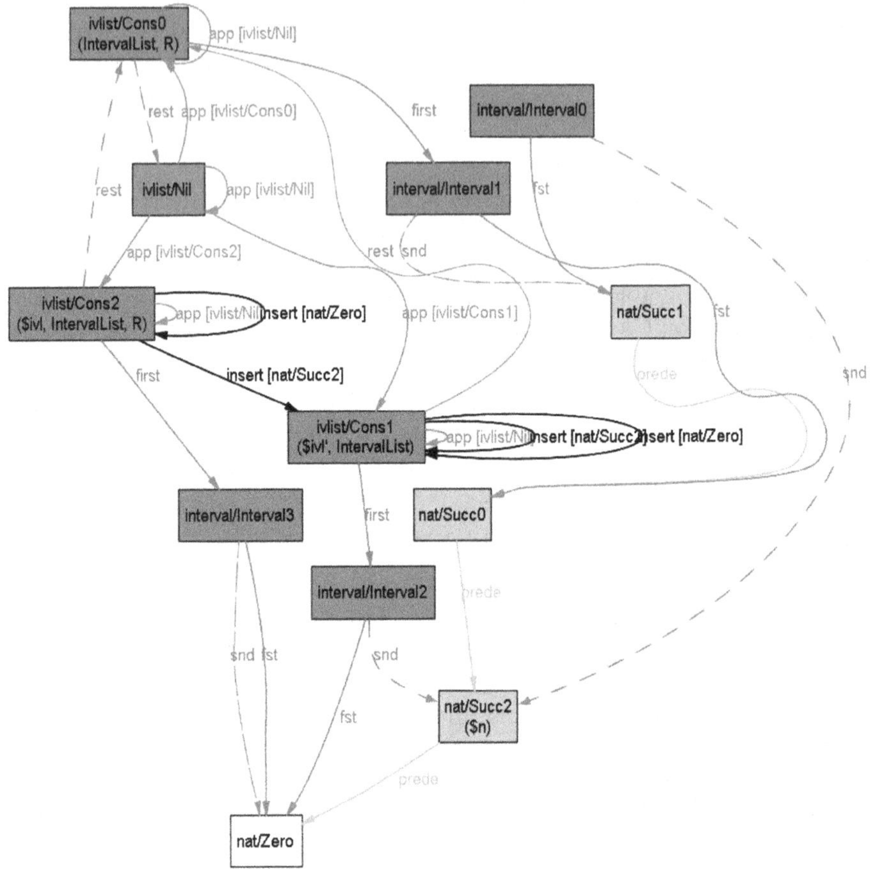

Fig. 6. Counter example generated by Alloy

6.1 Example: Lists of Intervals

As a nice nontrivial example we considered an implementation of sets of natural numbers by intervallists, that was used in [17] to demonstrate algebraic refinement via modules in KIV. The example has also been analyzed previously using KIV's own counter example generation mechanism described in [18]. We first describe the example, the results we got with Alloy and then give a short comparison of the results with KIV.

Sets of natural numbers can be implemented as lists of intervals, where an interval is simply a pair of numbers. For example the set $\{0, 1, 2, 4, 5, 7\}$ can be represented by the list of intervals $[(0, 2), (4, 5), (7, 7)]$ in a unique way. A typical application is the list of free blocks of dynamically allocated memory. A predicate R defines well-formed lists, e.g. $R([(0, 2)]) = true$, $R([(2, 0)]) = false$, $R([(0, 1), (1, 2)]) = false$. Further, an *insert* function is specified, which adds a number into a list of intervals. A correct specification of *insert* operation must satisfy following invariant:

$$\forall\, ivl_1, ivl_2 \in intervallist,\ n \in nat.\ R(ivl_1)\ \wedge\ ivl_2 = insert(ivl_1, n) \rightarrow R(ivl_2)$$

The original specification contained a bug in the definition of *insert* function: it failed to merge $[\_, n]$ and $[n+1, \_]$ into one interval when $n+1$ was inserted. As Table 1 shows, using our technique Alloy was able to identify the smallest counter example at the scope[4] of 4 in 2 seconds.

Table 1. Benchmark (berkmin SAT solver, 2.4 GHz Dual Core)

scope (model size)	counter example	clauses	time
1	no	2000	0.1 s
2	no	5000	0.3 s
3	no	13252	0.7 s
4	yes	83302	2 s

The invariant was violated for $ivl_1 = [(0,0),(2,3)]$, $ivl_2 = [(0,1),(2,3)]$ and $n = 1$. This instantiation can be read off from the model generated by Alloy, that is shown in Figure 6. It depicts a finite structure $M_0 = (I_0, L_0, N_0, \gamma)$ with atoms of sorts *interval*, *list* and *nat* together with corresponding relations between them. Alloy labels with marks $\$ivl, \$ivl'$, $\$n$ those atoms which violate invariant, i.e. *Cons1*, *Cons2* and *Succ2*. By tracing back constructor relations we rebuild corresponding terms and therewith identify values of ivl_1, ivl_2 and n.

The same example was tried using KIV's counter example generation. This roughly works as follows: first a proof attempt for (7) is done. Using heuristics KIV automatically creates a proof tree in 4 seconds, ending in an open goal. The user then has to analyze this goal and to decide, either that it is unprovable or which proof step to be apply next. In this case, the user will suspect rather soon, that it is unprovable and invoke counter example generation. This proof strategy exploits the fact, that constructing a counter example basically means to instantiate all variables x in the goal by constructor terms. Therefore it does a systematic search by instantiating all variables with all constructor terms and by applying rewrite rules. For the goal at hand the search stops after two seconds with an empty sequent, which is definitely unprovable (in unsuccessful cases the search does not terminate, and the user has to abort manually). KIV will then compute a counter example for the original goal, by examining the proof tree (the effort for doing this is negligible). For our goal the counter example will be $ivl_1 = [(0,1),(1,m)]$ with arbitrary m. The successful application critically depends on heuristics and that suitable rewrite rules have been designed. In summary, the 2 seconds that Alloy needs are a clear improvement compared to the 6 seconds + user analysis of a goal.

---

[4] Defines maximal number of atoms for each sort. The smallest counter example which is presented here needs at least 4 atoms of the *list* sort, i.e. $[]$, $[(2,3)]$, $[(0,0),(2,3)]$ and $[(0,1),(2,3)]$.

7 Conclusion

We have presented an automatic method which can be applied to a wide class of first-order logic formulas. We aim to integrate it into the theorem prover KIV. The method is restricted to universal-bounded existential sentences. The question whether a formula is amenable to the analysis can be answered by a simple syntactic check. This limitation is not a big drawback in our opinion as from our own experience non-UBE formulas are rather rare.

This work was our first experiment with Alloy tool and we achieved very promising results. Naturally, there are open issues. The main open question that remains is: when does the relation F_0 agree with $F\mid_{M_0}$? It seems that in a large number of cases it does, but we have not found a syntactic characterization of this class yet. Another assumption, that is too strong is that all functions are defined recursively. In practice it is also common to specify functions non-recursively using quantified formulas: e.g. a predicate $\in\,:\ elem \times list$ can be specified as $a \in x \leftrightarrow \exists y, z.\ y + a + z = x$.

The translation to Alloy language was done manually and we have to automate it. A new more powerful tool based on Alloy called Kodkod [22] has become available recently. It is implemented as an API rather than as a standalone application and can easily be incorporated as a backend of another tool. We plan to use it for more seamless integration in KIV's graphical user interface and better proof visualization. We also intend to investigate an extension of the method to non-freely generated data types (like arrays or sets).

References

1. Ahrendt, W., Beckert, B., Hähnle, R., Menzel, W., Reif, W., Schellhorn, G., Schmitt, P.: Integrating Automated and Interactive Theorem Proving. In: Bibel, W., Schmitt, P. (eds.) Automated Deduction – A Basis for Applications. Systems and Implementation Techniques, Interactive Theorem Proving, vol. II, Kluwer Academic Publishers, Dordrecht (1998)
2. Balser, M.: Verifying Concurrent Systems with Symbolic Execution. PhD thesis, Universität Augsburg, Fakultät für Informatik (2005)
3. Balser, M., Bäumler, S., Knapp, A., Reif, W., Thums, A.: Interactive verification of UML state machines. In: Davies, J., Schulte, W., Barnett, M. (eds.) ICFEM 2004. LNCS, vol. 3308, pp. 434–448. Springer, Heidelberg (2004)
4. Balser, M., Reif, W., Schellhorn, G., Stenzel, K.: KIV 3.0 for Provably Correct Systems. In: Hutter, D., Traverso, P. (eds.) FM-Trends 1998. LNCS, vol. 1641, Springer, Heidelberg (1999)
5. Balser, M., Reif, W., Schellhorn, G., Stenzel, K., Thums, A.: Formal system development with KIV. In: Maibaum, T.S.E. (ed.) FASE 2000. LNCS, vol. 1783, pp. 363–366. Springer, Heidelberg (2000)
6. de Nivelle, H., Meng, J.: Geometric resolution: A proof procedure based on finite model search. In: Furbach, U., Shankar, N. (eds.) IJCAR 2006. LNCS (LNAI), vol. 4130, pp. 303–317. Springer, Heidelberg (2006)

7. Fontaine, P., Marion, J.-Y., Merz, S., Nieto, L.P., Tiu, A.: Expressiveness + automation + soundness: Towards combining SMT solvers and interactive proof assistants. In: Hermanns, H., Palsberg, J. (eds.) TACAS 2006. LNCS, vol. 3920, pp. 167–181. Springer, Heidelberg (2006)
8. Harel, D., Kozen, D., Tiuryn, J.: Dynamic Logic. MIT Press, Cambridge (2000)
9. Harrison, J.: Inductive definitions: Automation and application. In: TPHOLs, pp. 200–213 (1995)
10. The Alloy Project, `http://alloy.mit.edu`
11. Jackson, D.: Automating first-order relational logic. In: SIGSOFT 2000/FSE-8: Proceedings of the 8th ACM SIGSOFT international symposium on Foundations of software engineering, pp. 130–139. ACM Press, New York (2000)
12. Kuncak, V., Jackson, D.: Relational analysis of algebraic datatypes. In: Joint 10th European Software Engineering Conference and 13th ACM SIGSOFT Symposium on the Foundations of Software Engineering (2005)
13. Meng, J., Quigley, C., Paulson, L.C.: Automation for interactive proof: First prototype. Inf. Comput. 204(10), 1575–1596 (2006)
14. Momtahan, L.: Towards a small model theorem for data independent systems in alloy. Electr. Notes Theor. Comput. Sci. 128(6), 37–52 (2005)
15. Ramananandro, T.: Mondex, an electronic purse: specification and refinement checks with the Alloy model-finding method. Formal Aspects of Computing 20(1), 21–39 (2008)
16. Reif, W., Schellhorn, G.: Theorem Proving in Large Theories. In: Bibel, W., Schmitt, P. (eds.) Automated Deduction—A Basis for Applications, vol. III, 2, Kluwer Academic Publishers, Dordrecht (1998)
17. Reif, W., Schellhorn, G., Stenzel, K.: Interactive Correctness Proofs for Software Modules Using KIV. In: COMPASS 1995 – Tenth Annual Conference on Computer Assurance, IEEE press, Los Alamitos (1995)
18. Reif, W., Schellhorn, G., Thums, A.: Flaw detection in formal specifications. In: Goré, R.P., Leitsch, A., Nipkow, T. (eds.) IJCAR 2001. LNCS (LNAI), vol. 2083, pp. 642–657. Springer, Heidelberg (2001)
19. Schellhorn, G.: Verification of Abstract State Machines. PhD thesis, Universität Ulm, Fakultät für Informatik (1999), `http://www.informatik.uni-augsburg.de/swt/Publications.htm`
20. Stenzel, K.: A formally verified calculus for full Java Card. In: Rattray, C., Maharaj, S., Shankland, C. (eds.) AMAST 2004. LNCS, vol. 3116, pp. 491–505. Springer, Heidelberg (2004)
21. Thums, A., Schellhorn, G., Ortmeier, F., Reif, W.: Interactive verification of statecharts. In: Ehrig, H., Damm, W., Desel, J., Große-Rhode, M., Reif, W., Schnieder, E., Westkämper, E. (eds.) INT 2004. LNCS, vol. 3147, pp. 355–373. Springer, Heidelberg (2004)
22. Torlak, E., Jackson, D.: Kodkod: A relational model finder. In: Grumberg, O., Huth, M. (eds.) TACAS 2007. LNCS, vol. 4424, pp. 632–647. Springer, Heidelberg (2007)

Static Analysis Via Abstract Interpretation of the Happens-Before Memory Model

Pietro Ferrara

École Polytechnique
F-91128 Palaiseau, France
Pietro.Ferrara@polytechnique.edu
Dipartimento di Informatica
Università Ca' Foscari di Venezia
I-30170 Venezia, Italy

Abstract. Memory models define which executions of multithreaded programs are legal. This paper formalises in a fixpoint form the happens-before memory model, an over-approximation of the Java one, and it presents a static analysis using abstract interpretation. Our approach is completely independent of both the programming language and the analysed property. It also appears to be a promising framework to define, compare and statically analyse other memory models.

Keywords: Static Analysis, Abstract Interpretation, Memory Model, Multithreaded Programs.

1 Introduction

While the improvement of single-core architectures is slowing down, many multi-core processors, like the family of Intel® Core^{TM}, are appearing in a broad market [10]. The only way to take advantage of this technology is to develop multithreaded programs that perform many parallel tasks.

The semantics of a programming language supporting multithreading must be defined well enough that developers can fully understand which behaviours are allowed during an execution, and which are not. In the literature, a common approach has been to consider as incorrect all the programs containing data races [19], i.e. in which two parallel threads access without any synchronisation action the same area of shared memory, and not to provide any semantics in this case. In this way, many static analyses have been aimed at proving the absence of data races [16,20]. Leaving completely unspecified the semantics of these programs is unsatisfying for modern programming languages, particularly those that are focused on security issues.

The attention on this topic has increased during the last years: for instance, the first specification of the Java Virtual Machine [12] was flawed [18], and only a following work [13] provided a correct definition. Nowadays, the specification of the memory model appears to be the "lingua franca" that can fill this lack on the semantics specification. In this context, two main but opposing approaches are

B. Beckert and R. Hähnle (Eds.): TAP 2008, LNCS 4966, pp. 116–133, 2008.

considered: (i) to restrict the non-deterministic behaviours in order to provide a simple reference to the developers; (ii) to allow as many compiler optimisations as possible, but that introduce non-deterministic behaviours.

On this topic, the debate is still in progress [2], and different ideas and solutions have recently been proposed [23].

Most state-of-the-art static analyses do not support multithreading, or they deal only with the possible interleavings of instructions; this is why they are not sound w.r.t. the memory model, as it usually allows more behaviours than the ones exposed by sequentially consistent executions.

Contribution: In this context, a static analyser able to approximate all the possible runtime behaviours of a multithreaded program w.r.t. a memory model seems to be particularly appealing, as it would help developers reason about compiler optimisations and all the possible interleavings due to the parallel execution of multiple threads [24]. Moreover, since the threads communicate implicitly through the shared memory, really subtle and unwanted interactions may arise, and a static analysis may trace and provide information about all these potential bugs. Some examples about these situations, like the one depicted by our running example, are presented by [13].

The happens-before memory model is an over-approximation of the Java one; for this reason, tuning a static analysis at this level will allow us to obtain sound results for Java multithreaded programs.

Our approach follows the abstract interpretation framework [4,5]. We first define the concrete trace semantics in a fixpoint form, aimed at formalising the happens-before memory model. Then we abstract it, proving the soundness of our analysis. Our analysis is generic to the programming language, as the happens-before memory model is. Moreover, our framework shall be used to formalise, compare, and statically analyse other memory models. The proposed analysis approximates all the possible multithreaded behaviours w.r.t. the happens-before memory model, starting from a given intra-thread domain and semantics. Our approach allows that the intra-thread semantics follows the sequential consistency rule (as most static analyses do); the multithreaded executions that are sensitive to compiler optimisations and threads' interleavings are obtained through the computation of a fixpoint.

The rest of the paper is organised as follows. In this section we present a running example. Section 2 introduces the happens-before memory model, and analyses it from a static analysis point of view. The concrete domain and semantics are defined by Section 3, while Section 4 depicts the abstract ones. Section 5 presents and discusses some related work, and Section 6 concludes.

1.1 The Running Example

The concepts in the rest of the paper are explained in the context of a simple example.Figure 1 depicts a Java-style program composed of two threads where variables `i` and `j` are shared between them. Supposing that at the beginning

Thread 1	Thread 2
`i=1;`	`if(j==1 && i==0)`
`j=1;`	`throw new Exception();`

Fig. 1. The running example

i and j are both equal to 0, which runtime behaviours are acceptable and consistent w.r.t. the memory model? And in particular: may the exception be thrown?

1.2 Abstract Interpretation

Abstract interpretation is a theory to define and soundly approximate the semantics of a program [4,5]. Roughly, a concrete semantics, aimed at specifying the runtime properties of interest, is defined; then it is approximated through one or more steps in order to finally obtain an abstract semantics that is computable, but still precise enough to capture the property of interest. In particular, the abstract semantics must be composed of an abstract domain, an abstract transfer function, and a widening operator in order to make the analysis convergent. Usually, each state of the concrete domain is composed of a set of elements (e.g. all the possible computational states), that is approximated by an unique trace in the abstract domain.

In our analysis, the concrete semantics is computed by a fixpoint that produces the set of all the possible finite executions of a multithreaded program; these executions respect the happens-before memory model. The abstract semantics computes, always through a fixpoint, an abstract element that approximates the concrete semantics. The soundness of the approach has been proved following the abstract interpretation framework.

2 The Happens-Before Memory Model

In the recent literature, the memory models have been aimed at formalising the behaviours that are allowed during the execution of a multithreaded program.

The Java Memory Model was presented by [18]. Its formalisation involves many different components, and all the run-time actions must be committed in a quite sophisticated way. In the same paper the happens-before memory model is formalised, as an over-approximation of the Java one, i.e. it allows a larger number of runtime behaviours. Its formalisation is simpler, and it allows us to reason in terms of static analysis.

The main components of this model are (we denote some rules with a specific name that will be used during the formalisation of the model in the fixpoint form):

- the program order, that, for each thread, totally orders the actions performed during its execution;

– a synchronises-with relation that relates two synchronised actions. For instance, the acquisition of a monitor synchronises-with all the previous releases of the same monitor. Moreover the first action of the execution of a thread is synchronised-with the action that launched it (rule IN);
– the happens-before order initially introduced by [11]. An action a_1 happens-before another action a_2 (rule HB) if (i) a_1 appears before a_2 in the program order; (ii) a_2 synchronises-with a_1; (iii) if you can reach a_2 by following happens-before edges starting from a_1 (i.e. the happens-before order is transitive).

Through the happens-before order, a consistency rule is defined. In particular, it states that a read r of a variable v is allowed to see a write w on v if: (i) r does not happens-before w (i.e. a read can not see a write that has to be executed after it); (ii) there is no write w' on v that happens-before r and w happens-before it (i.e. there is not any write on the same variable that has to be executed between the observed write and the read, overwriting it) (rule OW).

The happens-before memory model says nothing about what is a variable and its granularity (an object, a field, an array, a primitive value, ...).

2.1 Reasoning Statically

One point is not clear in these definitions: on one hand the definition of the happens-before consistency appears to be a static rule, but on the other hand the program order talks about a total order covering all the actions of an execution; this concept is clearly dynamic. Since our approach is parameterized on the abstract intra-thread transition relation, we suppose that it approximates this program order; in this way if a state appears before another one in the trace produced through this relation, it means that it will always be executed before it.

About the synchronises-with relation, threads generically synchronise on some elements (for instance in Java they synchronise on monitors defined on objects), and the mutual exclusion is guaranteed on them. In this way, they acquire a synchronisable element, keep it during some actions, and finally release it. In a static context, we do not know which thread acquires the synchronisable element. For instance, imagine the multithreaded program of Figure 2.

Thread 1	Thread 2

`acquire(o)`
`var=v1`
`var=v2`
`release(o)`
	`acquire(o)`
	`temp=var`
	`release(o)`

Fig. 2. An example

Which values may thread 2 read? The read action is synchronised on the same element of both writes in thread 1. It may read the initial value stored in `var`, or v2, but not v1, as its acquisition synchronises-with the release of thread 1, or vice versa its release is synchronised-with the acquisition of thread 1.

This consideration allows us to conclude that statically a read action is allowed to see all the values written by parallel threads, except the ones that are overwritten by a successive action and such that all the actions between them are synchronised at least on an element locked also in the state that is going to perform the read action. This is a straight consequence of the mutual exclusion principle.

All these concepts are formalised by the concrete semantics.

2.2 The Running Example

Let us apply these concepts to the running example depicted by section 1.1, and in particular to state if it is consistent that the exception may be thrown under the happens-before memory model. To answer this question, we evaluate which values may be read by the condition of the `if` statement of thread 2.

First of all, since there are no synchronisation actions, the synchronise-with order is empty, and all the actions of thread 1 do not happen-before the evaluation of the condition. So this instruction is allowed to see the initial value of variable `i` equal to zero, and the value written by the second instruction of thread 2 that assigns 1 to variable `j`. Therefore, it is consistent to evaluate this condition to `true`, and to throw the exception.

For instance, the exception is thrown if the two statements of thread 1 are switched by the compiler (since they are independent, this is allowed), a single-core processor executes `j=1`, and then the control switches to thread 2, in which the condition of the `if` evaluates to `true` .

2.3 Notation

We denote the sets of functions by capital Greek letters, the elements by a single lower-case letter, and the identifiers of sets always begin with a capital letter.

Concrete and abstract: The concrete sets and elements are denoted as just defined, while the abstract ones are over-lined; for instance, if S is a concrete set, the respective abstract set is denoted by $\overline{S}$. About the functions, if *fun* is the concrete one, its respective abstract version is denoted by $fun^{\#}$.

Trace semantics: Our concrete and abstract semantics are based on partial finite traces. Roughly, the execution of a thread is represented by a trace of states. ϵ denotes the empty trace, while $\sigma_0 \rightarrow \sigma_1 \rightarrow \cdots$ denotes a trace that begins with a state σ_0 followed by σ_1, and then there is an arbitrary number of successive states, denoted by $\cdots$. Given a transition function $\rightarrow: St \times St \mapsto \{\texttt{true}, \texttt{false}\}$, with an abuse of notation we denote the fact that $\rightarrow (\sigma_1, \sigma_2) = \texttt{true}$ by $\sigma_1 \rightarrow \sigma_2$. We denote by $St_{\rightarrow}$ the set of blocking states following the transition relation $\rightarrow$, i.e. such that $\forall \sigma_1 \in St_{\rightarrow} : \nexists \sigma_2 \in St :\rightarrow (\sigma_1, \sigma_2) = \texttt{true}$. Finally, let be S a generic set of elements, we denote by $S^{\vec{+}}$ the set of all the finite traces composed of elements in S.

3 Multithreaded Concrete Semantics

In this section we present the multithreaded concrete semantics. This semantics is aimed at formalising the happens-before memory model in a fixpoint form; it is completely parameterized by the concrete operational semantics that defines the behaviour of intra-thread atomic computational steps, and on some functions that given a state returns a part of it. In this way we completely separate the semantics of the language from its memory model.

Since the happens-before memory model refers only to finite executions, we consider only finite traces. Our multithreaded concrete semantics produces all the complete executions, i.e. in which the executions of all the threads end with a blocking state.

3.1 Required Elements

In order to define the happens-before memory model on the concrete semantics we need some sets and functions that extract information from the states.

For the sets, we denote by *TId* the set of the threads' identifiers, by *Sh* all the possible shared memories, by *Loc* the shared memory locations, by *Val* the values, by *Sync* all the shared elements on which a thread can synchronise, and by *St* the states that contain the memory and control state of a single thread. Moreover, as the happens-before memory model talks about the values read and written on the shared memory, we suppose that the shared memory relates each location to a value ($Sh : Loc \mapsto Val$).

We suppose that a transition function $\overset{\circ}{\rightarrow}: St \times St \mapsto \{\texttt{true}, \texttt{false}\}$ is provided, and that it defines the single step behaviours of the computation. We require that these steps are atomic at thread level, i.e. it is not possible for another thread to see an intermediate state during a single intra-thread transition.

We also require that the following functions are provided:

- $\mathit{shared} : St \mapsto Sh$, given a state it returns the shared memory contained in it;
- $\mathit{action} : St \mapsto \bot_a \cup (\{\texttt{r}, \texttt{w}\} \times Loc \times Val)$, given a state it returns the operation it is going to perform (reading from or writing on the shared memory), the shared location on which it operates and eventually the written value, or $\bot_a$ if it has performed another type of operation;
- $\mathit{synchronised} : St \mapsto \wp(Sync)$, given a state it returns all the elements of the memory state on which it is synchronised (for instance the set of all the monitors previously locked and not yet released); we do not specify what these elements are, since many different ways of synchronisation exist, and we are generic with respect to the programming language.

Finally, we require the function $\mathit{set\_shared} : St \times Sh \rightarrow St$, that given a state and a shared memory returns a state equal to the given one but in which the shared memory is replaced by the given one.

3.2 Thread Partitioned Concrete Domain

Our concrete domain is aimed at collecting information about the parallel execution of different threads. In this way we partition the trace of the execution relating each active thread to the trace of its execution. Moreover, we collect for each thread the one that has launched it, and the number of the state of its execution trace that is produced after this operation; for the main thread, that is launched by the system, we use a special value $\bot_\Omega$. In this way our concrete domain is composed by two functions, where the second one is just aimed at maintaining some information on the relations between threads. We collect the number of the state in order to restrict the execution trace only on the states successive to the launch of the thread, and so to respect the rule IN.

$$\begin{array}{l} \Psi : \mathit{TId} \rightarrow \vec{St^{+}} \\ \Omega : \mathit{TId} \rightarrow ((\mathit{TId} \times \mathit{Integer}) \cup \bot_\Omega) \end{array}$$

3.3 Single Step Definition

We define a *step* function that performs a single intra-thread step, consistent with respect to the happens-before memory model, and returns the set of the possible states obtained after it.

Definition 1 (*step* **function).** *Starting from the active thread, a multithreaded state containing the traces of the executions of all the threads, and an element of Ω, the step function returns the set of all the possible following states.*

In particular if the thread is not going to read from the shared memory, it computes the step while observing the sequential consistency rule (point (1)). Otherwise it may: (i) perform the step following the sequential consistency (point (2a)); (ii) select one visible value following the happens-before consistency and perform the step injecting this value in the shared memory (point (2b)).

Formally,

$$\begin{array}{ll} \mathit{step} : \mathit{TId} \times \Psi \times \Omega \mapsto \wp(St) & \\ \mathit{step}\ (t, f, s) = \{\sigma\} \text{ where } f(t) = \sigma_0 \rightarrow \cdots \rightarrow \sigma_i \text{ and} & \\ (1)\ \ \sigma_i \xrightarrow{\circ} \sigma & \text{if } \pi_1(\mathit{action}(\sigma_i)) \neq r \\ & \\ (2a)\ \sigma_i \xrightarrow{\circ} \sigma \vee & \text{if } \pi_1(\mathit{action}(\sigma_i)) = r \\ (2b)\ \exists v \in \mathit{visible}(t, \pi_2(\mathit{action}(\sigma_i)), \mathit{synchronised}(\sigma_i), f, s(t)) : & \\ \quad\quad \sigma' = \mathit{set\_shared}(\sigma_i, \mathit{shared}(\sigma_i)[l \mapsto v]), \sigma' \xrightarrow{\circ} \sigma & \end{array}$$

Definition 2 (*visible* **function).** *The visible function returns the values that are visible by the given thread. This set is built up by the values produced by the thread that launched the one that is reading, restricting it only on the part of the trace executed after the launch (point (1), rules IN), and the values produced by other threads (point (2)).*

$$\begin{array}{l} \mathit{visible} : \mathit{TId} \times \mathit{Loc} \times \wp(\mathit{Sync}) \times \Psi \times ((\mathit{TId} \times \mathit{Integer}) \cup \bot_\Omega) \mapsto \wp(\mathit{Val}) \\ \mathit{visible}\ (t, l, S, f, (t', i')) = \\ (1)\quad = \mathit{project}(l, \mathit{suffix}(f(t'), i'), S) \cup \\ (2)\quad\quad \{v : v \in \mathit{project}(l, f(t''), S) : t'' \in \mathit{dom}(f) \setminus \{t, t'\}\} \end{array}$$

Definition 3 (*suffix* **function).** *The suffix function, given a trace and an index, cuts the trace at the i-th element and returns the suffix of the trace. It supposes that the given index is between 0 and the length of the trace.*

$$suffix : \vec{St^+} \times Integer \mapsto \vec{St^+}$$
$$suffix\ (\sigma_0 \rightarrow \cdots \rightarrow \sigma_j, i) = \begin{cases} \sigma_i \rightarrow \cdots \rightarrow \sigma_j & \textit{if}\ i \geq 0 \wedge i < j \\ \epsilon & \textit{if}\ i = j \end{cases}$$

Definition 4 (*project* **function).** *The project function, given a location, a trace, a set of owned synchronisable elements, and the thread that is currently analysed, returns the set of visible values following the happens-before consistency in the given trace.*

$$project : Loc \times \vec{St^+} \times \wp(Sync) \mapsto \wp(Val)$$
$$project\ (l, \sigma_0 \rightarrow \cdots \rightarrow \sigma_i, S) = \{v : \exists j \in [0..i] : action(\sigma_j) = (w, l, v) \wedge$$
$$not\_synchronised(\sigma_j \rightarrow \cdots \rightarrow \sigma_i, S)\}$$

The first part of the condition of sh_j, i.e.,

$$action(\sigma_j) = (\mathtt{w}, l, v)$$

excludes the transitions that do not write on the shared memory, and the second part, i.e.,

$$not\_synchronised(\sigma_j \rightarrow \cdots \rightarrow \sigma_i, S)$$

the ones whose values are overwritten by a successive action following the happens-before order (rule OW).

Definition 5 (*not_synchronised* **function).** *The not_synchronised function, given a trace and a set of synchronisable elements, returns* **true** *if and only if the first state of the trace is not synchronised on an element in the given set (case (1)), or if there is no write action that writes on the same location of the first action of the given trace and that is synchronised-with it (case (2)).*

$$not\_synchronised : \vec{St^+} \times \wp(Sync) \mapsto \{\mathbf{true}, \mathbf{false}\}$$
$$not\_synchronised(\sigma_0 \rightarrow \cdots \rightarrow \sigma_i, S) = \mathbf{true}\ \textit{if and only if}$$
$$(1) S \cap synchronised(\sigma_0) = \emptyset \vee$$
$$(2) \nexists \sigma_j \in cut(\sigma_0 \rightarrow \cdots \rightarrow \sigma_i, S) : action(\sigma_j) = (w, l, v), action(\sigma_0) = (w, l_0, v_0),$$
$$l = l_0$$

Definition 6 (*cut* **function).** *The cut function, given a trace and a set of synchronisable elements, returns the trace cut to the first states that are all synchronised-with at least one of the given elements.*

$$cut : \vec{St^+} \times \wp(Sync) \mapsto \vec{St^+}$$
$$cut\ (\sigma_0 \rightarrow \cdots \rightarrow \sigma_i, S) = \begin{cases} \epsilon\ \textit{if}\ synchronised(\sigma_0) \cap S = \emptyset \\ \sigma_0 \rightarrow cut(\sigma_1 \rightarrow \cdots \rightarrow \sigma_i, S)\ \textit{otherwise} \end{cases}$$

3.4 Fixpoint Semantics

Through the *step* function we define the fixpoint concrete semantics in order to compute all the possible finite traces of a given multithreaded program.

Single-Thread Semantics. Given a thread and an element of the thread-partitioned domain, this semantics returns the traces of its possible partial finite executions, following the happens-before memory model, when the parallel executions of other threads are the ones represented by the given element of the thread-partitioned domain. It is the basic step that will be used to define the multithreaded semantics. This approach is classical in literature, as for instance the example 7.2.0.6.3 of [5].

Definition 7 ($\mathbb{S}^\circ$)

$$\begin{aligned}
&\mathbb{S}^\circ : \Psi \times \Omega \times TId \mapsto \wp(\vec{St^+}) \\
&\mathbb{S}^\circ\, [\![f, r, t]\!] = lfp_{\emptyset}^{\subseteq} \lambda T.\{\sigma_0\} \cup \{\, \sigma_0 \to \cdots \to \sigma_{i-1} \to \sigma_i : \sigma_0 \to \cdots \to \sigma_{i-1} \in T \\
&\qquad\qquad \wedge \sigma_i \in step(t, f, r)\}
\end{aligned}$$

Multithreaded Semantics. The multithreaded fixpoint semantics computes all the possible executions of a multithreaded program following the happens-before memory model.

It starts from an element of the thread-partitioned domain that relates each thread that is active at the beginning of the computation to an empty trace ϵ ($f_0 = \{[t \mapsto \epsilon : t \text{ is the identifier of an active thread}]\}$), and in the second component each active thread to $\bot_\Omega$, where

$$r_0 = \{[t \mapsto \bot_\Omega : t \text{ is the identifier of an active thread}]\}.$$

At each iteration it computes the semantics using the traces of the execution of different threads obtained at the previous step. The set of finite traces is restricted only to the traces that end with a blocking state; it is necessary in order to compute which values are visible through the *not_synchronised* function. In particular we want to discard all the elements that are overwritten during a set of transitions all synchronised-with the analysed read action; to do that, we need to consider only the traces that are complete, i.e. that end with a blocking state.

Definition 8 ($\mathbb{S}^\parallel$)

$$\begin{aligned}
&\mathbb{S}^\parallel : \Psi \times \Omega \mapsto \wp(\Psi \times \Omega) \\
&\mathbb{S}^\parallel\, [\![f_0, r_0]\!] = lfp_{\emptyset}^{\subseteq} \lambda \Phi.\{(f_0, r_0)\} \cup \{(f_i, r) : \exists (f_{i-1}, r) \in \Phi : \forall t \in dom(f_{i-1}) : \\
&\qquad\qquad f_i(t) \in S^\circ[\![f_{i-1}, r, t]\!], f_i(t) = \sigma_0 \to \cdots \to \sigma_i, \sigma_i \in St_{\underset{\to}{\circ}}\}
\end{aligned}$$

The intuition behinds this fixpoint definition is the following:

- at the first iteration it computes the complete semantics of each thread "in isolation" since the trace of the other threads is empty, and then the *step* function performs a step using the last state of the given thread and following the sequential consistency;

– at the second (or i-th) iteration it computes the complete semantics of each thread in which the visible values have been modified at most one (or i-1) times by other threads.

For instance to compute the multithreaded semantics of the following example when `x`, `y`, and `z` are equal to 0 at the beginning of computation:

Thread 1	Thread 2	Thread 3
`y=z;`	`z=x;`	`x=1;`

Informally, at the first iteration we obtained that in thread 1 `j=0`, in thread 2 `z=0`, and in thread 3 `x=1`.

At the second iteration we still obtain that in thread 1 `j=0` and in thread 3 `x=1`, while in thread 2 we may write the value 0 or 1 (as it may see the write action performed by thread 3 in the previous iteration) to variable `z`.

During the third iteration, thread 1 may write the value 0 or 1 to the variable `y`, as it may or may not see the value written by thread 2. The other two threads behave as in the previous iteration. Moreover we have reached a fixpoint and our computation ends.

In this simple example it is clear that we need to compute a fixpoint between the semantics of different threads in order to propagate the values written and read by threads. In a more complex situation, as for instance when a value written by a parallel thread may change the control flow of the thread, this interaction may be repeated many times, requiring a fixpoint computation.

3.5 Launching a Thread

The *step* function is not in position to launch a new thread, as it operates only intra-thread steps. So the multithreaded semantics must be extended to support this action. Since we are generic with respect to the programming language, we do not present the details; on the other hand, it is important to define it in order to make evidence of how the relations between threads are traced by the second component of the multithreaded domain.

In this context, we suppose that a function $launch : St \mapsto (TId \times St \times St) \cup \bot_l$ is provided; given a state, if its next action is the launch of a thread, it returns the identifier of the new thread, its initial state and the next state of the execution. Informally, the computational multithreaded step may be defined in the following way, where (f, r) is the previous state:

$$\begin{aligned}(f', r') : t \in dom(f), f(t) = \sigma_0 \to \cdots \to \sigma_i, launch(\sigma_i) = (t', \sigma'_0, \sigma_{i+1}),\\ f' = f[t \mapsto (\sigma_0 \to \cdots \to \sigma_i \to \sigma_{i+1}), t' \mapsto (\sigma'_0)], r' = r[t' \mapsto (t, i)]\end{aligned}$$

3.6 The Running Example

We apply all these definitions to the example presented in section 1.1. We focus only on the analysis of the condition of thread 2.

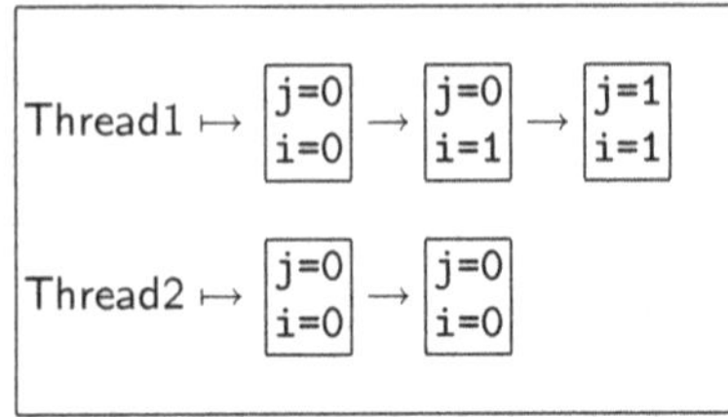

Fig. 3. The result of the first iteration of the multithreaded semantics computation

The result obtained by the first iteration of the computation of $\mathbb{S}^{\parallel}$ is depicted by figure 3 (we represent only the state of shared memory, ignoring the control state and the private memory). Note that, since the choice of which shared memory is visible is deterministic, it is composed only of an element of the concrete domain.

Which are the states of the shared memory returned by the *visible* function when we are evaluating the condition of thread 2 at the second iteration? In order to compute them, we need to consider which values are returned by the *project* function. We ignore the first use of this function ($project(suffix(f(t')), i)$, where t' is the thread that launched the current one), as we suppose there were two parallel threads at the beginning of the execution, and so that both are launched by the system. In the second case, we use the *project* function only with the execution trace of thread 1, as it is the only thread in the domain of our multithreaded state that is not the current thread. Since there is no synchronisation action, S is empty. In this situation, the read actions of variables `j` and `i` are both able to see the values 0 and 1, as 0 is sequentially consistent, while 1 has been written by thread 1 and may be returned by the *visible* function.

Finally, we are in position to check if, in this situation, the condition may be evaluated to `true`. The condition to be evaluated is $j == 1 \&\& i == 0$. If the read action on `i` sees the value sequentially consistent, and the one on `j` the value written by the second instruction of thread 1 (and returned by the *visible* function), the condition would be evaluated to `true`. This behaviour is sound w.r.t. the happens-before memory model, as pointed out by section 2.2.

4 Multithreaded Abstract Semantics

In order to develop a static analysis via abstract interpretation [4,5], we define the abstract semantics aimed at computing an approximation of the concrete one.

4.1 Required Elements

As we have done for the concrete semantics, in order to be generic with respect to the programming language we need some sets and functions.

In particular, the required sets are the following, with the same meaning as the ones introduced by the concrete semantics, but applied to abstract elements: $\overline{TId}$, $\overline{Sh}$, $\overline{Loc}$, $\overline{Sync}$, and $\overline{St}$. Moreover, we suppose that $\overline{Sh} : \overline{Loc} \mapsto \overline{Val}$.

In the same way the function $\xrightarrow{\circ}^{\#}: \overline{St} \times \overline{St} \mapsto \{\texttt{true}, \texttt{false}\}$ defines the abstract single step behaviours of the computation.

About the functions, we require the following, with the same meaning as the concrete semantics: $shared^{\#} : \overline{St} \mapsto \overline{Sh}$, $action^{\#} : \overline{St} \mapsto \overline{\bot}_a \cup (\{\texttt{r}, \texttt{w}\} \times \overline{Loc} \times \overline{Val})$, $synchronised^{\#} : \overline{St} \mapsto \wp(\overline{Sync})$, and $set\_shared^{\#} : \overline{St} \times \overline{Sh} \to \overline{St}$.

4.2 Trace Partitioned Abstract Domain

The abstract domain is similar to the concrete one: the only difference is that it deals with abstract sets, while the meaning is exactly the same.

$$\begin{array}{l}\overline{\Psi} : \overline{TId} \to \overline{St}^{\vec{+}} \\ \overline{\Omega} : \overline{TId} \to ((\overline{TId} \times Integer) \cup \overline{\bot}_{\Omega})\end{array}$$

4.3 Upper Bound Operator and Abstraction Function

We define the upper bound operator and the abstraction function on the domain just presented. We need the upper bound operator between two single-thread states ($\sqcup_{St}$) and between two values ($\sqcup_{Val}$), the abstraction functions $\alpha'_{ST} : St \mapsto \overline{St}$ (that given a concrete single-thread state returns its abstraction), and $\alpha'_{Tid} : TId \mapsto \overline{TId}$ (that given a concrete thread identifier returns its abstraction), are provided.

Note that in these definitions (and in the soundness proofs) we focus only on the first component of the domain (Ψ), as the second part just traces some relations between threads, and it can be linearly abstracted applying the α'_{TId} function.

Definition 9 (Upper bound operator on $\overline{\Psi}$)

$$\begin{array}{ll}\sqcup_f : & \overline{\Psi} \times \overline{\Psi} \mapsto \overline{\Psi} \\ \overline{f}_1 \sqcup_f \overline{f}_2 = & \{[\overline{t} \mapsto \overline{\tau}] : \overline{t} \in dom(\overline{f}_1) \cup dom(\overline{f}_2), \\ & \overline{\tau} = \begin{cases} \overline{f}_1(\overline{t}) \sqcup_\tau \overline{f}_2(\overline{t}) & if\, \overline{t} \in dom(\overline{f}_1) \cap dom(\overline{f}_2) \\ \overline{f}_1(\overline{t}) & if\, \overline{t} \in dom(\overline{f}_1) \setminus dom(\overline{f}_2) \\ \overline{f}_2(\overline{t}) & if\, \overline{t} \in dom(\overline{f}_2) \setminus dom(\overline{f}_1) \end{cases} \}\end{array}$$

Definition 10 (Upper bound operator on $\overline{St}^{\vec{+}}$)

$$\begin{array}{l}\sqcup_\tau : \overline{St}^{\vec{+}} \times \overline{St}^{\vec{+}} \mapsto \overline{St}^{\vec{+}} \\ (\overline{\sigma}_0 \to \cdots \to \overline{\sigma}_j) \sqcup_\tau (\overline{\sigma}'_0 \to \cdots \to \overline{\sigma}'_i) = \\ \quad = (\overline{\sigma}_0 \sqcup_{St} \overline{\sigma}'_0) \to \cdots \to (\overline{\sigma}_j \sqcup_{St} \overline{\sigma}'_j) \to (\overline{\sigma}'_{j+1}) \to (\overline{\sigma}'_i)\end{array}$$

supposing that $j \leq i$. Otherwise, $\sqcup_{St}$ is commutative and it is sufficient to commute the elements.

Definition 11 (Abstraction function of $\wp(\Psi)$)

$$\alpha_f : \wp(\Psi) \mapsto \overline{\Psi}$$
$$\alpha_f(\Phi) = \bigsqcup_{f \in \Phi}{}_{f} \, \alpha'_f(f)$$

$$\alpha'_f : \Psi \mapsto \overline{\Psi}$$
$$\alpha'_f(f) = \{[\overline{t} \mapsto \overline{\tau}] : \exists t \in dom(f) : \overline{t} = \alpha'_{TId}(t) \wedge \overline{\tau} = \alpha'_\tau(f(t))\}$$

Definition 12 (Abstraction function of $\wp(St^{\vec{+}})$)

$$\alpha_\tau : \wp(St^{\vec{+}}) \mapsto \overline{St}^{\vec{+}}$$
$$\alpha_\tau(T) = \bigsqcup_{\tau \in T}{}_{\tau} \, \alpha'_\tau(\tau)$$

$$\alpha'_\tau : St^{\vec{+}} \mapsto \overline{St}^{\vec{+}}$$
$$\alpha'_\tau(\sigma_0 \to \cdots \to \sigma_i) = \alpha'_{ST}(\sigma_0) \to \cdots \to \alpha'_{ST}(\sigma_i)$$

4.4 $step^{\#}$ Function

The $step^{\#}$ function is quite similar to the concrete one. If the action is not a read it just performs the step through the $\xrightarrow{\circ}{}^{\#}$ function. Otherwise it computes the step injecting into the read value the least upper bound of all the values returned by the *visible*$^{\#}$ function and of the sequential consistent value. The *visible*$^{\#}$ function is obtained as the abstraction of the *visible* function.

Definition 13 ($step^{\#}$ function)

$$step^{\#} : \overline{TId} \times \overline{\Psi} \times \overline{\Omega} \mapsto \overline{St}$$
$$step^{\#}(\overline{t}, \overline{f}, \overline{s}) = \sigma \text{ where } \overline{f}(\overline{t}) = \overline{\sigma}_0 \to \cdots \to \overline{\sigma}_i \text{ and}$$
$$\overline{\sigma}_i \xrightarrow{\circ}{}^{\#} \overline{\sigma} \qquad \text{if } \pi_1(action^{\#}(\overline{\sigma}_i)) \neq r$$

$$\overline{\sigma}'_i \xrightarrow{\circ}{}^{\#} \overline{\sigma} : \qquad \text{if } \pi_1(action^{\#}(\overline{\sigma}_i)) = r$$
$$\overline{V} = visible^{\#}(\overline{t}, \pi_2(action^{\#}(\overline{\sigma}_i)), synchronised^{\#}(\overline{\sigma}_i), \overline{f}, \overline{s}(\overline{t}))$$
$$\overline{v} = \bigsqcup_{\overline{v}' \in \overline{V}}{}_{Val} \, \overline{v}'$$
$$\overline{sh} = shared^{\#}(\overline{\sigma}_i), \overline{sh}' = \overline{sh}[\overline{l} \mapsto \overline{v} \sqcup_{Val} \overline{sh}(\overline{l})]$$
$$\overline{\sigma}'_i = set\_shared^{\#}(\overline{\sigma}, \overline{sh}')$$

In this definition, we focused on a situation in which the abstract domain for primitive values is non-relational; in this way, we do not support a relational domain as for instance octagons [15].

4.5 Fixpoint Semantics

We proceed as in section 3.4: we define the single trace semantics in fixpoint form basing it on the $step^{\#}$ function just presented, and then we present the multithreaded semantics.

Definition 14 (Single-thread semantics $\overline{\mathbb{S}}^{\circ}$)

$$\overline{\mathbb{S}}^{\circ} : (\overline{\Psi} \times \overline{\Omega} \times \overline{TId}) \mapsto \overline{St}^{\vec{+}}$$
$$\overline{\mathbb{S}}^{\circ} [\![\overline{f}, \overline{r}, \overline{t}]\!] = lfp_{\emptyset}^{\sqsubseteq} \lambda \overline{\tau}.\{\overline{\sigma}_0\} \sqcup_{\tau} \{\overline{\sigma}_0 \to \cdots \to \overline{\sigma}_{i-1} \to \overline{\sigma}_i : \overline{\sigma}_0 \to \cdots \to \overline{\sigma}_{i-1} = \overline{\tau} \wedge \overline{\sigma}_i = step^{\#}(\overline{t}, \overline{f}, \overline{r})\}$$

Definition 15 (Multithreaded semantics $\overline{\mathbb{S}}^{\parallel}$)

$$\overline{\mathbb{S}}^{\parallel} : \overline{\Psi} \times \overline{\Omega} \mapsto \overline{\Psi} \times \overline{\Omega}$$
$$\overline{\mathbb{S}}^{\parallel} [\![\overline{f}_0, \overline{r}_0]\!] = lfp_{\emptyset}^{\sqsubseteq} \lambda(\overline{f}, \overline{r}).\{(\overline{f}_0, \overline{r}_0)\} \sqcup_f \{(\overline{f}_i, \overline{r}) : \forall \overline{t} \in dom(\overline{f}) : \overline{f}_i(\overline{t}) = \overline{\mathbb{S}}^{\circ}[\![\overline{f}, \overline{t}]\!]\}$$

The intuition of these definitions is exactly the same of the concrete semantics: $\overline{\mathbb{S}}^{\circ}$ computes the semantics of a single thread given a multithreaded state (from which the $step^{\#}$ function extrapolates the visible values of the shared memory through the $visible^{\#}$ function), while $\overline{\mathbb{S}}^{\parallel}$ iterates this computation using the previous multithreaded state for each thread until a fixpoint is reached.

The definition of the multithreaded semantics may be straightforwardly extended in order to support widening and narrowing operators [4], which are required to guarantee the convergence of the analysis when the abstract domain is of infinite height.

Theorem 1 (Soundness of $\mathbb{S}^{\parallel}$). *The multithreaded semantics is sound, i.e. let* $\overline{\Psi}_{pre}$ *be the set of all the prefixpoints of* $\overline{F}^{\parallel}$, *then* $\forall \overline{f} \in \overline{\Psi}_{pre} : \alpha_f(\mathbb{S}^{\parallel})[\![\overline{f}]\!] \sqsubseteq_f \overline{\mathbb{S}}^{\parallel}[\![\overline{f}]\!]$.

4.6 Launching a Thread

The launch of a thread may be abstracted from the composition of the concrete definition presented by section 3.5 with the abstraction function.

4.7 Complexity

The proposed analysis requires the computation of two nested fixpoints. The complexity of this approach might appear too heavy in order to apply it to real programs, as the computation of a fixpoint is known to be an expensive operation. On the other hand, the multithreaded semantics may execute in parallel the single-thread semantics of different active threads; supposing that there is a number of processors at least equal to the number of active threads (looking at the current trend of the CPU market, with the appearance of multicore architectures, this supposition is not unreasonable), the complexity of each iteration of $\overline{\mathbb{S}}^{\parallel}$ corresponds to the most expensive computation of the active threads' semantics. In addition, there are interesting results in optimising the fixpoint computation [14].

A preliminary implementation of two nested fixpoints has been presented by [8]; note that this work does not implement the happens-before memory model, but it relies on two nested fixpoints in order to compute a sound approximation of a multithreaded program. Even if the computation of the fixpoint is sequential, the experimental results are quite promising: the analysis of 24 threads and more than 2.000 bytecode statements requires 1'07". Moreover, the execution time seems to grow linearly w.r.t. the number of analysed threads and statements.

In this context, our approach may be able to scale up; indeed, model checkers seem to be inadequate to analyse multithreaded programs because of the state explosion problem, which is particularly relevant when dealing with all the possible interleavings of threads' executions. In addition, partial order reduction techniques [17] do not improve significantly their performance when there are many interactions between threads.

Finally, since our approach is parametrised on the abstract intra-thread domain and semantics, we can also tune them in order to obtain a faster but less precise or a slower but more precise analysis.

4.8 The Running Example

We analyse the running example presented in section 1.1 supposing that we use the interval domain in order to catch information about integer variables.

At the first iteration we obtain the same results as the concrete semantics, completely described in section 3.6. The only difference is that now we deal with abstract values, and so we relate each integer variable to an interval value instead of an integer.

Then we analyse which abstract values are returned by the $\mathit{visible}^{\#}$ function when reading `i` and `j`. In particular, both the initial values (j and i equal to 0) and the values written by thread 1 (1 written both on j and on i) are visible. For both the variables the least upper bound of these elements returns the interval [0..1]. Then the condition of thread 2 ($j == 1 \&\& i == 0$) may be evaluated to `true`, and we conclude that the exception may be thrown. This result is sound w.r.t. the concrete semantics, and so to the happens-before memory model.

5 Related Works

Many approaches have been developed in order to statically analyse multithreaded programs; most of them deal with deadlock and data race detection [20]. In the last few years other approaches, analysing other and more generic properties, have been proposed [22,3,25,7]. Usually these approaches suppose that the execution is sequentially consistent, but this assumption is not legal under, for instance, the Java Memory Model.

[21] presents a semantics for Java multithreaded programs that respects an earlier version of the Java Memory Model. In particular it presents an executable

semantics that is sound and complete with respect to the Java Memory Model, and it verifies programs on it through model checking techniques. It is specific for the Java programming language, it deals with the memory model and also the semantics of the programming language, and it is affected by the state space explosion problem.

In a similar way, [9] develops a model checker sensitive to the .NET memory model [6]. It is specific for the C# language, and also in this case the experimental results show the effects of the state explosion problem.

[2] proposes a formalisation of the Java Memory Model through a semantics that combines the operational, denotational, and axiomatic approaches. It builds up a subset of the legal executions under the Java Memory Model. In this way this approach is similar to ours, since in order to obtain a sound static analysis we compute a superset of these executions. However it is specific to the Java programming language, and it does not propose any static analysis.

[23] presents a framework in order to formalise and study a memory model. This approach is generic w.r.t. the programming language, and it allows the comparison of different memory models. Indeed, it does not propose any static analysis.

In this research context, as far as we know our work appears to be the first one that combines a generic definition of a memory model and its static analysis.

6 Conclusion and Future Work

In this paper we present the formalisation of the happens-before memory model in a fixpoint form, and we build on top of it an abstraction in order to statically analyse a program w.r.t. this memory model. It is completely generic both to the programming language and to the analysed property, as it is parameterized by the concrete and abstract single-thread state, and semantics. In this way we completely split the formalisation of the memory model from the programming language. Moreover, at the abstract level the core of the happens-before memory model (i.e. the $\mathit{visible}^{\#}$ function) is obtained by linearly abstracting its concrete definition. In this way, we are in position to automatically build up a static analysis starting from the concrete specification of the core of a memory model.

Our approach may be easily applied to define and analyse other memory models, and also as an unifying framework in order to compare them: if we prove that a memory model is an abstraction of another one, we prove that all the analyses developed on the second one are sound in the first analysis.

We think that the idea of separating the memory model from the programming language on which it is applied is very promising, as it allows the reuse of analyses on different languages with different memory models. Until now, the only memory model that appears to have been studied deeply is the Java Memory Model, but it is not unrealistic to suppose that in the near future different models, like [6], will appear, to which our approach seems to be easily extendible.

On the other hand, the idea of reusing a memory model for a different programming language appears already near to reality. Behind the specification of a memory model there often is much work (sometimes many years of deep study, in order to understand the problems and how solve them), and so its reuse is not only a possibility, but sometimes a need. For instance, there is a draft [1] that depicts how to apply the Java Memory Model to the C++ programming language.

6.1 Future Works

Our aim is to develop a static analysis on Java bytecode for multithreaded programs. In this way, we are going to define the concrete and abstract intra-thread domain and semantics of this language, and some properties on it. We want also to extend our definitions in order to introduce volatile variables and the causality requirement of the Java Memory Model.

Acknowledgements. We would like to thank Mike Barnett, Agostino Cortesi, Radhia Cousot, Francesco Logozzo and the anonymous referees.

References

1. Alexandrescu, A., Boehm, H., Henney, K., Lea, D., Pugh, B.: Memory model for multithreaded c++. C++ standards committee paper WG21/N1680 (September 2004)
2. Cenciarelli, P., Knapp, A., Sibilio, E.: The java memory model: Operationally, denotationally, axiomatically. In: De Nicola, R. (ed.) ESOP 2007. LNCS, vol. 4421, pp. 331–346. Springer, Heidelberg (2007)
3. Chaumette, S., Ugarte, A.: A formal model of the java multi-threading system and its validation on a known problem. In: Proceedings of IPDPS 2001, IEEE Computer Society, Los Alamitos (2001)
4. Cousot, P., Cousot, R.: Abstract interpretation: a unified lattice model for static analysis of programs by construction or approximation of fixpoints. In: Proceedings of POPL 1977, pp. 238–252. ACM Press, New York (1977)
5. Cousot, P., Cousot, R.: Systematic design of program analysis frameworks. In: Proceedings of POPL 1979, pp. 269–282. ACM Press, New York (1979)
6. Standard ECMA-335. Common Language Infrastructure (CLI). ECMA, 4th edn. (June 2006)
7. Farzan, A., Madhusudan, P.: Causal dataflow analysis for concurrent programs. In: Grumberg, O., Huth, M. (eds.) TACAS 2007. LNCS, vol. 4424, pp. 102–116. Springer, Heidelberg (2007)
8. Ferrara, P.: A fast and precise analysis for data race detection. In: Proceedings of Bytecode 2008, vol. ENTCS, Elsevier, Amsterdam (2008)
9. Huynh, T.Q., Roychoudhury, A.: A memory model sensitive checker for c#. In: Misra, J., Nipkow, T., Sekerinski, E. (eds.) FM 2006. LNCS, vol. 4085, Springer, Heidelberg (2006)
10. Koch, G.: Discovering multi-core: extending the benefits of Moore's law. In: Technology Intel Magazine, July 2005, Intel (2005)
11. Lamport, L.: Time, clocks, and the ordering of events in a distributed system. In: Commun. ACM, vol. 21-7, pp. 558–565. ACM Press, New York (1978)

12. Lindholm, T., Yellin, F.: Java Virtual Machine Specification. Addison-Wesley Longman Publishing Co., Inc., Boston (1999)
13. Manson, J., Pugh, W., Adve, S.V.: The Java memory model. In: Proceedings of POPL 2005, pp. 378–391. ACM Press, New York (2005)
14. Méndez-Lojo, M., Navas, J., Hermenegildo, M.: Efficient, parametric fixpoint algorithm for analysis of java bytecode. In: Proceedings of Bytecode 2007, vol. ENTCS, Elsevier, Amsterdam (2007)
15. Miné, A.: The octagon abstract domain. Higher-Order and Symbolic Computation 19, 31–100 (2006)
16. Netzer, R.H.B., Miller, B.P.: What are race conditions?: Some issues and formalizations. ACM Lett. Program. Lang. Syst. 1, 74–88 (1992)
17. Peled, D.: Ten years of partial order reduction. In: Klette, R., Peleg, S., Sommer, G. (eds.) RobVis 2001. LNCS, vol. 1998, Springer, Heidelberg (2001)
18. Pugh, W.: The Java memory model is fatally flawed. Concurrency - Practice and Experience 12(6), 445–455 (2000)
19. Reynolds, J.C.: Towards a grainless semantics for shared-variable concurrency. In: Lodaya, K., Mahajan, M. (eds.) FSTTCS 2004. LNCS, vol. 3328, Springer, Heidelberg (2004)
20. Rinard, M.C.: Analysis of multithreaded programs. In: Cousot, P. (ed.) SAS 2001. LNCS, vol. 2126, Springer, Heidelberg (2001)
21. Roychoudhury, A., Mitra, T.: Specifying multithreaded java semantics for program verification. In: Proceedings of ICSE 2002, May 2002, ACM Press, New York (2002)
22. Ruys, T.C., Aan de Brugh, N.H.M.: Mmc: the mono model checker. In: Proceedings of Bytecode 2007, vol. ENTCS, Elsevier, Amsterdam (2007)
23. Saraswat, V.A., Jagadeesan, R., Michael, M., von Praun, C.: A theory of memory models. In: Proceedings of PPoPP 2007, pp. 161–172. ACM Press, New York (2007)
24. Sutter, H., Larus, J.: Software and the concurrency revolution. ACM Queue 3(7), 54–62 (2005)
25. Yang, Y., Gopalakrishnan, G., Lindstrom, G.: Rigorous concurrency analysis of multithreaded programs. In: Proceedings of CSJP 2004 (2004)

Pex–White Box Test Generation for .NET

Nikolai Tillmann and Jonathan de Halleux

Microsoft Research
One Microsoft Way, Redmond WA 98052, USA
{nikolait,jhalleux}@microsoft.com

Abstract. Pex automatically produces a small test suite with high code coverage for a .NET program. To this end, Pex performs a systematic program analysis (using dynamic symbolic execution, similar to path-bounded model-checking) to determine test inputs for Parameterized Unit Tests. Pex learns the program behavior by monitoring execution traces. Pex uses a constraint solver to produce new test inputs which exercise different program behavior. The result is an automatically generated small test suite which often achieves high code coverage. In one case study, we applied Pex to a core component of the .NET runtime which had already been extensively tested over several years. Pex found errors, including a serious issue.

1 Overview

Pex [24] is an automatic white-box test generation tool for .NET. Starting from a method that takes parameters, Pex performs path-bounded model-checking by repeatedly executing the program and solving constraint systems to obtain inputs that will steer the program along different execution paths, following the idea of dynamic symbolic execution [12,6]. Pex uses the theorem prover and constraint solver Z3 [3] to reason about the feasibility of execution paths, and to obtain ground models for constraint systems.

While the concept of dynamic symbolic execution is not new, Pex extends the previous work in several ways:

- Pex can build faithful symbolic representations of constraints that characterize execution paths of *safe* .NET programs. In other words, Pex contains a complete symbolic interpreter for safe programs that run in the .NET virtual machine. (And the constraint solver Z3 comes with decision procedures for most such constraints.)
- Pex can reason about a commonly used set of *unsafe* features of .NET. (*Unsafe* means unverifiable memory accesses involving pointer arithmetic.)
- Pex employs a set of search strategies with the goal to achieve high statement coverage in a short amount of time.

We have integrated Pex into Visual Studio as an add-in. Pex can generate test-cases that can be integrated with various unit testing frameworks, including NUnit [20] and MSTest [22]. Pex is an extensible dynamic program analysis

B. Beckert and R. Hähnle (Eds.): TAP 2008, LNCS 4966, pp. 134–153, 2008.

platform; one recent plug-in is DySy [7], an invariant inference tool based on dynamic symbolic execution. We are working towards making the symbolic execution analysis compositional [1].

We have conducted a case study in which we applied Pex to a core component of the .NET architecture which had already been extensively tested over five years by approximately 40 testers. The component is the basis for other libraries, which are used by thousands of developers and millions of end users. Pex found errors, including a serious issue. Because of proprietary concerns, we cannot identify the .NET component on which this case study was based. We will refer to it as the "core .NET component" in the following.

The rest of the paper is structured as follows: Section 2 contains an introduction to Pex. Section 3 discusses the implementation of Pex in more detail. Section 4 shows a particular application of Pex to unsafe .NET code. Section 5 presents the results of applying Pex to a core .NET component. Section 6 compares Pex with other related technologies, and Section 7 concludes.

2 An Introduction to Pex

2.1 Parameterized Unit Testing

At its core, Pex is a test input generator. A test input generator is only useful in practice

- if we have a program to generate test inputs for, and
- if we have a test oracle that decides whether a program execution was successful for some given test inputs.

For Pex, we have adopted the notion of *parameterized unit tests* [28,29] which meet both requirements. A parameterized unit test is simply a method that takes parameters, performs a sequence of method calls that exercise the code-under-test, and asserts properties of the code's expected behavior.

For example, the following parameterized unit test written in C# creates an array-list with a non-negative initial capacity, adds an element to the list, and then asserts that the added element is indeed present.

```
[PexMethod]
public void AddSpec(
    // data
    int capacity, object element) {
    // assumptions
    PexAssume.IsTrue(capacity >= 0);
    // method sequence
    ArrayList a = new ArrayList(capacity);
    a.Add(element);
    // assertions
    Assert.IsTrue(a[0] == element);
}
```

Here, `AddSpec` is decorated with the *custom attribute* `[PexMethod]`, which Pex uses to distinguish parameterized unit tests from ordinary methods.

2.2 The Testing Problem

Starting from parameterized unit tests as specification, we formulate the testing problem as follows.

> Given a sequential program P with statements S, compute a set of program inputs I such that for all reachable statements s in S there exists an input i in I such that $P(i)$ executes s.

Remarks:

- By *sequential* we mean that the program is single-threaded.
- We consider failing an assertion, or violating an implicit contract of the execution engine (e.g. `NullReferenceException` when `null` is dereferenced) as special statements.

2.3 The Testing Problem in Practice

In general, the reachability of program statements is not decidable. Therefore, in practice we aim for a good approximation, e.g. high coverage of the statements of the program. Instead of statement coverage, other coverage metrics such as arc coverage can be used.

In a system with dynamic class loading such as .NET, it is not always possible to determine the statements of the programs ahead of time. In the worst case, the only way to determine all *reachable statements* is an incremental analysis of all possible behaviors of the program.

The analysis of all possible program behaviors, i.e. all execution paths, may take an infinite amount of time. In practice, we have only a limited amount of time available, so we aim for an analysis that can produce test inputs for most reachable statements fast.

Another problem arises from the fact that most interesting programs interact with the environment. In other words, the semantics of some program statements may not be known ahead of time. Most static analysis tools make conservative assumptions in such cases and may produce many *false positives*, e.g. test-cases that supposedly may exhibit an error, but in practice do not. For test generation tools it is more appropriate to take into account environment interactions in order to filter out false positives.

In the remainder of this section we describe the foundations on which Pex tries to address the testing problem, and the next section describes Pex' implementation in more detail, including how heuristic search strategies often solve the problem of achieving high coverage fast.

2.4 Symbolic Execution

Pex implements a white box test input generation technique that is based on the concept of *symbolic execution*. Symbolic execution works similar to concrete execution, only that symbolic variables are used for the program inputs instead of concrete values. When a program variable is updated to a new value during program execution, then this new value may be an expression over the symbolic variables. When the program executes a conditional branch statement where the condition is an expression over the symbolic variables, symbolic execution has to consider two possible continuations, since the condition may evaluate to either `true` or `false`, depending on the program inputs. For each path explored by symbolic execution in this way, a *path condition* is built over symbolic variables. The path condition is the conjunction of the expressions that represent the branch conditions of the program. In this manner all constraints are collected which are needed to deduce what inputs cause an execution path to be taken.

A constraint solver or automatic theorem prover is used to decide the feasibility of individual execution paths, and to obtain concrete test inputs as representatives of individual execution paths.

2.5 Dynamic Symbolic Execution

Pex explores the reachable statements of a parameterized unit test using a technique called *dynamic symbolic execution* [12,6]. This technique consists in executing the program, starting with very simple inputs, while performing a symbolic execution in parallel to collect symbolic constraints on inputs obtained from predicates in branch statements along the execution. Then Pex uses a constraint solver to compute variations of the previous inputs in order to steer future program executions along different execution paths. In this way, all execution paths will be exercised eventually.

Dynamic symbolic execution extends conventional static symbolic execution [16] with additional information that is collected at runtime, which makes the analysis more precise [12,11]. While additional information is collected by monitoring concrete traces, each of these traces is representative of an execution path, i.e. the equivalence class of test inputs that steer the program along this particular execution path. By taking into account more details of structure of the program (e.g. boundaries of basic blocks or functions), even bigger equivalences classes can be analyzed at once [12,1].

Algorithm 2.1 shows the general dynamic symbolic execution algorithm implemented in Pex. The choice of the new program inputs i in each loop iteration decides in which order the different execution paths of the program are enumerated.

Pex uses several heuristics that take into account the structure of the program and the already covered statements when deciding on the next program inputs. While the ultimate goal of Pex is to discover all reachable statements, which is an undecidable problem, in practice Pex attempts to achieve high statement coverage fast. This simplifies the configuration of Pex greatly: the user just has to set a time limit or another rough exploration bound. Other dynamic symbolic execution tools ([12,11,12,6]) perform an exhaustive search of all the execution paths in a fixed order, within bounds on the size and structure of the input given by the user. In the case of Pex the inputs are often richly structured object graphs for which it is a difficult problem to define practical and useful bounds.

Algorithm 2.1. Dynamic symbolic execution

Set $J := \emptyset$	(intuitively, J is the set of already
loop	analyzed program inputs)
Choose program input $i \notin J$	(stop if no such i can be found)
Output i	
Execute $P(i)$; record path condition C	(in particular, $C(i)$ holds)
Set $J := J \cup C$	(viewing C as the set $\{i \mid C(i)\}$)
end loop	

2.6 More Reasons for *Dynamic* Symbolic Execution

Symbolic execution was originally proposed [16] as a static program analysis technique, i.e. an analysis that only considered the source code of the analyzed program. This approach works well as long as all decisions about the feasibility of execution paths can be made on basis of the source code alone. It becomes problematic when the program contains statements that cannot be reasoned about easily (e.g. memory accesses through arbitrary pointers, or floating point arithmetic), or when parts of the program are actually unknown (e.g. when the program communicates with the *environment*, for which no source code is available, and whose behavior has not been specified rigorously).

It is not uncommon for .NET programs to use unsafe .NET features, i.e. using pointer arithmetic to access memory for performance reasons, and most .NET programs interact with other unmanaged (i.e. non-.NET) components or the Windows API for legacy reasons.

While static symbolic execution algorithms do not use any information about the environment into which the program is embedded, dynamic symbolic execution can leverage dynamic information that it observes during concrete program executions, i.e. the memory locations which are actually accessed through pointers and the data that is passed around between the analyzed program and the environment.

As a result, Pex can prune the search space. When the program communicates with the environment, Pex builds a model of the environment from the actual data that the environment receives and returns. This model is an under-approximation of the environment, since Pex does not know the conditions under which the environment produces its output. The resulting constraint systems that Pex builds may no longer accurately characterize the program's behavior. In practice this means that for a computed input the program may not take the predicted execution path. Since Pex does not have a precise abstraction of the program's behavior in such cases, Pex may not discover all reachable execution paths, and thus all reachable statements.

In any case, Pex always maintains an under-approximation of the program's behavior, which is appropriate for testing.

3 Pex Implementation Details

3.1 Instrumentation

Pex monitors the execution of a .NET program through code instrumentation. Pex plugs into the .NET profiling API [21]. It inspects the instructions of a method in the intermediate language [15] which all .NET compilers target. Pex rewrites the instructions just before they are translated into the machine code at runtime. The instrumented code drives a "shadow interpreter" in parallel to the actual program execution. The "shadow interpreter"

- constructs symbolic representations of the executed operations over logical variables instead of the concrete program inputs;
- maintains and evolves a symbolic representation of the entire program's state at any point in time;
- records the conditions over which the program branches.

Pex' "shadow interpreter" models the behavior of all verifiable .NET instructions precisely, and models most unverifiable (involving unsafe memory accesses) instructions as well.

3.2 Symbolic Representation of Values and Program State

A symbolic program state is a predicate over logical variables together with an assignment of expressions over logical variables to locations, just as a concrete program state is an assignment of values to locations. For Pex, the locations of a state consist of static fields, instance fields, method arguments, local variables, and positions on the operand stack.

Pex' expression constructors include primitive constants for all basic .NET data types (integers, floating point numbers, object references), and functions over those basic types representing particular machine instructions, e.g. addition and multiplication. Pex uses tuples to represent .NET value types ("structs") as well as indices of multi-dimensional arrays, and maps to represent instance fields and arrays, similar to the heap encoding of ESC/Java [10]: An instance field of an object is represented by a *field map* which associates object references with field values. (For each declared field in the program, there is one location in the state that holds current field map value.) An array type is represented by a class with two fields: a length field, and a field that holds a mapping from integers (or tuples of integers for multi-dimensional arrays) to the array elements. Constraints over the .NET type system and virtual method dispatch lookups are encoded in expressions as well. Predicates are represented by boolean-valued expressions.

We will illustrate the representation of the state with the following class.

```
class C {
    int X;
    int GetXPlusOne() { return this.X + 1; }
    void SetX(int newX) { this.X = newX; }
}
```

Symbolically executing the method `c.GetXPlusOne()` with the receiver object given by the object reference `c` will yield the expression `add(select(X_Map,c), 1)` where the `select` function represents the selection of `c`'s `X`-field value from the current field map `X_Map`. After symbolically executing `c.SetX(42)`, the final state will assign the expression `update(X_Map,c,42)` to the location that holds the current field map of `X`. `X_Map` denotes the value of the field map of `X` before the execution of the method.

Pex implements various techniques to reduce the enormous overhead of the symbolic state representation. Before building a new expression, Pex always applies a set of reduction rules which compute a normal form. A simple example of a reduction rule is constant folding, e.g. $1 + 1$ is reduced to 2. All logical connectives are transformed into a binary decision diagram (BDD) representation with if-then-else expressions [5]. All expressions are hash-consed, i.e. only one instance is ever allocated in memory for all structurally equivalent expressions. Map updates, which are used extensively to represent the evolving heap of a program, are compactly stored in tries, indexed over unique expression indices.

Based on the already accumulated path condition, expressions are further simplified. For example, if the path condition already established that $x > 0$, then $x < 0$ simplifies to `false`.

3.3 Symbolic Pointers

Pex represents pointers as expressions as well. Pex distinguishes the following pointer constructors.

- Pointer to nowhere. Represents an invalid pointer, or just `null`.
- Pointer to value. Represent a pointer to an immutable value, e.g. a pointer to the first character of a string.
- Pointer to static field.
- Pointer to instance field map. Represents a pointer to the mapping of an instance field that associates object references with field values.
- Pointer to method argument or local variable.
- Pointer to element. Given a pointer to a mapping and an index expression, represents a pointer to the indexed value.

While the pointers in safe, managed .NET programs are guaranteed to be either `null` or pointing to a valid memory location, unsafe .NET code that is sufficiently trusted to bypass .NET's byte code verifier does not come with such a guarantee. Thus, when the user enables Pex' strict pointer checking mode, Pex builds a verification condition whenever the program is about to perform an indirect memory access through a pointer. In particular, given a pointer to an element of an array, the condition states that the index must be within the bounds of the array.

In practice, the verification conditions can verify most uses of unsafe pointers. For example, the following code shows a common use of pointers, with the intention of simply avoiding the overhead of repeated array-bounds checking.

```
public unsafe bool BuggyContainsZero(byte[] a) {
    if (a == null || a.Length == null) return false;
    fixed (byte* p = a)
        for (int i = 0; i <= a.Length; i++)
            if (p[i] == 0) return true;
    return true;
}
```

This code contains an error: The loop condition should be `i < a.Length` instead of `i <= a.Length`. This error might not be detected with conventional testing, since reading beyond the bounds of an array with a pointer often does not trigger an exception (the allocated memory is usually advanced to another block of allocated memory).

While the problem of buffer overflows has been well studied, e.g. in the context of C programs that are compiled to machine code directly, we are not aware of a thorough checker in the context of managed execution environments, in particular .NET.

Pex can not only detect the error in strict pointer-checking mode, Pex will even steer the program towards obscure program behaviors by test input generation through dynamic symbolic execution.

However, Pex cannot symbolically reason about all operations that involve pointers. In particular, Pex does not track when the content of a memory is reinterpreted, e.g. a pointer to an array of bytes is cast to a pointer of an integer, and when the memory was obtained from the environment, e.g. through a call to a Windows API.

3.4 Search Strategy

Deciding reachability of program statements is a hard problem. In a system with dynamic class loading and virtual method dispatch the problem does not become easier. As discussed earlier, Pex' approach based on dynamic symbolic execution enumerates feasible execution paths, where information from previously executed paths is used to compute test inputs for the next execution paths. Most earlier approach to dynamic symbolic execution [12,27,26,6] in fact only use information from the last execution path to determine test inputs that will exercise the next path. This restriction forces them to use a fixed "depth-first, backtracking" search order, where the next execution path would always share the longest possible prefix with the previous execution path. As a result, a lot of time may be spent analyzing small parts of the program before moving on. These approaches require well defined bounds on the program inputs to avoid unfolding the same program loop forever, and they may discover "easy" to cover statements only after an exhaustive search. (To avoid getting stuck in the depth-first search, these earlier approaches frequently inject random test inputs to steer the search towards other parts of the program. However, this prevents any deep symbolic analysis.)

Pex uses the information of all previously executed paths: During exploration, Pex maintains a representation of the explored execution tree of the program, whose paths are the explored execution paths. In each step of the test generation algorithm, Pex picks an outgoing unexplored branch of the tree, i.e. the prefix of a feasible execution path plus an outgoing branch that has not been exercised yet. The next test inputs are the solution (if any) of the constraint system that is built from the conjunction of the path condition of the feasible path prefix, and the condition of the unexercised outgoing branch. If the constraint system has no solution, or it cannot be computed by the constraint solver, the search marks the branch as infeasible and moves on.

In earlier experiments, we tried well-known search strategies to traverse the execution tree, such as breadth-first search. While this strategy does not get stuck in the same way as depth-first search, it does not take into account the structure of the program either.

The program consists of building blocks such as methods and loops, which may get instantiated and unfolded many times along each execution path, giving rise to multiple branch instances in the execution path (and tree). For our ultimate goal, to cover all reachable statements, the number of unfoldings is irrelevant, although a certain number of unfoldings might be required to discover that a statement is reachable. How many and which unfoldings are required is undecidable.

In order to avoid getting stuck in a particular area of the program by a fixed search order, Pex implements a fair choice between all such unexplored branches of the explored execution tree. Pex includes various fair strategies which partition all branches into equivalence classes, and then pick a representative of the least often chosen class. The equivalence classes cluster branches by mapping them

- to the branch statement in the program of which the execution tree branch is an instance (each branch statement may give rise to multiple branch instances in the execution tree, e.g. when loops are unfolded),
- to the stack trace at the time the brach was recorded,
- to the overall branch coverage at the time the branch was recorded,
- to the depth of the branch in the execution tree.

Pex combines all such fair strategies into a meta-strategy that performs a fair choice between the strategies.

Creating complex objects. When an argument of a parameterized unit test is an object that has non-public fields, Pex will still collect constraints over the usage of that field. Later, new test inputs may be computed which assign particular values to those fields. But then Pex may not know how to create an object through the publicly available constructors such that the object's private fields are in the desired state. (Of course, Pex could use .NET's reflection mechanism to set private fields in arbitrary ways, but then Pex might violate the (implicit) class invariant.)

In such cases, Pex selects a constructor of the class (the user may configure which constructor is chosen), and Pex includes this constructor in the exploration of the parameterized unit test. As a result, Pex will first try to find a non-exceptional path through the control-flow of the constructor, and then use the created object to further explore the parameterized unit test that required the object. In other words, Pex tries to avoid the backward search to find a way to reach a target state; instead, it will perform a forward search that is compatible with dynamic symbolic execution.

In this way, directed object graphs can easily be created, where arguments to constructors can refer to earlier constructed objects. Cyclic object graphs can only result if a constructor updates a field of an argument to point to the constructed object.

As an alternative to employing only existing constructors to configure objects, the user may also provide factory methods, which could invoke a sequence of method calls to construct and configure a new object, possibly creating cyclic references as well.

3.5 Constraint Solving

For each chosen unexplored branch, Pex builds a formula that represents the condition under which this branch may be reached. Pex performs various pre-processing steps to reduce the size of the formula before handing it over to the constraint solver, similar to constraint caching, and independent constraint optimization [6].

Pex employs Z3 as its constraint solver. Pex faithfully encodes all constraints arising in safe .NET programs such that Z3 can decide them with its built-in decision procedures for propositional logic, fixed sized bit-vectors, tuples, arrays, and quantifiers. Arithmetic constraints over floating point numbers are approximated by a translation to rational numbers. Pex also encodes the constraints of the .NET type system and virtual method dispatch lookups as universally quantified formulas.

3.6 Pex Architecture

Internally, Pex consists of several libraries:

Microsoft.ExtendedReflection. Extended Reflection (ER) is a library that enables the monitoring of .NET applications at the instruction level. It uses the unmanaged profiling API to instrument the monitored .NET program with callbacks to the managed ER library. The callbacks are used to drive the "shadow interpreter" mentioned in Section 3.1.

Microsoft.Pex.Framework. This library is serves as a front-end for the user to configure Pex. It defines a number of .NET custom attributes, including the `PexMethod` attribute that we used in the earlier example.

Microsoft.Pex. The Pex engine implements the search for test inputs, by repeatedly executing the program while monitoring it, and building constraint systems to obtain new test inputs.

Microsoft.Z3. [3] is the constraint solver that Pex uses.

Pex is built from individual components, that are organized in three layers:

1) A set of components is alive for the entire lifetime of the Pex engine. 2) In addition, a set of components is created and kept alive for the duration of the exploration of a single parameterized unit test. 3) In addition, a set of components is created and kept alive for each execution path that is executed and monitored.

Pex' monitoring library, ER, is a quite general monitoring library that can be used in isolation. In addition to Pex itself, we have built PexCop on top of ER, a dynamic program analysis application which analyzes individual execution traces, looking for common programming errors, e.g. resource leaks.

Pex itself provides an extension mechanism, where a user can hook into any of the three component layers of Pex (engine, exploration, path). For example, DySy [7], an invariant inference tool based on dynamic symbolic execution, uses this extension mechanism to analyze all execution path of a parameterized unit test.

3.7 Limitations

There are certain situations in which Pex cannot analyze the code properly:

Nondeterminism. Pex assumes that the analyzed program is deterministic; this means in particular that all environment interactions should be deterministic. Pex detects non-determinism by comparing the program's actual execution path with the predicted execution path. When non-deterministic behavior is detected, Pex prunes the test inputs that caused it. Pex also gives feedback to the user, showing the program branches where monitored execution paths began to deviate from the prediction. The user can decide to ignore the problems, or the user can change the code to make it more testable.

To alleviate the problem, Pex has a mechanism for substituting methods that have a known non-deterministic behavior with deterministic alternatives. For example, Pex routinely substitutes the `TickCount` property of the `System.Environment` class that measures time with a constant alternative. Substitutions are easy to write by users; they are applied by Pex through name matching.

```
namespace __Substitutions.System {
    public static class Environment {
        public static int get_TickCount___redirect() {
            return 0;
        }
    }
}
```

Concurrency. Today, Pex does not handle multithreaded programs. Pex only monitors the main thread of the program. Other threads may cause non-deterministic behavior of the main thread, which results in feedback to the user just like other non-deterministic program behavior.

Native Code, .NET code that is not instrumented. Pex does not monitor native code, e.g. x86 instructions called through the P/Invoke mechanism of .NET. Also, since instrumentation of managed code comes with a significant performance overhead, Pex instruments code only selectively. In both cases, the effect is the same: constraints are lost. However, even if some methods are implemented in native code or are uninstrumented, Pex will still try to cover the instrumented code as much as possible.

The concept of redirecting method calls to alternative substitution methods is also used sometimes to give managed alternatives to native methods, so that Pex can determine the constraints of native methods by monitoring the managed alternative.

Symbolic Reasoning. Pex uses an automatic constraint solver (Z3) to determine which values are relevant for the test and the program-under-test. However, the abilities of the constraint solver are, and always will be, limited. In particular, Z3 cannot reason about floating point arithmetic, and Pex imposes a configurable memory and time consumption limit on Z3.

Language. Pex can analyze arbitrary .NET programs, written in any .NET language. Today, the Visual Studio add-in and the test code generation only support C#.

4 Application

Pex is integrated into Visual Studio as an add-in. The user writes parameterized unit tests as public instance methods decorated the custom attribute `PexMethod`, as shown in the following example.

```
[PexMethod]
public void ParameterizedTest(int i) {
    if (i == 123)
        throw new ArgumentException("i");
}
```

Then, the user simply right-clicks the parameterized unit test, and selects the **Pex It** menu item.

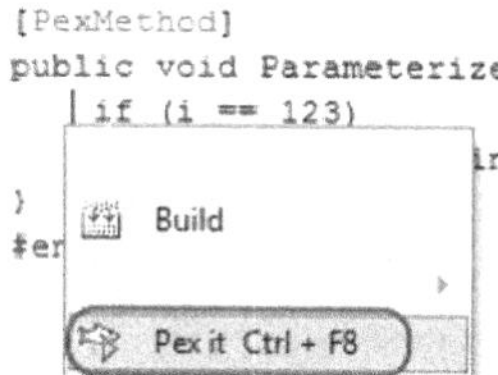

Pex will then launch a process in the background which analyzes the code, executing it multiple times. The results are shown in a **Pex Results** window, that lists the computed parameter values in a table for each parameterized unit test.

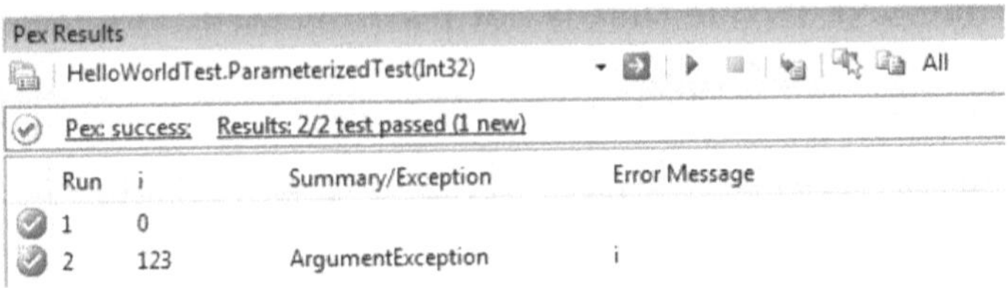

Pex Results

HelloWorldTest.ParameterizedTest(Int32) All

Pex success: Results: 2/2 test passed (1 new)

Run	i	Summary/Exception	Error Message
1	0		
2	123	ArgumentException	i

As expected, Pex generated 2 tests to cover `ParameterizedTest`. The first tests uses the "default" value 0 for an integer, and Pex records the constraint `i!=123`. The negation of this constraint leads to the second test, where `i==123`, which triggers the branch that throws a `ArgumentNullException`.

In the following example, we show that Pex can analyze unsafe managed .NET code. We wrote the following parameterized unit test, that obtains an unsafe pointer from a (safe) byte array, then passes the pointer to the .NET `UnmanagedMemoryStream`, which is in turn given to the `ResourceReader`.

```
[PexClass]
...
public partial class ResourceReaderTest {
    [PexMethod]
    public unsafe void ReadEntriesFromUnmanagedMemoryStream(
        [PexAssumeNotNull]byte[] data) {
        fixed (byte* p = data)
            using (UnmanagedMemoryStream stream =
                new UnmanagedMemoryStream(p, data.Length)) {
                ResourceReader reader =
                    new ResourceReader(stream);
                readEntries(reader);
            }
    }

    private static void readEntries(ResourceReader reader) {
        int i = 0;
        foreach (DictionaryEntry entry in reader) {
            PexAssert.IsNotNull(entry.Key);
            i++;
        }
    }
}
```

We further decorate the test with the following attributes, to suppress certain exceptions that the documentation deems acceptable, and to enable Pex' strict checking of unsafe memory accesses.

```
[PexInjectExceptionsOnUnverifiableUnsafeMemoryAccess]
[PexAllowedException(typeof(BadImageFormatException))]
[PexAllowedException(typeof(IOException))]
[PexAllowedException(typeof(NotSupportedException))]
```

From the parameterized unit test, Pex generates several test inputs. After around one minute, and executing the parameterized unit tests for 576 times with different inputs, Pex generates test-cases such as the following. (Most of the generated test-cases represent invalid resource file, but some represent legal resource files with one or more entries. The byte array shown here is an illegal resource file.)

```
public void ReadEntriesFromUnmanagedMemoryStream_576() {
    byte[] bs0 = new byte[56];
    bs0[0] = (byte)206;
    bs0[1] = (byte)202;
    bs0[2] = (byte)239;
    bs0[3] = (byte)190;
    bs0[7] = (byte)64;
    bs0[12] = (byte)2;
    bs0[16] = (byte)2;
    bs0[24] = (byte)192;
    bs0[25] = (byte)203;
    bs0[26] = (byte)25;
    bs0[27] = (byte)176;
    bs0[28] = (byte)1;
    bs0[29] = (byte)145;
    bs0[30] = (byte)88;
    bs0[40] = (byte)34;
    bs0[41] = (byte)128;
    bs0[42] = (byte)132;
    bs0[43] = (byte)113;
    bs0[44] = (byte)132;
    bs0[46] = (byte)168;
    bs0[47] = (byte)5;
    bs0[48] = (byte)172;
    bs0[49] = (byte)32;
    this.ReadEntriesFromUnmanagedMemoryStream(bs0);
}
```

Pex deduced the entire file contents from the `ResourceReader` implementation. Note that the first four bytes represent a magic number which the `ResourceReader` expects. The later bytes form resource entries. The following code is part of the resource reader implementation. `ReadInt32` combines four bytes to a 32-bit integer through bitwise operations.

```
// Read ResourceManager header
// Check for magic number
// _store wraps the input stream
int magicNum = _store.ReadInt32();
if (magicNum != ResourceManager.MagicNumber)
    throw new ArgumentException("Resource file not valid!");
```

5 Evaluation

We applied Pex on a core .NET component that had already been extensively tested over several years.

We used a version of the component which contains assertion checks that the developers of the component embedded into the code. These checks are very expensive, and they are removed from the retail version of the component that is normally deployed by the users. These additional consistency checks, realized by conditional branch instructions, greatly increase the number of potential execution paths that must be analyzed. As a result, Pex analysis takes at least an order of magnitude longer than it does when applied on the retail version.

We used the Pex Wizard to generate individual parameterized unit tests for each public method of all public classes. These automatically generated unit tests do not contain any additional assertion validation; they simply pass the arguments through to the method-under-test. Thus, the test oracle only consists of the assertions that are embedded in the product code, and the pattern that certain exceptions should not be thrown by any code, e.g. access violation exceptions that indicate that an unsafe operation has corrupted the memory. In addition, we wrote about ten parameterized unit tests by hand which exercise common call sequences.

For example, for a method `Parse` that creates a data type `DataType` instance by parsing a string, the Wizard generates parameterized unit tests such as the following.

```
[PexMethod]
public void Parse(string s) {
    DataType result = DataType.Parse(s);
    PexValue.AddForValidation("result", result);
}
```

The parameterized unit test calls `DataType.Parse` with a given string and stores the result in a local variable. The call to `PexValue.AddForValidation` logs the result of the call to `Parse`, and it the test suite which Pex creates will include verification code that can be used in future regression testing to ensure that the `Parse` will not change its behavior but always return the same output as when Pex explored it.

We ran Pex on about 10 machines (different configurations, similar to P4, 2GHz, 2GB RAM) for three days; each machine was processing one class at a time.

In total, the analysis involved more than 10,000 public methods with more than 100,000 blocks and more than 100,000 arcs. When executing the code as part of the analysis, Pex created a sand-box with security permissions "Internet", i.e. permissions that correspond to the default policy permission set suitable for content from unknown origin, which means in particular that most operations involving the environment, e.g. file accesses, were blocked, Starting from the public methods, Pex achieved about 43% block coverage and 36% arc coverage. We do not know how many blocks and arcs are actually reachable.

Table 1. Automatically achieved coverage on selected classes of the core .NET component

Class	Blocks	Block Coverage	Arcs	Arc Coverage
A (mostly stateless methods)	>300	95%	>400	90%
B (mostly stateless methods)	>100	97%	>200	94%
C (stateful)	>200	76%	>300	65%
D (parsing code)	>500	81%	>800	73%
E (numerical algorithms)	>400	71%	>600	67%
F (numerical algorithms)	>100	82%	>200	79%
G (numerical algorithms)	>100	98%	>100	97%
H (numerical algorithms)	>200	71%	>200	61%
I (numerical algorithms)	>200	97%	>300	96%

Because of the restricted security permissions, and the fact that Pex was only testing one method at a time, the overall coverage numbers clearly can be improved. However, Pex did very well on many classes which do not require many method calls to access their functionality. Table 1 shows a selection of classes of the core .NET component on which Pex fully automatically achieved high block and arc coverage. Only lower bounds for the block and arc numbers are given for proprietary reasons.

One category of errors that Pex found contains test cases that trigger rather benign exceptions, e.g. `NullReferenceException` and `IndexOutOfRangeException`. Another more interesting category of 17 unique errors involves the violation of assertions which the developers wrote in the code, and the exhaustion of memory, and other serious issues.

Most of the errors that Pex found required very carefully chosen argument values (e.g. a string of length 100 filled with particular characters), and it is unlikely that a random test input generator would find them. While some of the errors could be found by assertion-targetting techniques, e.g. [18], the branch conditions that guarded the errors were usually quite complex (involving bitvector arithmetic, indirect memory accesses) and were spread over multiple methods, and incorporated values obtained from the environment (here, the Windows API). It requires a dynamic analysis (to obtain the values from the environment) with a precise symbolic abstraction of the program's behavior to find these errors.

6 Related Work

Pex performs path-bounded model-checking of .NET programs. Pex is related to other program model checkers, in particular JPF [2] and XRT [14] which also operate on managed programs (Java and .NET). Both JPF and XRT have extensions for symbolic execution. However, both can only perform *static* symbolic execution, and they cannot deal with stateful environment interactions. Also, in the case of JPF, only some aspects of the program execution can be encoded symbolically (linear integer arithmetic constraints), while others must always be explored explicitly (constraints over indirect memory accesses).

The idea of symbolic execution was pioneered by [16]. Later work on dynamic test generation, e.g. [17,18], mainly discussed the generation of test inputs to determine whether a particular execution path or branch was feasible. While Pex' search strategies try to exercise individual execution paths in a particular (heuristically chosen) sequence, the strategies are complete and will eventually exercise all execution paths. This is important in an environment such as .NET where the program can load new code dynamically, and not all branches and assertions are known ahead of time.

Dynamic symbolic execution was first suggested in DART [12]. Their tool instruments C programs at the source code level, and it tracks linear integer arithmetic constraints. CUTE [27] follows the approach of DART, but it can track and reason about not only linear integer arithmetic, but also pointer aliasing constraints. jCUTE [26] is an implementation of CUTE for Java, a managed environment without pointers. EXE [6] is another implementation of C source code based dynamic symbolic execution, and EXE implements a number of further improvements, including constraint caching, independent constraint optimization, bitvector arithmetic, and tracking indirect memory accesses symbolically. Each of these approaches is specialized for a particular source language, and they only include certain operations in the symbolic analysis. Also, their search order is not prioritized to achieve high coverage quickly, which forces the user to precisely define bounds on the size of the program inputs and to perform an exhaustive search. Pex is language independent, and it can symbolically reason about pointer arithmetic as well as constraints from object oriented programs. Pex search strategies aim at achieving high coverage fast without much user annotations.

Another language agnostic tool is SAGE [13], which is used internally at Microsoft. It virtualizes a Windows process on the x86 instruction level, and it tracks integer constraints as bitvectors. While operating at the instruction level makes it a very general tool, this generality also comes with a high instrumentation overhead which is significantly smaller for Pex.

Several improvements have been proposed recently to improve the scalability of dynamic symbolic execution, by making it compositional [11,19], and demand-driven [19,8]. We are working on related improvements in Pex [1] with encouraging early results.

Randoop [23] is a tool that generates new test-cases by composing previously found test-case fragments, supplying random input data. Randoop was also used internally in Microsoft to test core .NET components. While Pex and Randoop found some of the same errors, the error findings were generally different in that Randoop found errors that needed two or more method calls, while most of the errors that Pex found involved just a single method calls, but with very carefully chosen argument values.

The commercial tool AgitarOne from Agitar [4] generates test-cases for Java by analyzing the source code, using information about program invariants obtained in a way similar to [9]. Similar to idea of parameterized unit testing [25], work building on Agitar proposes a concept called theories [25] to write and explore general test-cases.

7 Conclusion

Pex [24] is an automatic white-box test generation tool for .NET that explores the code-under test by dynamic symbolic execution. Pex analyzes safe, managed code, and it can validate unsafe memory accesses on individual execution paths. We applied Pex on a extremely well tested core .NET component, and found errors, including a serious issue. The automatically achieved results are encouraging. However, the combined coverage of the test-cases that Pex generated fully automatically clearly show that there is room for future research, e.g. leveraging information about the structure of the program to construct method call sequences automatically.

Acknowledgements

We would like to thank Wolfram Schulte for his support, our interns Thorsten Schuett, Christoph Csallner and Saswat Anand for their work to improve Pex, Nikolaj Bjorner and Leonardo de Moura for Z3, the developers and testers of the core .NET component for their support and advice, as well as Patrice Godefroid, and the anonymous reviewers for their comments.

References

1. Anand, S., Godefroid, P., Tillmann, N.: Demand-driven compositional symbolic execution. Technical Report MSR-TR-2007-138, Microsoft Research, Redmond, WA (October 2007)
2. Anand, S., Pasareanu, C.S., Visser, W.: Jpf-se: A symbolic execution extension to java pathfinder. In: Grumberg, O., Huth, M. (eds.) TACAS 2007. LNCS, vol. 4424, pp. 134–138. Springer, Heidelberg (2007)
3. Bjorner, N., de Moura, L.: Z3: An efficient SMT solver (2007), `http://research.microsoft.com/projects/Z3`
4. Boshernitsan, M., Doong, R., Savoia, A.: From daikon to agitator: lessons and challenges in building a commercial tool for developer testing. In: ISSTA 2006: Proceedings of the 2006 international symposium on Software testing and analysis, pp. 169–180. ACM Press, New York (2006)
5. Brace, K.S., Rudell, R.L., Bryant, R.E.: Efficient implementation of a BDD package. In: DAC 1990: Proceedings of the 27th ACM/IEEE conference on Design automation, pp. 40–45. ACM Press, New York (1990)
6. Cadar, C., Ganesh, V., Pawlowski, P.M., Dill, D.L., Engler, D.R.: Exe: automatically generating inputs of death. In: CCS 2006: Proceedings of the 13th ACM conference on Computer and communications security, pp. 322–335. ACM Press, New York (2006)

7. Csallner, C., Tillmann, N., Smaragdakis, Y.: Dysy: Dynamic symbolic execution for invariant inference. Technical Report MSR-TR-2007-151, Microsoft Research, Redmond, WA (November 2007)
8. Engler, D., Dunbar, D.: Under-constrained execution: making automatic code destruction easy and scalable. In: ISSTA 2007: Proceedings of the 2007 international symposium on Software testing and analysis, pp. 1–4. ACM, New York (2007)
9. Ernst, M.D., Perkins, J.H., Guo, P.J., McCamant, S., Pacheco, C., Tschantz, M.S., Xiao, C.: The Daikon system for dynamic detection of likely invariants. Science of Computer Programming (2007)
10. Flanagan, C., Leino, K.R.M., Lillibridge, M., Nelson, G., Saxe, J.B., Stata, R.: Extended static checking for Java. In: Proc. the ACM SIGPLAN 2002 Conference on Programming language design and implementation, pp. 234–245. ACM Press, New York (2002)
11. Godefroid, P.: Compositional dynamic test generation. In: POPL 2007: Proceedings of the 34th annual ACM SIGPLAN-SIGACT symposium on Principles of programming languages, pp. 47–54. ACM Press, New York (2007)
12. Godefroid, P., Klarlund, N., Sen, K.: DART: directed automated random testing. SIGPLAN Notices 40(6), 213–223 (2005)
13. Godefroid, P., Levin, M.Y., Molnar, D.: Automated whitebox fuzz testing. Technical Report MSR-TR-2007-58, Microsoft Research, Redmond, WA (May 2007)
14. Grieskamp, W., Tillmann, N., Schulte, W.: XRT - Exploring Runtime for .NET - Architecture and Applications. In: SoftMC 2005: Workshop on Software Model Checking, July 2005. Electronic Notes in Theoretical Computer Science (2005)
15. E. International. Standard ECMA-335, Common Language Infrastructure (CLI) (June 2006)
16. King, J.C.: Symbolic execution and program testing. Commun. ACM 19(7), 385–394 (1976)
17. Korel, B.: A dynamic approach of test data generation. In: IEEE Conference On Software Maintenance, November 1990, pp. 311–317 (1990)
18. Korel, B., Al-Yami, A.M.: Assertion-oriented automated test data generation. In: Proc. the 18th international conference on Software engineering, pp. 71–80. IEEE Computer Society, Los Alamitos (1996)
19. Majumdar, R., Sen, K.: Latest: Lazy dynamic test input generation. Technical Report UCB/EECS-2007-36, EECS Department, University of California, Berkeley (Mar 2007)
20. Two, M.C., Poole, C., Cansdale, J., Feldman, G., Newkirk, J.W., Vorontsov, A.A., Craig, P.A.: NUnit, `http://www.nunit.org/`
21. Microsoft. Net framework general reference - profiling (unmanaged api reference), `http://msdn2.microsoft.com/en-us/library/ms404386.aspx`
22. Microsoft. Visual Studio Team System, Team Edition for Testers, `http://msdn2.microsoft.com/en-us/vsts2008/products/bb933754.aspx`
23. Pacheco, C., Lahiri, S.K., Ernst, M.D., Ball, T.: Feedback-directed random test generation. In: ICSE 2007, Proceedings of the 29th International Conference on Software Engineering, Minneapolis, MN, USA, May 23–25 (2007)
24. Pex development team. Pex (2007), `http://research.microsoft.com/Pex`
25. Saff, D., Boshernitsan, M., Ernst, M.D.: Theories in practice: Easy-to-write specifications that catch bugs. Technical Report MIT-CSAIL-TR-2008-002, MIT Computer Science and Artificial Intelligence Laboratory, Cambridge, MA, January 14 (2008)

26. Sen, K., Agha, G.: CUTE and jCUTE: Concolic unit testing and explicit path model-checking tools. In: Ball, T., Jones, R.B. (eds.) CAV 2006. LNCS, vol. 4144, pp. 419–423. Springer, Heidelberg (2006)
27. Sen, K., Marinov, D., Agha, G.: Cute: a concolic unit testing engine for c. In: ESEC/FSE-13: Proceedings of the 10th European software engineering conference held jointly with 13th ACM SIGSOFT international symposium on Foundations of software engineering, pp. 263–272. ACM Press, New York (2005)
28. Tillmann, N., Schulte, W.: Parameterized unit tests. In: Proceedings of the 10th European Software Engineering Conference held jointly with 13th ACM SIGSOFT International Symposium on Foundations of Software Engineering, pp. 253–262. ACM, New York (2005)
29. Tillmann, N., Schulte, W.: Unit tests reloaded: Parameterized unit testing with symbolic execution. IEEE Software 23(4), 38–47 (2006)

Non-termination Checking for Imperative Programs

Helga Velroyen[1] and Philipp Rümmer[2]

[1] Department of Computer Science
RWTH Aachen University of Technology
helga.velroyen@rwth-aachen.de
[2] Department of Computer Science and Engineering,
Chalmers University of Technology and Göteborg University
philipp@chalmers.se

Abstract. While termination checking tailored to real-world library code or frameworks has received ever-increasing attention during the last years, the complementary question of *disproving* termination properties as a means of debugging has largely been ignored so far. We present an approach to automatic non-termination checking that relates to termination checking in the same way as symbolic testing does to program verification. Our method is based on the automated generation of invariants that show that terminating states of a program are unreachable from certain initial states. Such initial states are identified using constraint-solving techniques. The method is fully implemented on top of a program verification system and available for download. We give an empirical evaluation of the approach using a collection of non-terminating example programs.

1 Introduction

Termination properties of programs are crucial for liveness and safety: a piece of software which does not terminate can have vast consequences, especially when employed in critical environments or wide-spread. The latter concerns in particular library code or frameworks, whose specific use is often unknown at the time of development. Non-termination bugs can be very subtle and hide long before they take effect in productivity situations.

Although the concept of formally proving termination properties has been known and investigated for a long time, the last years have seen intensified research on how to check the termination of real-world code [1,2]. During the same time, however, the complementary field of showing the potential *non-termination* of programs as a means of debugging has largely been ignored. This is a surprising situation, because programs under development are prone to contain defects. In this context, direct attempts to find those bugs might be more successful and more useful than to learn from failed correctness or termination proofs.

Traditional dynamic techniques of testing program behavior by means of concrete execution are not adequate to show non-termination (they can nevertheless

B. Beckert and R. Hähnle (Eds.): TAP 2008, LNCS 4966, pp. 154–170, 2008.

provide valuable hints). As a consequence, although the purpose of non-termination analysis is more related to testing than to program verification, in most cases the usage of symbolic reasoning cannot be avoided. In the present paper, we introduce an approach to automatic non-termination checking that relates to termination checking in the same way as symbolic testing does to program verification. The method has been implemented on top of a general-purpose program verification system. Experiments using a database of non-terminating programs indicate that it can be a useful tool for detecting termination defects early during software development.

Showing the non-termination of a program consists of two parts: (i) to prove that a potential loop in a program is reachable from some initial state, and (ii) to prove that the potential loop can indeed cause non-termination. We use constraint solving techniques to achieve the first part, following the approach described in [3]. For the second part, we introduce an algorithm to synthesise invariants that show that the found loop is never exited and that terminating states of the program are therefore unreachable. Our approach is based on two main techniques, a template method for generating invariants (together with constraint solving) and refinement (strengthening) of invariants based on counterexamples. Because our experiments show that invariants for proving non-termination are typically much smaller than invariants for proving partial correctness, we believe that this yields a practical procedure for constructing non-termination proofs.

The paper is organised as follows: In Sect. 2 we define the programming language that is analysed in the whole paper. Sect. 3 introduces the logic and the calculus that we use to reason about programs, which is the basis for an effective algorithm in Sect. 4. An empirical evaluation of our approach is given in Sect. 5. Finally, we list related work in Sect. 6 and conclude in Sect. 7.

2 Preliminaries

We assume that the reader is familiar with classical first-order logic and Gentzen-style sequent calculi, see [4] for an introduction. For sake of simplicity, all considerations of this paper are done in the context of a simple while-language that operates on the (infinite) domain of integers. The generalisation to other imperative languages is mostly straightforward, and, in our experience, occurring problems tend to be orthogonal to the task of proving non-termination. More details are given in [5,3].

In order to introduce the while-language, we first assume a fixed vocabulary Σ of functions and predicates (with fixed arity) that describe the native side-effect-free operations that are available, as well as a fixed set V_p of program variables. The set Σ is supposed to contain at least literals and the standard operations on integers $(0, 1, -1, \ldots, +, -, \cdot, =, <, \leq)$. Ground terms, ground formulae and programs are then inductively defined by the following grammars:

$$\begin{aligned} t_g &::= v \mid f(t_g, \ldots, t_g) \\ \phi_g &::= \mathit{true} \mid \mathit{false} \mid \phi_g \wedge \phi_g \mid \neg\phi_g \mid \cdots \mid p(t_g, \ldots, t_g) \\ \alpha &::= \alpha \,;\, \ldots \,;\, \alpha \mid v = t_g \mid \textbf{if } (\phi_g)\ \alpha \textbf{ else } \alpha \mid \textbf{while } (\phi_g)\ \alpha \end{aligned}$$

where $f \in \Sigma$ ranges over functions, $p \in \Sigma$ over predicates and $v \in V_p$ over program variables.

Semantics of Programs. Because only the integers are considered as domain, a *structure* is a pair $S = (\mathbb{Z}, I)$ consisting of the set $\mathbb{Z}$ of integers and an *interpretation* I with $I(f) : \mathbb{Z}^n \to \mathbb{Z}$ if $f \in \Sigma$ is a function of arity n and $I(p) \subseteq \mathbb{Z}^n$ if $p \in \Sigma$ is a predicate of arity n. Only those structures are considered in which the standard integer operations from above (like $0, 1, -1, +, \ldots$) have their usual meaning. A *program variable assignment* is a mapping $\gamma : V_p \to \mathbb{Z}$. The space of all program variable assignments is denoted by $PA = V_p \to \mathbb{Z}$. While-programs α are evaluated in structures S and denote partial mappings $[\![\alpha]\!]^S : PA \rightharpoonup PA$ from program variable assignments to program variable assignments:

$$[\![\alpha]\!]^S(\gamma) = \begin{cases} \gamma' & \alpha \text{ terminates in state } \gamma' \text{ when started in } \gamma \\ \bot & \alpha \text{ does not terminate when started in } \gamma \end{cases}$$

Given an evaluation function $val_{S,\gamma}$ for ground terms and formulae, which is defined as is common for first-order logic (cf. [4]), the concrete definition of $[\![\alpha]\!]^S$ follows the lines of denotational semantics (for instance, [6]).

3 Proving Non-termination: The Calculus Level

We introduce our approach to non-termination detection in two parts: in this section, we describe the logic and the calculus to reason about programs. Based on this declarative framework, Sect. 4 defines an algorithm (a proof procedure) for automatically detecting non-termination.

Dynamic Logic for the While-Language (WhileDL). First-order dynamic logic (DL) [7] is a multi-modal extension of first-order predicate logic, in which modal operators are labelled with programs. Most importantly, given a program α and a formula ϕ, a *box-formula* $[\alpha]\,\phi$ expresses that ϕ holds in each final state of α. This paper uses a version of dynamic logic for the simple while-language [7] that is enriched with an explicit operator for simultaneous substitutions called *updates* [8, Sect. 3]. Updates allow us to present some of the techniques of this papers in a simpler way, but also simplify the generalisation to more involved languages like Java [5,3,8].

We assume the same vocabulary Σ and the same set V_p of program variables as in Sect. 2, but in addition we define a disjoint set V_l of *logical variables* that can occur in formulae and terms (outside of programs). Because some of our rules need to introduce fresh function symbols, we assume that Σ contains infinitely many functions for each arity n. Extending the grammar from Sect. 2, arbitrary terms, formulae and updates are then defined by:

$$\begin{aligned} t &::= t_g \mid x \mid f(t, \dots, t) \mid \{U\}\, t \\ \phi &::= \phi_g \mid \phi \wedge \phi \mid \neg\phi \mid \cdots \mid p(t, \dots, t) \mid [\alpha]\, \phi \mid \{U\}\, \phi \\ U &::= v := t \mid U, \dots, U \end{aligned}$$

where $f \in \Sigma$ ranges over functions, $p \in \Sigma$ over predicates, $x \in V_l$ over logical variables and $v \in V_p$ over program variables.

In order to define the semantics of terms, formulae and updates, besides structures $S = (\mathbb{Z}, I)$ and program variable assignments $\gamma \in PA$ we also need *logical variable assignments* $\beta : V_l \to \mathbb{Z}$. The denotation $[\![U]\!]^{S,\beta} : PA \to PA$ of an update U is a total operation on program variable assignments:

$$[\![v_1 := t_1, \dots, v_k := t_k]\!]^{S,\beta}(\gamma)(w) = \begin{cases} val_{S,\beta,\gamma}(t_i) & w = v_i \text{ and} \\ & \quad w \notin \{v_{i+1}, \dots, v_k\} \\ \gamma(w) & w \notin \{v_1, \dots, v_k\} \end{cases}$$

This means that the assignments of an update are executed in parallel, and that assignments that syntactically occur later can override the effects of earlier assignments ($v_j := t_j$ will override $v_i := t_i$ for $v_i = v_j$ and $j > i$).

The evaluation $val_{S,\beta,\gamma}$ of terms and formulae is mostly defined as it is common for first-order predicate logic. Formulae are mapped into a Boolean domain, where tt stands for semantic truth. The cases for programs and updates are:

$$\begin{aligned} val_{S,\beta,\gamma}([\alpha]\, \phi) &= \begin{cases} val_{S,\beta,[\![\alpha]\!]^S(\gamma)}(\phi) & \text{if } [\![\alpha]\!]^S(\gamma) \text{ is defined} \\ \mathrm{tt} & \text{otherwise} \end{cases} \\ val_{S,\beta,\gamma}(\{U\}\, \phi) &= val_{S,\beta,[\![U]\!]^{S,\beta}(\gamma)}(\phi) \end{aligned}$$

We interpret free logical variables $x \in V_l$ existentially: a formula ϕ is *valid* iff for each structure S and each program variable assignment $\gamma \in PA$ there is a variable assignment $\beta : V_l \to D$ such that $val_{S,\beta,\gamma}(\phi) = \mathrm{tt}$. Likewise, a sequent $\Gamma \vdash \Delta$ is called valid iff $\bigwedge \Gamma \to \bigvee \Delta$ is valid. Free variables are used to express symbolic program inputs and as parameters in loop invariants and serve as an interface to constraint solving (see below for more details).

Characterisation of Non-Termination. Because box-formulae $[\alpha]\, \phi$ are trivially rendered true by a diverging program α, we can express non-termination by asserting *false* as post-condition: $[\alpha]\, \mathit{false}$. This means that, given a structure S, $val_{S,\gamma}([\alpha]\, \mathit{false}) = \mathrm{tt}$ holds for exactly those initial states $\gamma \in PA$ for which α diverges.

In order to express non-termination for some *arbitrary* initial state, it is necessary to quantify the variables occurring in α existentially, following the approach from [3]. For the while-language, this is done by prefixing the formula from above with an update that assigns arbitrary values to all program variables in α:

$$\{v_1 := x_1, \dots, v_n := x_n\}\, [\alpha]\, \mathit{false} \tag{1}$$

where $v_1, \ldots, v_n \in V_p$ are the variables occurring in α and $x_1, \ldots, x_n \in V_l$ are fresh logical variables. (1) is valid iff there are initial states from which α diverges.

A Sequent Calculus for WhileDL. To reason formally about the non-termination of programs, we introduce a Gentzen-style sequent calculus for WhileDL that follows closely the calculi in [3,8]. Fig. 1 contains the most important calculus rules, which can be categorised as program-independent *first-order rules* (the upper part of the figure) and *symbolic execution rules.*

The rule Assign turns assignments into updates, which subsequently can be merged with the former preceding update U and simplified. The simplification and application of updates is performed by the rewriting rules in Fig. 2, which propagate updates in formulae or terms downwards until they can be applied to program variables like substitutions.

In If, a case analysis for an if-statement is performed by splitting on the branch predicate ψ evaluated in the current program state U. The invariant rule While is a simplified version of the rule for Java defined in [8, Chap. 3]. In While, the erasure of side formulae is avoided with the help of *anonymising updates* A_1, A_2 that assign unspecified values to all variables that can be modified by the loop body α. More formally, given that (i) $v_1, \ldots, v_n \in V_p$ are the variables that occur as left-hand sides of assignments in α, that (ii) $x_1, \ldots, x_m \in V_l$ are the logical variables that occur in U, ϕ, or *Inv*, and that (iii) $f_1, \ldots, f_n$ are fresh function symbols, we say that the update

$$v_1 := f_1(x_1, \ldots, x_m), \ \ldots, \ v_n := f_n(x_1, \ldots, x_m)$$

is a fresh anonymising update for α with respect to U, ϕ, Inv. Note, that we need to inject the logical variables $x_1, \ldots, x_m$ as arguments of the functions $f_1, \ldots, f_n$ for exactly the same reasons as in the standard Skolemisation rule (cf. [4]).

Finally, *theory rules* are necessary to handle equality, integers, etc. in the calculus, we refer the reader to [9] for more details. An example proof using the WhileDL calculus is shown below.

When inspecting the calculus rules, it can be observed that all rules but While are local equivalence transformations: for all structures, program variable assignments and logical variable assignments, the conclusion of a rule holds iff all premisses hold. This property is important for us, because it implies that countermodels of an open goal are also countermodels of the initial conjecture (unless While has been applied). In Sect. 4, we use counterexamples that were extracted from open proof goals to refine invariant candidates.

Incremental Closure of Proofs. In order to close a proof tree that contains free logical variables, we have to show that the variables can be given values (depending on the considered structure) such that all remaining goals are turned into obviously valid sequents. We apply the idea of *incremental closure* [4,10] together with the arithmetic constraint language from [3, Sect. 4] to check the existence of such values. The rules in Fig. 3 are responsible for introducing closure

$$\frac{*}{\Gamma \vdash true, \Delta}\ \text{TRUE-RIGHT} \qquad \frac{\Gamma \vdash \Delta}{\Gamma, true \vdash \Delta}\ \text{TRUE-LEFT}$$

$$\frac{\Gamma \vdash \phi, \Delta \quad \Gamma \vdash \psi, \Delta}{\Gamma \vdash \phi \land \psi, \Delta}\ \land\text{-RIGHT} \qquad \frac{\Gamma, \phi, \psi \vdash \Delta}{\Gamma, \phi \land \psi \vdash \Delta}\ \land\text{-LEFT}$$

$$\frac{\Gamma, \phi \vdash \Delta}{\Gamma \vdash \neg\phi, \Delta}\ \neg\text{-RIGHT} \qquad \frac{\Gamma \vdash \phi, \Delta}{\Gamma, \neg\phi \vdash \Delta}\ \neg\text{-LEFT}$$

$$\dots$$

$$\frac{\Gamma \vdash \{U\}\phi, \Delta}{\Gamma \vdash \{U\}[\,]\phi, \Delta}\ \textsc{Skip} \qquad \frac{\Gamma \vdash \{U\}\{v := t\}[\dots]\phi, \Delta}{\Gamma \vdash \{U\}[v = t\,;\ \dots]\phi, \Delta}\ \textsc{Assign}$$

$$\frac{\Gamma \vdash \{U\}(\psi \to [\alpha_1\,;\ \dots]\phi), \Delta \qquad \Gamma \vdash \{U\}(\neg\psi \to [\alpha_2\,;\ \dots]\phi), \Delta}{\Gamma \vdash \{U\}[\mathbf{if}\ (\psi)\ \alpha_1\ \mathbf{else}\ \alpha_2\,;\ \dots]\phi, \Delta}\ \textsc{If}$$

$$\frac{\begin{array}{l}\Gamma \vdash \{U\}\,Inv, \Delta \\ \Gamma \vdash \{U\}\{A_1\}\,(Inv \land \psi \to [\alpha]\,Inv), \Delta \\ \Gamma \vdash \{U\}\{A_2\}\,(Inv \land \neg\psi \to [\dots]\phi), \Delta\end{array}}{\Gamma \vdash \{U\}[\mathbf{while}\ (\psi)\ \alpha\,;\ \dots]\phi, \Delta}\ \textsc{While}$$

(A_1, A_2 are fresh anonymising updates for α w.r.t. U, ϕ, Inv)

Fig. 1. Sequent calculus for WhileDL. In the last four rules, the update $\{U\}$ can also be empty and disappear.

$$\begin{array}{rcll}
\{v_1 := t_1, \dots, v_k := t_k\}\,v_i & \to & t_i & \text{if } v_i \notin \{v_{i+1}, \dots, v_k\} \\
\{v_1 := t_1, \dots, v_k := t_k\}\,t & \to & t & \text{if } v_1, \dots, v_k \text{ do not occur in } t \\
\{U\}\,f(t_1, \dots, t_n) & \to & f(\{U\}\,t_1, \dots, \{U\}\,t_n) & \\
\{U\}\,p(t_1, \dots, t_n) & \to & p(\{U\}\,t_1, \dots, \{U\}\,t_n) & \\
\{U\}\,\neg\phi & \to & \neg\{U\}\,\phi & \\
\{U\}\,(\phi \land \psi) & \to & \{U\}\,\phi \land \{U\}\,\psi & \\
\{U\}\,\{v_1 := t_1, \dots, v_k := t_k\}\,\phi & \to & \{U,\ v_1 := \{U\}\,t_1,\ \dots,\ v_k := \{U\}\,t_k\}\,\phi & \\
\{\dots, v := s, \dots, v := t, \dots\}\,\phi & \to & \{\dots, v := t, \dots\}\,\phi &
\end{array}$$

Fig. 2. The main application rules for updates in WhileDL. Further rules to simplify updates can be formulated (cf. [8, Chap. 3]), but are not shown here.

$$\frac{[\,s = t\,]}{\Gamma \vdash s = t, \Delta}\ =\text{-RIGHT} \qquad \frac{[\,s \le t\,]}{\Gamma \vdash s \le t, \Delta}\ \le\text{-RIGHT} \qquad \frac{[\,s \ge t\,]}{\Gamma \vdash s \ge t, \Delta}\ \ge\text{-RIGHT}$$

$$\frac{[\,s \ne t\,]}{\Gamma, s = t \vdash \Delta}\ =\text{-LEFT} \qquad \frac{[\,s > t\,]}{\Gamma, s \le t \vdash \Delta}\ \le\text{-LEFT} \qquad \frac{[\,s < t\,]}{\Gamma, s \ge t \vdash \Delta}\ \ge\text{-LEFT}$$

Fig. 3. Closure rules for the WhileDL sequent calculus

constraints for proof goals. If it is possible, in this way, to find compatible closure constraints for *all* proof goals (i.e., the conjunction of the constraints is valid), then it is sound to close the proof.

Example. We illustrate the usage of the sequent calculus by proving the non-termination of the following program:

$$\text{LCM} \quad = \quad \begin{cases} a = a_0\ ;\ b = b_0\ ; \\ \texttt{while}\ (a \neq b)\ \{ \\ \qquad \texttt{if}\ (a > b)\ b = b + b_0\ \texttt{else}\ a = a + a_0 \\ \} \end{cases}$$

In case of termination, the post-value of a and b is the least common multiple of the two integers a_0, b_0. The program fails, however, to handle negative inputs correctly: if the signs of a_0 and b_0 are different, for instance, the program does not terminate. To prove this formally, we instantiate (1) with LCM and construct a proof tree (Fig. 4).

The only step in the course of the proof that requires creativity is the choice of the formula *Inv* that is used as invariant when applying the rule WHILE (our technique for synthesising such formulae is described in the next section). In terms of the program execution, *Inv* has to describe a set of program states that (i) is entered when LCM reaches the while-loop, (ii) is not left during the execution of the loop, and (iii) does not contain any states in which the loop guard becomes false. We chose $a < b$ as invariant in this example, but similar proofs can be given for the invariants $a < 0 \wedge b > 0$ or $a \neq b$. In all cases, the technique of incremental closure has to be used to determine some initial state (i.e., values of the variables a_0, b_0) for which the chosen formula *Inv* actually *is* an invariant and the proof can be closed. The closing constraint in Fig. 4 is $[\, x_a < 1 \wedge x_a < x_b \,]$, which means that we have proven the non-termination for initial states (a_0, b_0) like $(0,1), (0,2), (-10,-5)$, etc.

4 Automatically Detecting Non-termination

In our work, we developed an algorithm to identify non-terminating programs automatically. It has two components, an invariant generator and a theorem prover. The theorem prover is used to prove formulae which state the non-termination of a program. This done by construction of proof trees using the calculus rules and incremental closure, described in Sect. 3. The other component, the invariant generator, is used to provide and refine invariants for the theorem prover. It was used to construct the invariant $a < b$ from the previous section in a systematic way.

The idea of the algorithm is to construct a non-termination proof as described in the preceding section. The essential part of a non-termination proof is the invariant which is used in the application of the WHILE rule. Our algorithm tries to find this invariant by repeatedly constructing proof attempts. In each iteration a different invariant is used, starting with the formula *true*, representing that the

$$
\begin{array}{c}
[\,x_a < x_b\,] \\ \hline
x_a \geq x_b \ \vdash \quad \geq\text{-LEFT} \\ \hline
\vdash\ x_a < x_b \quad (*) \\ \hline
\vdash\ \{U_0, a := x_a, b := x_b\}\ a < b \quad \overset{*}{\rightarrow} \qquad \textit{Inv. Preservation} \qquad \textit{Inv. Usage} \\ \hline
\vdash\ \{U_0, a := x_a, b := x_b\}\ [\mathtt{while}\ (a \neq b)\ \beta]\,\mathit{false} \quad \text{WHILE} \\ \hline
\vdash\ \{U_0, a := x_a, b := x_2\}\ [b = b_0\ ;\ \mathtt{while}\ (a \neq b)\ \beta]\,\mathit{false} \quad \text{ASSIGN}, \overset{*}{\rightarrow} \\ \hline
\vdash\ \{U_0, a := x_1, b := x_2\}\ \{a := a_0\}\ [b = b_0\ ;\ \mathtt{while}\ (a \neq b)\ \beta]\,\mathit{false} \quad \overset{*}{\rightarrow} \\ \hline
\vdash\ \{a_0 := x_a, b_0 := x_b, a := x_1, b := x_2\}\ [a = a_0\ ;\ b = b_0\ ;\ \ldots]\,\mathit{false} \quad \text{ASSIGN} \\ \hline
\vdash\ \{a_0 := x_a, b_0 := x_b, a := x_1, b := x_2\}\ [\text{LCM}]\,\mathit{false}
\end{array}
$$

$$
\begin{array}{c}
[\,x_a < 1\,] \\ \hline
f_a \leq f_b - 1, f_a \geq f_b - x_a, x_a \geq 1 \ \vdash \quad \geq\text{-LEFT} \\ \hline
f_a \leq f_b - 1 \ \vdash\ f_a + x_a < f_b \quad (*) \\ \hline
f_a \leq f_b - 1 \ \vdash\ \{U_0, a := f_a + x_a, b := f_b\}\ [\,]\ a < b \quad \text{SKIP}, \overset{*}{\rightarrow} \\ \hline
f_a \leq f_b - 1 \ \vdash\ \{U_0, a := f_a, b := f_b\}\ [a = a + a_0]\ a < b \quad \text{ASSIGN}, \overset{*}{\rightarrow} \\ \hline
f_a \leq f_b - 1 \ \vdash\ f_a \not> f_b \rightarrow \{U_0, a := f_a, b := f_b\}\ [a = a + a_0]\ a < b \quad (*) \\ \hline
f_a \leq f_b - 1 \ \vdash\ \{U_0, a := f_a, b := f_b\}\ (a \not> b \rightarrow [a = a + a_0]\ a < b) \quad \overset{*}{\rightarrow} \qquad \begin{array}{c} * \\ \vdots\ (*) \end{array} \\ \hline
f_a \leq f_b - 1 \ \vdash\ \{U_0, a := f_a, b := f_b\}\ [\mathtt{if}\ (a > b)\ \ldots\ \mathtt{else}\ \ldots]\ a < b \quad \text{IF} \\ \hline
\vdash\ f_a < f_b \wedge f_a \neq f_b \rightarrow \{U_0, a := f_a, b := f_b\}\ [\beta]\ a < b \quad (*) \\ \hline
\vdash\ \{U_0, a := x_a, b := x_b\}\ \{a := f_a, b := f_b\}\ (a < b \wedge a \neq b \rightarrow [\beta]\ a < b) \quad \overset{*}{\rightarrow} \\ \hline
\textit{Inv. Preservation}
\end{array}
$$

$$
\begin{array}{c}
* \\ \hline
\vdash\ g_a < g_b \wedge g_a = g_b \rightarrow \{U_0, a := g_a, b := g_b\}\ [\,]\,\mathit{false} \quad (*) \\ \hline
\vdash\ \{U_0, a := x_a, b := x_b\}\ \{a := g_a, b := g_b\}\ (a < b \wedge a = b \rightarrow [\,]\,\mathit{false}) \quad \overset{*}{\rightarrow} \\ \hline
\textit{Inv. Usage}
\end{array}
$$

Fig. 4. Proof for the (potential) non-termination of the program LCM using the invariant $a < b$. The proof can be closed with the constraint $[\,x_a < 1 \wedge x_a < x_b\,]$, which describes a set of initial states that causes LCM to diverge. We write β for the body of the while-loop, f_a, f_b, g_a, g_b as abbreviation for the Skolem terms $f_a(x_a, x_b)$, $f_b(x_a, x_b)$, $g_a(x_a, x_b)$, $g_b(x_a, x_b)$, and U_0 as abbreviation for the update $a_0 := x_a, b_0 := x_b$. Rewriting steps to apply updates are denoted by $\overset{*}{\rightarrow}$, whereas $(*)$ means that rules for propositional and arithmetic reasoning are applied which are not shown in detail.

It.	cur. Inv.	Open goals	Queue after step 5 of algorithm
1	*true*	$a = b \vdash$	$b > a$, $b < a$, $b < U_b$, $a < U_a$, $b > L_b$, $a > L_a$, $a \neq b$
2	$b > a$	none	$b < a$, $b < U_b$, ...

Fig. 5. Application of the algorithm on LCM. Technically, a and b in the open goals are Skolem terms like $f_a(x_a, x_b)$ in Fig. 4, which have to be translated back to obtain invariants in terms of the program variables. In iteration 2, the non-termination proof can be closed with the constraint $[\,x_a < x_b \wedge x_a < 1\,]$. The result expresses that LCM does not terminate if the initial value of a_0 is less than that of b_0 and not positive.

prover has no knowledge about the invariant at start up. After each failed proof attempt, the incomplete proof tree is examined. The retrieved information from this examination is then used to refine the invariant. There are several ways of refinement of which one uses template variables for the invariants.

A positive result of the algorithm is a successful non-termination proof of the program together with a description of a set of input values for which the loop of the program runs forever.

Note on Nested Loops. The algorithm as it is described here is only applicable to single, unnested loops. As it is always possible to transform nested loops into unnested ones, this is no real restriction. Besides, in [5] we describe how our algorithm can be adapted so that it directly works on nested loops.

Outline of the Algorithm. Let α be the program whose termination is in question. The input of the algorithm is α's source code, which is inserted into a WhileDL formula ϕ (formula (1) in Sect. 3) which states that there are inputs for which α does not terminate.

Initialisation

1. The formula ϕ is handed over to the theorem prover. The proof procedure is invoked and constructs a proof tree in which the program is symbolically executed until the execution reaches the loop.

Iteration

2. The proof procedure applies the invariant rule WHILE (Fig. 1). The invariant Inv_{cur} which is used in the invariant rule's application is chosen from a queue of invariants. Initially there is only $Inv_{cur} \equiv true$ in the queue.
3. The proof procedure keeps on constructing the proof as far as possible without human interaction.
4. If the proof procedure can close the proof, the algorithm terminates with the result that the program does not terminate. If the proof cannot be closed, the open goals of the proof are extracted and handed over to the invariant generator.
5. The invariant generator inspects the formulae of the open goals. The obtained information is used to refine the invariant candidate to create one or more new candidates, which are then added to the queue.

The algorithm repeats step 2 to 5 iteratively, each time using one of the invariant candidates from the invariant queue. The iterations are carried out until one of these events occurs: the proof can be closed with the help of the invariant candidate, the algorithm runs out of new invariant candidates or a maximum number of iterations is reached. In case of a successful termination of the algorithm, it outputs the invariant used for the final proof, together with the (consistent) closing constraint.

There are three parts of step 5 of the algorithm that we like to describe in more detail. The first is the actual creation of the invariants.

Invariant Creation. There are different methods to create new invariants from the open goals of failed proofs. Assume that we obtained the open goal

$$\phi_1, \ldots, \phi_n \vdash \psi_1, \ldots \psi_m$$

where ϕ_i and ψ_i are WhileDL-formulae. Given such an open goal, the invariant generator creates invariant fragments ρ which are conjunctively added to the invariant Inv_{cur} which was used in the current iteration to obtain a new invariant $Inv_{new} = Inv_{cur} \wedge \rho$. The invariant fragments are created by the following operations:

- ADD. A formula ψ_i in the succedent states a situation in which there is a problem with the non-termination proof when ψ_i does not hold. Most often that means that in this situation the loop actually terminates. We exclude this situation by setting $\rho = \psi_i$.
- NEGADD. A formula ϕ_i in the antecedent means that there is a problem with the non-termination in the situation where ϕ_i holds. Here, the same idea applies as for formulae in the succedent, but in this case we have to negate it before we add it to the old invariant, which means $\rho = \neg\phi_i$.
- INEQ. In case a formula ϕ_i of the antecedent is of form $\phi_i \equiv a = b$, we do not only add the negation as in NEGANDADD, but an inequality. That means from $a = b$ we obtain two fragments $\rho_1 \equiv a \geq b$ and $\rho_2 \equiv a \leq b$, yielding two different new invariants.
- INEQVAR. Often it is useful to express that *there are* upper or lower bounds for an expression rather than specifically setting one like in INEQ. This is done through the introduction of free logical variables. Those variables stand for particular but not yet specified values. For each term in the open goal, we provide two new variables U and L, one for the upper and one for the lower bound. Thus, for each term t_k occurring in one ϕ_i, we obtain two fragments $\rho_k^u \equiv t_k \leq U_k$ and $\rho_k^l \equiv t_k \geq L_k$. The values for the new variables are estimated by the constraint solver of the proof procedure.

The latter two creation methods are of course only applicable if a, b and t_k are expressions of an ordered type, in our case integers.

Invariant Filtering. In the process of invariant creation, sometimes invariant candidates are created that are not helpful in the search of a non-termination invariant. This is due to the fact that these methods are applied "blindly" without actually examining the old invariant candidate. Therefore, after the creation of invariants in step 5 of the algorithm, we filter out those candidates which are obviously useless:

- *Inconsistent Invariant.* A newly created invariant candidate can be equivalent to the formula *false*. Because the first property of non-termination invariants is that the invariant must hold before the loop execution, it is dismissed.

– *Equivalence to Previous Invariants.* A new invariant candidate can be equivalent to a candidate that was already created and/or used in an earlier iteration. Dismissal of these candidates avoid unnecessary calculations and thus save resources.
– *Impossible Closure of the Init-branch.* The application of the invariant rule makes the proof branch into three branches. The first branch proves that the invariant holds when the loop is reached in the execution of the program. In the refinement process, invariant candidates might be created that do not hold in the beginning of the loop, even if they are satisfiable in general. Once we have created an invariant candidate which prevents the first branch from closing, it does not make sense to refine any further: refinement would only strengthen the candidate even more.[1]
– *Complexity.* For performance reasons, we set a limit on the complexity of formulae to keep the runtime at a reasonable level.

Invariant Scoring. In each iteration of the algorithm, when the invariant candidates are created and filtered in step 5 still a lot of invariants can remain. In order to traverse the search space of invariants in a reasonable way, we have to queue invariants according to their probable usefulness for non-termination proofs.

We estimate this usefulness by several criteria and express it in a score, which is a real number between 0 and 1. The lower the score is, the more the invariant is preferred in the queue. The score is calculated as a weighted average of scores for each of the following criteria.

– *Complexity.* In order to find the most general description of a set of critical inputs, we prefer simple invariants to complex ones. The complexity is measured in both the term depth and the number of operators of the invariant.
– *Existence of Free Variables.* The creation method InEqVar is a strong tool (and sometimes the only effective one) to find the desired invariant. The problem with free variables is that in cases where they do *not* lead to a closed proof, they tend to lead to even bigger open proofs. It is reasonable to prefer invariant candidates that do not contain free variables to those who do in order to keep the number of newly created candidates as low as possible.
– *Multiple Occurrence of Formulae.* In an open proof, sometimes the same formulae occur in several open goals. We prefer invariant candidates made from those formulae to others, because if the candidate makes the algorithm close branches, it will close several branches in the same proof.
– *Reoccurring Formulae.* Formulae which occurred in open proofs in several iterations of the algorithm might be suitable candidates for the next invariant, because they hint to situations where the non-termination proof repeatedly failed.

[1] The filtering of inconsistent invariants is subsumed in this filter. We kept it in the list of filters, because checking for inconsistency is easier than for closure of the initial branch. So, for performance reasons it is useful to first check only for consistency before examining the closability of the first branch.

– *Proof Size.* We presume that the smaller an open proof is (measured in the number of open goals) the closer it is to being closed. Therefore we prefer formulae which come from small open proofs to those from big open proofs.

Experiments have shown that the choice and weighting of the criteria is extremely important for the search in the space of invariants. In our work, we ran several experiments to test the impact of different heuristics, the results of which are given in Sect. 5 and [5].

Examples. We apply our algorithm to the example programs FIB and LCM, of which the latter one was introduced in Sect. 3 already. For the sake of simplicity, we assume that for scoring of the invariants only the criteria of complexity is applied.

Example LCM. Fig. 5 shows how the algorithm works on LCM. In this case all presented creation methods are used.

Example FIB. Given a Fibonacci number n as input, FIB calculates how many calculation steps are necessary in the series of Fibonacci numbers to reach n. The result is stored in variable c. In case n is not a Fibonacci number, the program does not terminate.

$$\text{FIB} \quad = \quad \begin{cases} i = 0 \ ; \ j = 1 \ ; \ t = 0 \ ; \ c = 2 \ ; \\ \texttt{while} \ (j \neq n) \ \{ \\ \qquad t = j + i \ ; \ i = j \ ; \ j = t \ ; \ c = c + 1 \\ \} \end{cases}$$

In contrast to LCM, the algorithm needs several refinement steps (Fig. 6) to prove the non-termination of FIB. The input variable n is associated with the free logical variable x_n. This time, we used only the creation methods ADD, NEGADD, INEQ, together with the complexity scoring criterion. We abstained from showing the creation method INEQVAR, because it increases the number of necessary iterations too much to be shown here. However, we did run the same experiment with INEQVAR and will present the results in the following section.

Properties of the algorithm. We would like to have a closer look at the properties of the algorithm which we presented here.

– *Soundness.* The algorithm is sound for non-termination: it will never identify a terminating program as non-terminating. This is an immediate consequence of the soundness of the calculus from Sect. 3, because non-termination is only reported if it was possible to construct a proof for it. Applied to a terminating program, the algorithm will fail to find such a proof and will output that it was not able to prove non-termination.
– *Incompleteness.* Unfortunately, but expectedly, both our calculus and the algorithm are not complete for non-termination: there are programs that

do not terminate for some inputs, but there is no proof of this fact in the calculus from Sect. 3. This is implied by the soundness, because the set of programs that do not terminate for some inputs is not recursively enumerable.[2] Because the algorithm is based on heuristics, it might also fail to find existing non-termination proofs for a program, of course.
- *Automation.* The algorithm works fully automatic, in the sense that no manual "human" actions are necessary to obtain the results.
- *Determinism.* The algorithm is deterministic, because for the same input it always produces the same results. The indeterministic calculus which forms the base of the prover is made deterministic by choice of heuristics and prioritisation.
- *Termination.* Our algorithm itself always terminates. This is ensured by setting an upper limit for the number of iterations, and by limiting the size of proofs in the calculus from Sect. 3 that are constructed. Of course these limits have to be chosen carefully, because the lower they are the fewer non-terminating programs can be identified.

5 Experiments

We implemented the algorithm, which we presented in Sect. 4 in particular we wrote the part of the invariant generator and used the software KeY [8] as theorem prover. Both are written in Java. Since there was no publicly available standardised example set of non-terminating programs, we built up one to estimate the quality of our approach and test different heuristics.

Example Set. Our example set consists of 55 programs, of which 53 are known to be non-terminating for all or some input values, one whose termination behavior is not fully known and one which is terminating. All programs are written in a fragment in Java, which captures the functionality of the While language which we described in Sect. 2. They have between one and five variables and up to 25 lines of code. We chose them either because they represent typical programming errors or because they reveal very tricky non-termination behavior.

Results of the Experiments. We tested different settings concerning creation and scoring of invariants in several experiments [5]. Our software could solve 41 of the 55 examples automatically, but not more than 37 with one setting. This fact shows how sensitive the algorithm's heuristics are.

Some of the experiments were used to estimate the usefulness of the different creation methods of Sect. 4, in particular the method IneqVar. Experiments who included free logical variables as invariant templates could solve about 20% more problems than those who did not. Free variables are obviously a strong tool (and sometimes the only one) which leads to successful non-termination proofs. Unfortunately, they increase the complexity of proofs in case they do not lead

[2] Note that the set of programs that terminate for *all* possible inputs is not recursively enumerable either.

It.	cur. Inv.	Open goals
1	$Inv_1 \equiv true$	$j = x \vdash$
2	$Inv_2 \equiv j > x$	$x \geq 1 \vdash$, $j \leq x - i, i \leq -1, j \geq 1 + x \vdash$
3	$Inv_3 \equiv j < x$	$x \leq 1 \vdash$, $i \geq 1, j \geq x - i, j \leq -x \vdash$
4	$Inv_4 \equiv j \neq x$	$x = 1 \vdash$, $j = x - i, i = 0 \vdash$
5	$Inv_5 \equiv j > x \land x < 1$	$x \geq 1 \vdash$, $j \leq x - i, x \leq 0, i \leq -1, j \geq 1 + x \vdash$
6	$Inv_6 \equiv j > x \land x > -1$	none

The next invariants to be tried:

$Inv_7 \equiv j < x \land x > 1$	$Inv_{14} \equiv j \neq x \land j > x - i$
$Inv_8 \equiv j < x \land i < 1$	$Inv_{15} \equiv j > x \land x < 1 \land x > 0$
$Inv_9 \equiv j \neq x \land i = 0$	$Inv_{16} \equiv j > x \land j > x - i$
$Inv_{10} \equiv j \neq x \land x > 1$	$Inv_{17} \equiv j < x \land j < x - i$
$Inv_{11} \equiv j \neq x \land x < 1$	$Inv_{18} \equiv j \neq x \land j \neq x - i$
$Inv_{12} \equiv j \neq x \land x \neq 1$	$Inv_{19} \equiv j > x \land x < 1 \land j > x - i$
$Inv_{13} \equiv j > x \land x < 1 \land i > -1$	

Fig. 6. Application of the algorithm on example FIB. Again, technically, i and j in the open goals are Skolem terms like $f_a(x_a, x_b)$ in Fig. 4. In iteration no. 6, the non-termination proof can be closed with the constraint $[x_n < 1 \land -2 < x_n]$ for the free variables. This result expresses that for n being 0 or -1, FIB does not terminate. The following invariants were dismissed by the filters because of inconsistency: $j > x_n \land j < 1 + x_n$, $j < x_n \land j > x_n - 1$, and $j > x_n \land x_n < 1 \land j < 1 + x_n$.

to a closed proofs. In some cases this led to the situation that the algorithm reached the limit of iterations before a suitable invariant was found. This is also the case when the target program is actually terminating for all initial states. The average number of iterations in successful cases (that means a suitable invariant was found) lay between 1.5 and 3.5 depending on the heuristics.

The example LCM of Sect. 4 was solved in all experiments. The number of necessary iterations lay between 2 and 8 iterations. The example FIB was solved by some of the experiments and their number of iterations was between 6 and 39 iterations. The best run is illustrated in Fig. 6. Using the creation method INEQVAR, the number of iteration raises (depending on the heuristics). An invariant which was found in this case is $j > L_j \land i > L_i$, where the proof was closed with the (simplified) constraint $[L_j = -1 \land L_i = -1 \land x < 0]$. Invariant and constraint describe the situation where the input value n is negative and the variables j and i are non-negative (which is always the case).

The example set and the implementation of the software is publicly available at `http://www.key-project.org/nonTermination/`.

6 Related Work

Although the development of *termination checkers* is a flourishing research subject, we only know of two methods (and implementations) that are directly comparable to the *non-termination* analysis presented in this paper:

The more similar approach is [11], which uses concolic program execution to search for lassos (loops) in a program, and constraint solving for proving the feasibility of lassos. The latter part is similar to the invariant generation method shown in the present paper, but it does not make use of counterexamples to refine invariant candidates. Because we use purely symbolic reasoning to determine critical initial program states, it can also be expected that our approach is able to derive more general descriptions of such input states than [11], at the cost of being less scalable.

Secondly, the AProVE system [12] is able to prove both the termination and non-termination of term rewrite systems [13] and is in principle also applicable to imperative programs: such programs can be analysed after a suitable translation to rewrite systems [2]. So far, existing translations are incomplete, however, which means that the resulting rewrite system might be non-terminating even if the original program is terminating.

Construction of invariants using invariant templates and constraint solving is an approach that is employed in many contexts, e.g., [14,15]. The principle is usually not embedded in a program logic as it is done in the present paper.

The iterative refinement of invariants described in this paper has some similarities to iterative backwards-propagation of assertions, which is described in [16] but can, in some form or another, be found in many static program analysis techniques.

7 Conclusion and Future Work

We have introduced a novel approach to automated detection of non-termination defects in software programs. The approach is built on the basis of a sequent calculus for dynamic logic and works by generating invariants that prove the unreachability of terminating states. In experiments, the majority of our example programs could automatically be proven non-terminating. Furthermore, when experimenting with more complex non-terminating Java programs [5], we found that also here it is often possible to find small and simple invariants that witness non-termination. The intuitive explanation for this is that (i) the usage of the invariant rule WHILE (with anonymising updates) allows to ignore those parts of the program state that are not changed in the loop, and that (ii) the precise character of state changes caused by a loop can be ignored in the invariant as well, as long as non-termination is preserved. Although further investigations concerning such programs are necessary, this indicates that our method is also applicable to programs that operate on heap data structures.

When moving from the while-language to actual Java-like programs, one modification of the algorithm that appears helpful is to automatically add heap-wellformedness conditions to the invariant candidates. Partly, this is a consequence of using dynamic logic for Java [8, Sect. 3], in which properties like "attributes of allocated objects only point to allocated objects" are non-trivial and can be difficult to synthesise for the invariant generator. Another aspect that becomes more central with Java programs is the detection of the variables and heap locations that a loop can assign to. It might be useful to determine also these locations incrementally and simultaneously with the loop invariant, based on failed proof attempts.

As a prerequisite for more extensive experiments, we want to develop an implementation of our non-termination checker that is more tightly integrated with the program verification tool used. This way, we expect to achieve a significantly higher performance. On the more theoretic level, we are in the process of investigating the usage of closure constraints (Sect. 3) more systematically in order to define fragments of first-order logic with integer arithmetic for which the calculus is complete, and in order to further develop the approach.

Acknowledgements

We like to thank the following people for constructive feedback and support: Richard Bubel, Prof. Reiner Hähnle, Mattias Ulbrich, Benjamin Weiss and all others of the KeY-group. Besides we like to thank Prof. Giesl for supporting the diploma thesis which was the base for this paper.

References

1. Cook, B., Podelski, A., Rybalchenko, A.: Terminator: Beyond safety. In: Ball, T., Jones, R.B. (eds.) CAV 2006. LNCS, vol. 4144, pp. 415–418. Springer, Heidelberg (2006)
2. Sondermann, M.: Automatische Terminierungsanalyse von imperativen Programmen. Master's thesis, RWTH Aachen University, Aachen, Germany (2006)
3. Rümmer, P., Shah, M.A.: Proving programs incorrect using a sequent calculus for Java Dynamic Logic. In: Gurevich, Y., Meyer, B. (eds.) TAP 2007. LNCS, vol. 4454, pp. 41–60. Springer, Heidelberg (2007)
4. Fitting, M.C.: First-Order Logic and Automated Theorem Proving, 2nd edn. Springer, New York (1996)
5. Velroyen, H.: Automatic non-termination analysis of imperative programs. Master's thesis, Chalmers University of Technology, Aachen Technical University, Göteborg, Sweden and Aachen, Germany (2007)
6. Winskel, G.: The Formal Semantics of Programming Languages. MIT Press, Cambridge (1993)
7. Harel, D., Kozen, D., Tiuryn, J.: Dynamic Logic. MIT Press, Cambridge (2000)
8. Beckert, B., Hähnle, R., Schmitt, P.H. (eds.): Verification of Object-Oriented Software. LNCS (LNAI), vol. 4334. Springer, Heidelberg (2007)
9. Rümmer, P.: A sequent calculus for integer arithmetic with counterexample generation. In: Proceedings of 4th International Verification Workshop (VERIFY 2007). CEUR, vol. 259 (2007), `http://ceur-ws.org/`
10. Giese, M.: Incremental closure of free variable tableaux. In: Goré, R.P., Leitsch, A., Nipkow, T. (eds.) IJCAR 2001. LNCS (LNAI), vol. 2083, pp. 545–560. Springer, Heidelberg (2001)
11. Gupta, A., Henzinger, T.A., Majumdar, R., Rybalchenko, A., Xu, R.-G.: Proving non-termination. In: Necula, G.C., Wadler, P. (eds.) ACM Symposium on Principles of Programming Languages (POPL), San Francisco, USA, pp. 147–158. ACM, New York (2008)

12. Giesl, J., Schneider-Kamp, P., Thiemann, R.: Aprove 1.2: Automatic termination proofs in the dependency pair framework. In: Furbach, U., Shankar, N. (eds.) IJCAR 2006. LNCS (LNAI), vol. 4130, pp. 281–286. Springer, Heidelberg (2006)
13. Giesl, J., Thiemann, R., Schneider-Kamp, P.: Proving and disproving termination of higher-order functions. In: Gramlich, B. (ed.) FroCos 2005. LNCS (LNAI), vol. 3717, pp. 216–231. Springer, Heidelberg (2005)
14. Kapur, D.: Automatically generating loop invariants using quantifier elimination. In: Baader, F., Baumgartner, P., Nieuwenhuis, R., Voronkov, A. (eds.) Deduction and Applications. Dagstuhl Seminar Proceedings, Schloss Dagstuhl, Germany, vol. 05431 (2006)
15. Colón, M., Sankaranarayanan, S., Sipma, H.: Linear invariant generation using non-linear constraint solving. In: Hunt Jr., W.A., Somenzi, F. (eds.) CAV 2003. LNCS, vol. 2725, pp. 420–432. Springer, Heidelberg (2003)
16. Bjørner, N., Browne, A., Manna, Z.: Automatic generation of invariants and intermediate assertions. Theor. Comput. Sci. 173(1), 49–87 (1997)

Parameterized Unit Testing with Pex
(Tutorial)

Jonathan de Halleux and Nikolai Tillmann

Microsoft Research
One Microsoft Way, Redmond WA 98052, USA
{jhalleux,nikolait}@microsoft.com

Abstract. This hands-on tutorial will teach the principles of Parameterized Unit Testing [5,4] with Pex [2], an automatic test input generator for .NET which performs a systematic program analysis, similar to path bounded model-checking.

A parameterized unit test is simply a method that takes parameters, calls the code under test, and states assertions.

1 Unit Tests

A *unit test* is a self-contained program that checks an aspect of the implementation under test. A unit is the smallest testable part of the program.

Here is a typical unit test of the array list that describes the normal behavior of the Add method with respect to the indexing operator `[]`.

```
public void SomeAddTest() {
    // exemplary data
    object element = new object();
    ArrayList list = new ArrayList(1);
    // method sequence
    list.Add(element);
    // assertions
    Assert.IsTrue(list[0] == element);
}
```

We partition each unit test into three parts.

- Unit tests take *exemplary data* as test inputs that are passed to the called methods.
- Unit tests consist of a *method sequence* which represents a typical scenario for the usage of an API.
- *Assertions* encode the test oracle of a unit test. The test fails if any assertion fails or an exception is thrown but not caught.

The above unit test specifies the behavior of the array list by example. Strictly speaking, this unit test only says that by adding a new object to an empty array list, this object becomes the first element of the list. What about other array lists and other objects?

B. Beckert and R. Hähnle (Eds.): TAP 2008, LNCS 4966, pp. 171–181, 2008.

2 Parameterized Unit Tests (PUTs)

A straightforward extension is to allow parameters for unit tests. Here is a parameterized version of the array list unit test. Under the condition that a given array list is not `null`, this parameterized unit test asserts that after adding an element to the list, the element is indeed present at the end of the list:

```
public void SomeAddSpec(
    // data
    ArrayList list, object element) {
    // assumptions
    PexAssume.IsTrue(list != null);
    // method sequence
    int len = list.Count;
    list.Add(element);
    // assertions
    PexAssert.IsTrue(list[len] == element);
}
```

This test is more general than the original test. It states that for all non-null array lists, and all objects, after adding the object to the array list, it is contained at the end.

Parameterized unit tests like this one can be called with various input values, perhaps drawn from an attached database. Unit testing frameworks that support parameterized unit tests sometimes refer to them as data-driven tests (e.g. in [2]).

Unlike many other forms of specification documents, PUTs are written on the level of the actual software APIs, in the programming language of the software project. This allows PUTs to evolve naturally with the code against which they are written.

2.1 Separation of Concerns

Splitting the specification and test cases by parameterized unit testing is a *separation of concerns*:

- Firstly, we specify the intended external behavior of the software as PUTs; only human beings can perform this specification task.
- Secondly, a tool like Pex can automatically create a test suite with high code coverage by determining test inputs which exercise different execution paths of the implementation.

2.2 Coverage through Test Generation

Adding parameters to a unit test improves its expressiveness as a specification of intended behavior, but we lose concrete test cases. We can no longer execute a parameterized test by itself. We need actual parameters. But which values must be provided to ensure sufficient and comprehensive testing?

Let's look at the code that implements `Add` and the indexing operator in the .NET base class library.

```
public class ArrayList
...
 {
    private Object[] _items;
    private int _size, _version;
    ...
    public virtual int Add(Object value) {
        if (_size == _items.Length)
        EnsureCapacity(_size + 1);
        _items[_size] = value;
        _version++;
        return _size++;
    }
}
```

There are two cases of interest. One occurs when adding an element to an array list that already has enough room for the new element (i.e. the array list's capacity is greater than the current number of elements in the array list). The other occurs when the internal capacity of the array list must be increased before adding the element.

Let's assume that the library methods invoked by the `ArrayList` implementation are themselves correctly implemented, i.e., `EnsureCapacity` guarantees that the `_items` array is resized so its length is greater or equal `_size + 1`, and let's not consider possible integer overflows.

Then we only need to run two test cases to check that the assertion embedded in `SomeAddSpec` holds for all array lists and all objects given the existing .NET implementation.

```
[TestMethod]
public void TestAddNoOverflow() {
    SomeAddSpec(new ArrayList(1), new object());
}

[TestMethod]
public void TestAddWithOverflow() {
    SomeAddSpec(new ArrayList(0), new object());
}
```

We don't need any other input to test `Add`, since any other input will execute exactly the same paths as the two inputs mentioned above.

3 Dealing with the Environment

3.1 Unit Testing Is not Integration Testing

Each unit test, whether parameterized or not, should test a single feature, so that a failing unit test identifies the broken feature as concisely as possible. Also, the fewer system components a test interacts with, the faster it will run.

However, in practice it is often difficult to test features in isolation: The code may take a file name as its input, and use the operating system to read in the contents of the file. Or the test may need to connect to another machine to fulfill its purpose.

The first step towards making the code testable is to introduce abstraction layers. For example, the following `Parse` method is not testable in isolation, since it insists on interacting with the file system.

```
public void Parse(string fileName) {
    StreamReader reader = File.OpenText(fileName);
    string line;
    while ((line = reader.ReadLine()) != null) {
        ...
    }
}
```

The parser in the following code is better testable, since the actual parsing logic can be driven from any implementation of the abstract `StreamReader` class. In particular, it is no longer necessary to go through the file system to test the main code.

```
public void Parse(string fileName) {
    this.Parse(File.OpenText(fileName));
}

public void Parse(StreamReader reader) {
    string line;
    while ((line = reader.ReadLine()) != null) {
        ...
    }
}
```

Abstraction from the environment is necessary to systematically apply Pex.

3.2 Mock Objects

When the code is written with abstraction layers, mock objects [1] can be used to substitute parts of the program that are irrelevant for a tested feature. Mock objects answer queries with fixed values similar to those that the substituted program would have computed.

Today, developers usually define the behavior of mock objects by hand. (By *behavior*, we mean the return values of mocked methods, what exceptions they should throw, etc.) Several frameworks [6] exist which provide stubs, i.e. trivial implementations of all methods of an interface or a class; these stubs don't perform any actions by themselves and usually just return some default value. The behavior of the stubs must still be programmed by the developer. (A capture-replay approach is used in [3] to distill actual behavior of an existing program into mock objects.)

3.3 Parameterized Mock Objects

When manually writing mock objects, one of the main questions is: What values should the mock object return? How many versions of a mock object do I need to write to test my code thoroughly?

We have seen earlier how parameterized unit tests are a way to write general tests that do not have to state particular test inputs. In a similar way, *parameterized mock objects* are a way to write mock objects which do not have just one particular, fixed behavior.

Consider the method `AppendFormat` of the `StringBuilder` class in the .NET base class library. Given a string with formatting instructions, and a list of values to be formatted, it computes a formatted string. For example, formatting the string `"Hello {0}!"` with the single argument `"World"` yields the string `"Hello World!"`.

```
public StringBuilder AppendFormat(
  IFormatProvider provider,
  string format, object[] args) {
    ...
}
```

The first parameter of type `IFormatProvider` "provides a mechanism for retrieving an object to control formatting" according to the MSDN documentation:

```
public interface IFormatProvider {
    object GetFormat(Type fmtType);
}
```

A non-trivial test case calling `AppendFormat` needs an object that implements `IFormatProvider`. Pex can automatically generate a mock type with stubs that implements the interface:

```
[PexMock]
public class MFormatProvider : IFormatProvider {
    public object GetFormat(Type fmtType) {
        IPexMethodCallOracle call = PexOracle.Call(this);
        return call.ChooseResult<object>();
    }
}
```

The mock method `GetFormat` obtains from the global `PexOracle` a handle called `call` that represents the current method call. The `PexOracle` provides the values which define the behavior of the mocked methods, e.g. their return values.

When the test case is executed, `ChooseResult` will initially return some simple value, e.g. `null` for reference types. Pex performs a dynamic symbolic analysis that tracks how the value obtained from `ChooseResult` is used by the program. (This is similar to how Pex tracks all other test inputs.) Depending on the conditions that the program checks on the value obtained from `ChooseResult`, Pex will execute the test case multiple times, trying other values that will be different from `null`.

For example, the following call to `GetFormat` occurs in `AppendFormat` after checking `provider!=null`:

```
cf = (ICustomFormatter)provider.GetFormat(
                                  typeof(ICustomFormatter)
                                      );
```

Depending on the result of `GetFormat`, the cast to `ICustomFormatter` might fail. Pex understands this type constraint, and Pex generates a test case with the following mock object behavior.

```
MFormatProvider m = new MFormatProvider();
PexOracle.NewTest()
    .OnCall(0, typeof(MFormatProvider), "GetFormat",
            typeof(Type)
          )
    .Returns(m);
```

Here, Pex creates a mock object and instructs the oracle that during the execution of a unit test the first call to `m.GetFormat` should return the mock object itself! (The test cases that Pex generate are always *minimal*, this is an example of how Pex tries to use as few objects as possible to trigger a particular execution path.) This particular mock object behavior will cause the cast to fail, since `MFormatProvider` does not implement `ICustomFormatter`.

3.4 Parameterized Mock Objects with Assumptions

Unconstrained mock objects can cause the code to behave in unexpected ways. Just as you can state assumptions on the arguments of parameterized unit tests, you can state assumptions on the results of mock object calls. For example, the author of the `IFormatProvider` interface probably had the following contract in mind:

```
public object GetFormat(Type fmtType) {
    IPexMethodCallOracle call = PexOracle.Call(this);
    object result = call.ChooseResult<object>();

    // constraining result
    PexAssume.IsTrue(result != null);
    PexAssume.IsTrue(
        fmtType.IsAssignableFrom(result.GetType())
                    );

    return result;
}
```

4 Exercises

Exercise 1: Getting started with Pex in Visual Studio

Part 1: Adding Pex to a Project

1. Add a reference to the `Microsoft.Pex.Framework.dll` assembly to the test project. In the **Add Reference** dialog, select the **.NET** pane, then scroll down to `Microsoft.Pex.Framework`,

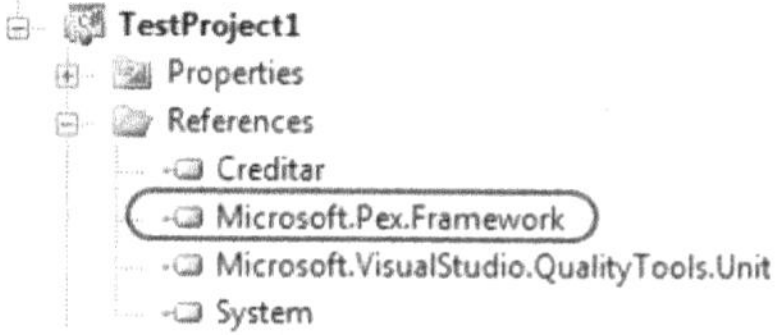

Part 2: Creating a Parameterized Unit Test

1. In the `HelloWorldTest`, add a new public instance method `ParameterizedTest` that takes an `int` parameter. Mark this method with the `PexMethodAttribute`.

```
[PexMethod]
public void ParameterizedTest(int i) {
    if (i == 123)
        throw new ArgumentException("i");
}
```

Part 3: Run the Parameterized Unit Test

1. Move the mouse cursor inside the `ParameterizedTest` method, right-click and select the **Pex It** menu item.

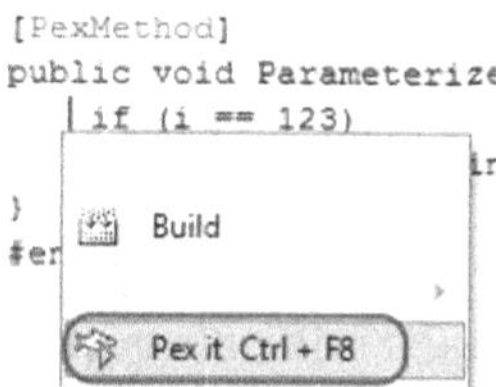

2. Pex automatically displays the **Pex Results** window. Most of your interactions with Pex will be through this window.

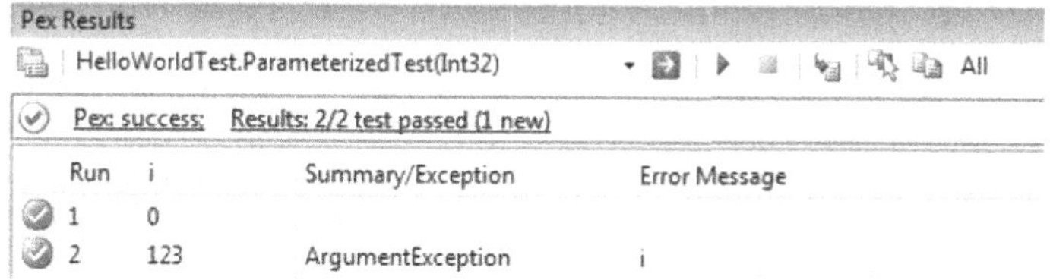

3. Each row in the table corresponds to a generated test for the current exploration. Each row contains
   - an icon describing the status of the test (passing, failing),
   - a number indicating how often Pex had to execute the parameterized unit test with different input values in order to arrive at this test,
   - a summary of the exception that occurred, if any

   Pex also automatically logs the values of the input parameters of the test. Note that often Pex runs the parameterized unit test for several times until it outputs a test. The rationale behind this behavior is that Pex explores different execution paths of the program, but it only outputs a new test when this test increases the coverage (arc coverage, to be precise). Many execution paths might have the same coverage.

4. When exploring the `ParameterizedTest` that we wrote earlier, Pex generates two unit tests. Each unit test can be accessed by selecting the corresponding row and clicking on the **Go to generated test** link.

```
[TestMethod]
public void ParameterizedTest_Int_71114_003426_0_00() {
    this.ParameterizedTest(0);
}
[TestMethod, ExpectedException(typeof(ArgumentException))]
public void ParameterizedTest_Int_71114_003427_0_02() {
    this.ParameterizedTest(123);
}
```

Exercise 2: Instrumentation Configuration. Pex can only generate a test suite with high code coverage if Pex monitors the relevant parts of the code. Therefore, it is most important to configure correctly which types Pex should instrument.

Consider the following parameterized unit test.

```
[PexMethod(MaxBranches = 2000)]
public void Test(string s) {
    DateTime dt = DateTime.Parse(s);
    PexValue.Add("dt", dt);
}
```

When Pex generates tests, it will only generate a single test at first. However, we do get a warning that some methods were not instrumented.

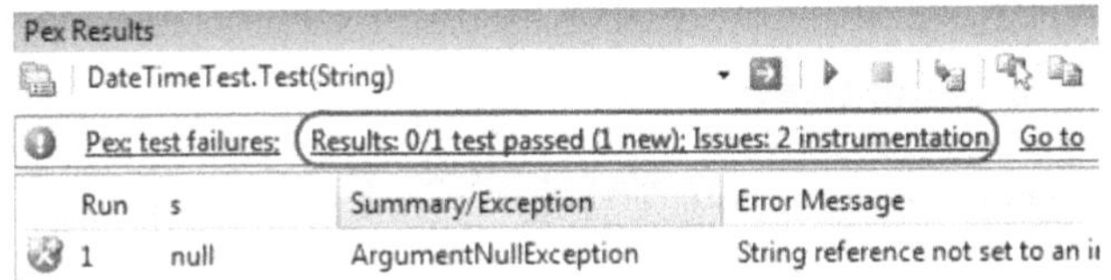

In the log view, Pex lists the uninstrumented methods. (You can switch between the parameter table and the log view by clicking on the **Results: ... Issues: ... instrumentation** link in the link menu.)

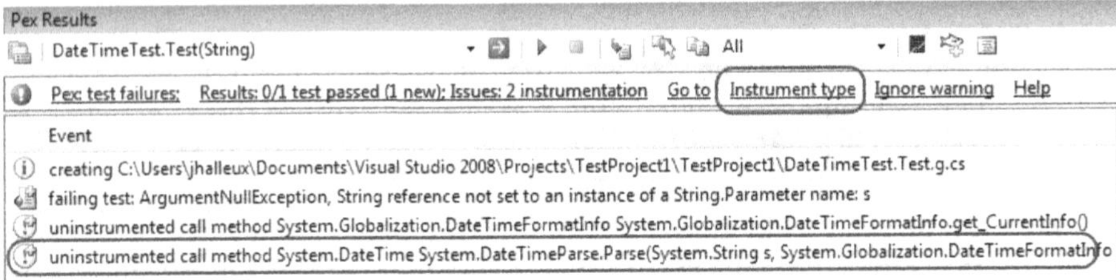

We can select one of them, and click on the link “Instrument type” to tell Pex that it should instrument this type in the future. Pex will insert custom attributes such as the following for you.

```
using Microsoft.Pex.Framework.Instrumentation;
[assembly: PexInstrumentType("mscorlib",
                             "System.DateTimeParse")]
[assembly: PexInstrumentType("mscorlib",
                             "System.__DTString")]
```

After you instruct Pex to instrument a type, you have to re-run Pex to see the effects of more instrumentation. In turn, you might get more uninstrumented method warnings.

Exercise 3: Path Conditions and Symbolic Values. The following method `Complicated` checks that its input parameter `x` stands in an obscure relation to its input parameter `y`.

```
int Complicated(int x, int y) {
    if (x == Obfuscate(y))
        throw new RareException();
    return 0;
}

int Obfuscate(int y) {
    return (100 + y) * 567 % 2347;
}
```

Part 1: Solving constraints Call `Complicated` from a parameterized unit test, and inspect which values Pex uses as test inputs.

Part 2: Observing constraints Pex generates test input by performing a symbolic analysis of the code under test. You can use the method `GetPathConditionString` of the `PexSymbolicValue` class to obtain a textual representation of the current path condition, a predicate that characterizes an execution path. The following code will add a column to the parameter table, and fill it in with the path condition.

```
int Complicated(int x, int y) {
    if (x == Obfuscate(y))
        throw new RareException();

    // logging the path condition
    string pc = PexSymbolicValue.GetPathConditionString();
    PexValue.Add("pc", pc);

    return 0;
}
```

The ToString method of the PexSymbolicValue class gives a textual representation of how a value was derived from the test inputs:

```
int Complicated2(int x, int y) {
    if (x == Obfuscate(y)) {
        // logging the path condition
        string obfuscateY =
            PexSymbolicValue.ToString(Obfuscate(y));
        PexValue.Add("obfuscate(y)", obfuscateY);
        throw new RareException();
    }
    return 0;
}
```

Exercise 4: Heap Constraints. Consider the following type

```
public class C { public int F; }
```

that is used in the following method.

```
public void AliasChallenge(C x, C y) {
    if (x != null)
        if (y != null) {
            x.F = 42;
            y.F = 23;
            // if (x.F == 42) throw new Exception("boom");
        }
}
```

How many execution paths will Pex have to explore? (Pex only generates different test inputs when they exercise different execution paths.)

Exercise 5: Implicit Branches. The following method has two execution paths.

```
public void ImplicitNullCheck(int[] a) {
    int x = a.Length;
}
```

How many paths will Pex explore in the following method? (Note that Pex checks for each possible exception type separately, and considers checks for different exception types as different branches.)

```
public void ImplicitIndexOutOfRangeCheck(int[] a) {
    int x = a[0];
}
```

Pex understands checked code as well. Pex finds inputs that will cause the following method to throw an OverflowException.

```
public void ImplicitOverflowCheck(int x, int y) {
    int z = checked(x + y);
}
```

Can you write a parameterized unit test that could cause an exception of type `InvalidCastException`?

References

1. Mackinnon, T., Freeman, S., Craig, P.: Endotesting: Unit testing with mock objects. In: XP 2000 (May 2000)
2. Pex development team. Pex (2007), `http://research.microsoft.com/Pex`
3. Saff, D., Artzi, S., Perkins, J.H., Ernst, M.D.: Automatic test factoring for Java. In: Proc. 20th ASE, pp. 114–123. ACM Press, New York (2005)
4. Saff, D., Boshernitsan, M., Ernst, M.D.: Theories in practice: Easy-to-write specifications that catch bugs. Technical Report MIT-CSAIL-TR-2008-002, MIT Computer Science and Artificial Intelligence Laboratory, Cambridge, MA, January 14 (2008)
5. Tillmann, N., Schulte, W.: Parameterized unit tests. In: Proceedings of the 10th European Software Engineering Conference held jointly with 13th ACM SIGSOFT International Symposium on Foundations of Software Engineering, pp. 253–262. ACM, New York (2005)
6. Wiki. Mock objects, `http://www.mockobjects.com`

Integrating Verification and Testing of Object-Oriented Software

Christian Engel, Christoph Gladisch, Vladimir Klebanov, and Philipp Rümmer

www.key-project.org

Abstract. Formal methods can only gain widespread use in industrial software development if they are integrated into software development techniques, tools, and languages used in practice. A symbiosis of software testing and verification techniques is a highly desired goal, but at the current state of the art most available tools are dedicated to just one of the two tasks: verification or testing. We use the KeY verification system (developed by the tutorial presenters) to demonstrate our approach in combining both.

1 What KeY Is

KeY is an approach and a system for the deductive verification of object-oriented software. It aims for integrating design, implementation, and quality assurance of software as seamlessly as possible. The intention is to provide a platform that allows close collaboration between conventional and formal software development methods.

Recently, version 1.0 of the KeY system has been released in connection with the KeY book [2]. The KeY system is written in JAVA and runs on all common architectures. It is available under GPL and can be downloaded from `www.key-project.org`.

1.1 Towards Integration of Formal Methods

Formal methods can only gain widespread use in industrial software development if they are integrated into software development techniques, tools, and languages used in practice. KeY integrates with (currently two) well-known CASE tools: Borland Together and the Eclipse IDE. Users can develop a whole software project, comprised of specifications as well as implementations, entirely within either of the mentioned CASE tools. The KeY plugin offers then the *extended functionality* to generate proof obligations from selected parts of specifications and verify them with the KeY prover. The core of the KeY system, the KeY verification component, can also be used as a stand-alone prover, though.

The KeY project is constantly working on techniques to increase the returns of using formal methods in the industrial setting. Recent efforts in this area concentrate on applying verification technology to traditional software processes. These have resulted in development of such approaches as symbolic debugging

B. Beckert and R. Hähnle (Eds.): TAP 2008, LNCS 4966, pp. 182–191, 2008.

and verification-based testing. The latter is the central topic of this tutorial with Section 3 explaining why and how to utilise synergies between verification and testing.

1.2 Full Coverage of a Real-World Programming Language

To ensure acceptance among practitioners it is essential to support an industrially relevant programming language as the verification target. We chose JAVA Card source code [5] because of its importance for security- and safety-critical applications.

For specification, KeY supports both the OMG standard Object Constraint Language (OCL) [20] and the Java Modeling Language (JML) [16], which is increasingly used in the industry. In addition, KeY features a syntax-directed editor for OCL that can render OCL expressions in several natural languages while they are being edited.

The KeY prover and its calculus [2] support the full JAVA CARD 2.2.1 language. This includes all object-oriented features, JAVA CARD's transaction mechanism, the (finite) JAVA integer types, abrupt termination (local jumps and exceptions) and even a formal specification (both in OCL [15] and JML[1]) of the essential parts of the JAVA CARD API. In addition, some JAVA features that are not part of JAVA CARD are supported as well: multi-dimensional arrays, JAVA class initialisation semantics, `char` and `String` types. In short, if you have a sequential JAVA program without dynamic class loading and floating point types, then it is (in principle) possible to verify it with KeY.

To a certain degree, KeY allows to customise the assumed semantics of JAVA CARD. For instance, the user can choose between different semantics of the primitive JAVA integer types. Options are: the mathematical integers (easy to verify, but not a faithful model of JAVA and, hence, unsound), mathematical integers with overflow check (sound, reasonably easy to verify, but incomplete for programs that depend on JAVA's finite ring semantics), and a faithful semantics of JAVA integers (sound and complete, but difficult to verify).

2 Foundations of KeY

2.1 The Logic

KeY is a *deductive verification* system, meaning that its core is a theorem prover, which proves formulae of a suitable logic. Different deductive verification approaches vary in the choice of the used logic. The KeY approach employs a logic called JAVA CARD DL, which is an instance of *Dynamic Logic* (DL) [12]. DL, like Hoare Logic [14], has the advantage of transparency with respect to the program to be verified. This means, programs are neither abstracted away into a less expressive formalism such as finite-state machines nor are they embedded into a general purpose higher-order logic. Instead, the logic and the calculus "work"

[1] See `http://www.cs.ru.nl/~woj/software/software.html`

directly on the Java Card source code. This transparency is extremely helpful for proving problems that require a certain amount of human interaction.

DL itself is a particular kind of *modal logic*. Different parts of a formula are evaluated in different worlds (states), which vary in the interpretation of functions and predicates. DL differs, however, from standard modal logic in that the modalities are "indexed" with pieces of program code, describing how to reach one world (state) from the other. Syntactically, DL extends full first-order logic with two additional (mix-fix) operators: $\langle . \rangle .$ (diamond) and $[.] .$ (box). In both cases, the first argument is a *program*, whereas the second argument is another DL formula. Under program we understand a sequence of Java Card statements.

A formula $\langle p \rangle \varphi$ is true in a state s if execution of p terminates normally when started in s and results in a state where φ is true. As for the other operator, a formula $[p]\varphi$ is true in a state s if execution of p, when started in s, does *either* not terminate normally *or* results in a state where φ is true.[2]

A frequent pattern of DL formulae is $\varphi \rightarrow \langle p \rangle \psi$, stating that the program p, when started from a state where φ is true, terminates with ψ being true afterwards. The formula $\varphi \rightarrow [p]\psi$, on the other hand, does not claim termination, and has exactly the same meaning as the Hoare triple $\{\psi\}\ p\ \{\phi\}$.

The following is an example of a Java Card DL formula:

$$\texttt{o1.f} < \texttt{o2.f} \rightarrow \langle \texttt{int t=o1.f; o1.f=o2.f; o2.f=t;} \rangle\, \texttt{o2.f} < \texttt{o1.f}$$

It says that, when started in any state where the integer field `f` of `o1` has a smaller value than `o2.f`, the statement sequence "`int t=o1.f; o1.f=o2.f; o2.f=t;`" terminates, and afterwards `o2.f` is smaller than `o1.f`.

The main advantage of DL over Hoare logic is increased expressiveness: one can express not merely program correctness, but also security properties, correctness of program transformations, or the validity of assignable clauses. Also, a pre- or postcondition can contain programs themselves, for instance to express that a linked structure is acyclic. A full account of Java Card DL is found in the KeY book [2].

2.2 Verification as Symbolic Execution

The actual verification process in KeY can be viewed as *symbolic execution* of source code. Unbounded loops and recursion are either handled by induction over data structures occurring in the verification target or by specifying loop invariants and variants. Symbolic execution plus induction as a verification paradigm was originally suggested for informal usage by Burstall [4]. The idea to use Dynamic Logic as a basis for mechanising symbolic execution was first realised in the Karlsruhe Interactive Verifier (KIV) tool [13]. Symbolic execution is very well suited for interactive verification, because proof progress corresponds

[2] These descriptions have to be generalised when non-deterministic programs are considered, which is not the case here.

to program execution, which makes it easy to interpret intermediate stages in a proof and failed proof attempts.

Most program logics (e.g., Hoare Logic, wp-calculus) perform substitutions on formulae to record state changes of a program. In the KeY approach to symbolic execution, the application of substitutions is *delayed* as much as possible; instead, the state change effect of a program is made *syntactically explicit* and accumulated in a construct called *updates.* Only when symbolic execution has completed are updates turned into substitutions. For more details about updates we refer to [2].

The second foundation of symbolic execution, next to updates, is *local program transformation.* JAVA (Card) is a complex language, and the calculus for JAVA Card DL performs program transformations to resolve all the complex constructs of the language, breaking them down to simple effects that can be moved into updates. For instance, in the case of `try-catch` blocks, symbolic execution proceeds on the "active" statement *inside* the `try` block, until normal or abrupt termination of that block triggers different transformations.

2.3 Automated Proof Search

For automated proof search, a number of predefined strategies are available in KeY, which are optimised, for example, for symbolically executing programs or proving pure first-order formulae.

In order to better interleave interactive and automated proof construction, KeY uses a proof confluent sequent calculus, which means that automated proof search does not require backtracking over rule applications. The automated search for quantifier instantiations uses meta variables that are place-holders for terms. Instead of backtracking over meta-variable instantiations, instantiations are postponed to the point where the whole proof can be closed, and an incremental global closure check is used. Rule applications requiring particular instantiations (unifications) of meta variables are handled by attaching unification constraints to the resulting formulas [11].

KeY also offers an SMT-LIB backend[3] for proving near-propositional proof goals with external decision procedures.

2.4 User-Friendly Graphical User Interface

Despite a high degree of automation (see Sect. 2.3), in many cases there are significant, non-trivial tasks left for the user. For that purpose, the KeY system provides a user-friendly graphical user interface (GUI). When proving a property which is too involved to be handled fully automatically, certain rule applications need to be performed in an interactive manner, in dialogue with the system. This is the case when either the automated strategies are exhausted, or else when the user deliberately performs a strategic step (like a case distinction) manually, *before* automated strategies are invoked (again). In the case of human-guided

[3] See `http://combination.cs.uiowa.edu/smtlib/`

rule application, the user is asked to solve tasks like: *selecting a proof rule* to be applied, *providing instantiations for* the proof rule's *schema variables*, or *providing instantiations for quantified variables* of the logic. These tasks are supported by dynamic context menus and drag-and-drop.

Other supported forms of interaction in the context of proof construction are the inspection of proof trees, the pruning of proof branches, stepwise backtracking, and the triggering of proof reuse.

3 Integrating Verification and Testing

3.1 Why Integrate

Although deductive verification can achieve a level of reliability of programs that goes beyond most other analysis techniques, there are reasons to augment fully-symbolic reasoning about programs with execution of concrete tests. We distinguish two classes of reasons.

The first class involves failing or inapplicable verification. In many common cases it is impossible to apply verification successfully: be it because no full formal specification is available, because verification is too costly, or simply because the program at hand proves to be incorrect. Moreover, once a verified program is (even slightly) changed, existing correctness proofs become invalid and have to be repeated. We will show how verification technology can be applied also in such situations by generating test-cases based on symbolic execution of programs [10,1], and by turning proof search into a systematic bug search [18].

The second class is due to principal shortcomings of formal verification. Symbolic reasoning about programs on the source code level does not take all phenomena into account that can occur during the actual program execution. It happens routinely that a Java Card application works perfectly on the desktop emulator, but behaves erroneously once deployed on the card. This is typically because the card does not provide a Java Card virtual machine that fully complies with the semantic model used for the verification. As it is simply too complex to formally specify and verify compilers, protocols, smart card operating systems, virtual machine implementations, etc., testing is essential even if a complete proof has been found. The KeY system can automatically generate test-cases from proofs and thus simplifies testing after verification.

3.2 Generating Test Cases from Proofs

The KeY tool integrates all necessary steps for generating comprehensive JUnit tests for white-box testing. The major steps are (1) computation of path conditions with verification technology, (2) generation of concrete test data by constraint solving, and (3) generation of test oracles. The KeY tool can also be combined with existing black-box tools by outsourcing the second and third steps and achieving synergy effects between the tools.

In the following, we assume that we have a program under test p (PUT) and its specification ϕ, which can be a contract (i.e., a pre- and a postcondition) or an invariant. Even very simple specifications yield useful test cases: A specification of total correctness with a postcondition *true* is sufficient to generate tests detecting uncaught exceptions.

3.3 Test-Case Generation by Bounded Symbolic Execution

The proof obligation resulting from the program p and the property ϕ is input into the KeY system, which symbolically executes p for up to a fixed number of steps. This produces a bounded symbolic execution tree, from which feasible execution paths and branches with the corresponding path and branch conditions are easily extracted. With the help of external arithmetics decision procedures like Simplify [9] or Cogent [8], concrete models for these path conditions are computed. These serve as test inputs for p. The property ϕ is translated into a test oracle. Thus, we obtain a test case for every feasible execution path of p (below the bound). The output of the process is a complete JUnit test case suite that requires no further modifications.

Let us consider a simple example program:

```
/*@ public normal_behavior
  @   ensures (
  @     \forall int i; 0<=i && i<arr.length; arr[i]<=\result);
  @*/
public int getMax(int[] arr){
  int max = arr[0];
  for(int i=1; i<arr.length; i++){
    if(arr[i]<max) max = arr[i];
  }
  return max;
}
```

The JML specification requires that `getMax()` terminates normally (without raising an exception) and the returned result is greater or equal than each of `arr`'s entries. This postcondition is translated by KeY into a test oracle, with universal quantifiers mimicked by loops:

```
private boolean oracle(int result, int[] arr){
  boolean b = true
  for(int i=0; i<arr.length; i++){
    b = b && arr[i]<=result;
  }
  return b;
}
```

Since we made no assumptions on `arr.length`, the number of loop iterations is bounded only by `Integer.MAX_VALUE`. Since the number of feasible execution paths through the loop is $2^{\texttt{arr.length}}$ (due to the `if` statement), it is technically not possible to create a test satisfying full feasible path coverage.

Nonetheless, we still get useful test cases if we symbolically execute the code by unrolling the `for` loop a bounded number of times, for instance just once.

These tests already catch both implementation bugs contained in `getMax()`. We now describe this in more detail.

The evaluation of the first statement `max = arr[0];` induces the following case distinction:

(1) $\texttt{arr} \neq \texttt{null} \wedge \texttt{arr.length} \geq 1$: The execution proceeds normally. The path condition on this execution path is feasible.
(2) $\texttt{arr} = \texttt{null}$: A `NullPointerException` is raised, but this branch condition is contradictory to the implicit JML assumption that arguments of a method are not **null**, unless declared `nullable`. KeY recognises this infeasibility and does not generate a test case.
(3) $\texttt{arr.length} < 1$: An `ArrayIndexOutOfBoundsException` is raised. This branch condition is feasible, and a test generated for this path detects that the implementation is erroneous, since we required normal termination of `getMax()`.

The symbolic execution now proceeds on the path (1) with unrolling the **for** loop once. After the first iteration of the loop we end up with an open proof tree containing 4 different feasible execution paths (of which 2 have not yet terminated) with path conditions:

(4) $\texttt{arr.length} < 1$: This path is identical to the path (3) above.
(5) $\texttt{arr.length} = 1$: The loop is never entered, since the loop guard is false.
(6) $\texttt{arr.length} > 1 \wedge \texttt{arr[1]} < \texttt{arr[0]}$: The guard `arr[i]<max` of the **if** statement is true, and `max` is set to `arr[1]`. This violates the postcondition.
(7) $\texttt{arr.length} > 1 \wedge \texttt{arr[1]} \geq \texttt{arr[0]}$: The guard of the **if** statement is false. The postcondition is also possibly violated on this path, namely in case $\texttt{arr[1]} \neq \texttt{arr[0]}$.

The four test cases generated from this proof tree exercise `getMax()` on the paths (4)–(7). The test for (4) initialises `arr` with `new int[0]` and reports an error due to an exception thrown by `getMax()`. The test for (5) succeeds, while the tests for (6) and (7) report failures due to results not accepted by the test oracle.

3.4 Test-Case Generation from Method Specifications and Loop Invariants

An obvious deficiency of bounded symbolic execution is that it only explores a part of all program behaviours. The following example shows the problematic situation.

```
class Bar {
  final int[] arr = new int[16];
  void foo() {
    int max = getMax(arr);
    if(max<0) { A(); }
  }
}
```

We assume a correct implementation of `getMax()`, which is applied to a fixed-length buffer. In order to compute a path condition for the execution of the method `A()` the unwinding bound for symbolic execution of the loop in `getMax()` must be at least 16. This value, in general, is not practicable due to the exponential growth of execution trees. Even worse, the minimal unwinding bound of a loop for executing a certain branch is generally unknown.

An extension of the bounded approach allows generation of test cases based on loop invariants and method specifications in combination with symbolic execution. A loop or a method call is in this case replaced by the invariant resp. the method specification. With this technique we can compute precise conditions for entering a branch, even if the path passes through a loop or a method invocation.

For example the desired path condition for executing the method `A()` in the code above is: $\forall i.\ 0 \leq i \wedge i < 16 \rightarrow \texttt{arr[}i\texttt{]} < 0$. This path condition is computed with our approach by using the branch condition $\texttt{max} < 0$ and the postcondition of `getMax()`.

3.5 White-Box Testing by Combining Specification Extraction and Black-Box Testing

Existing black-box testing tools [7,3,6,17] can be augmented by KeY to provide white-box testing capabilities. In this case, the external tool generates the test inputs and the oracle, while KeY provides information about program structure.

This information is extracted from the symbolic execution tree and input into the black-box testing tool as a part of the program specification. We call this process "structure-preserving specification extraction". The whole approach is illustrated in Figure 1.

Depending on the methods used for its extraction, the specification may not cover iterations of loops above a certain limit. However, by combining the extracted specification with a given requirement specification, black-box testing methods can generate tests that exercise random amounts of loop iterations including those not covered by the extracted specification alone. In this way, it is also possible to achieve a combination of code coverage and data coverage criteria from both techniques.

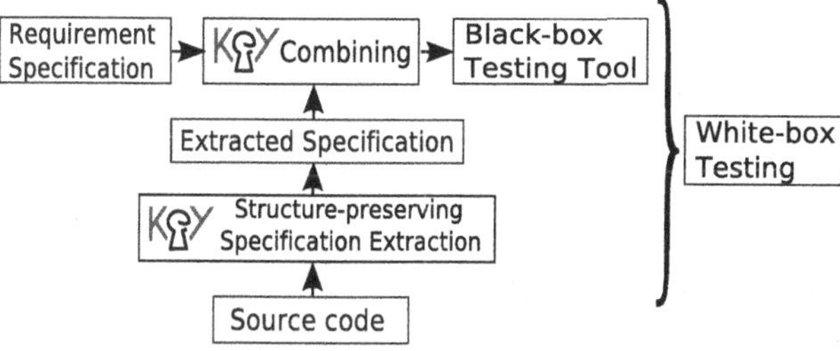

Fig. 1. White-box testing as black-box testing with path extraction

3.6 Proving Incorrectness of Programs

All approaches to find program defects that have been described so far make use of the symbolic execution and reasoning capabilities of KeY without actually aiming at the construction of a complete proof. Due to the generality of JAVA CARD DL, however, the problem can also be approached head-on by simply proving the incorrectness of a program [18]. This is done by showing a negated and existentially quantified correctness formula:

$$\exists\, \textit{pre-state}.\ \neg\big(\textit{preconditions} \rightarrow \langle\, \textit{statements}\, \rangle\ \textit{postconditions}\big) \tag{1}$$

in which *statements* represents the program in question and $\exists\, \textit{pre-state}.$ existentially quantifies all variables, class members and array components that can be read by the program. Formula (1) is true if and only if there is a pre-state in which the preconditions hold, the program fragment does not terminate, or terminates and the postconditions do not hold in the final state. With the help of meta variables (Sect. 2.3) for handling the existential quantifier, symbolic execution and the proof search strategy mechanism, KeY is quite capable to discharge such *disproving obligations* automatically.

Like the discovery of a failing test case, the ability to prove (1) reveals a program defect.[4] The program state for which this happens can be recovered by analysing the proof and extracting the values that were chosen when eliminating the quantifier in (1). Because only symbolic execution of the program is involved, this can even yield descriptions of whole classes of states, in the style of: "the program fails whenever x is greater than y." For the program `getMax()` on page 187, for instance, KeY can automatically find the counterexamples $\texttt{arr.length} = 1$, $\texttt{arr.length} = 2 \wedge \texttt{arr[0]} < \texttt{arr[1]}$ and $\texttt{arr.length} = 3 \wedge \texttt{arr[0]} < \texttt{arr[1]} \wedge \texttt{arr[0]} \leq \texttt{arr[2]}$.

Symbolic incorrectness proofs can also discover defects that are inaccessible to normal testing, for instance the divergence of programs [19]. In order to show that a program does not terminate (for a particular pre-state), it has to be proven that no terminal state is reachable. This can be done by synthesising an invariant that approximates the set of reachable states, and which excludes all terminal states.

References

1. Beckert, B., Gladisch, C.: White-box testing by combining deduction-based specification extraction and black-box testing. In: Gurevich, Y. (ed.) Proceedings, Testing and Proofs, Zürich, Switzerland. LNCS, Springer, Heidelberg (2007)
2. Beckert, B., Hähnle, R., Schmitt, P.H. (eds.): Verification of Object-Oriented Software. LNCS (LNAI), vol. 4334. Springer, Heidelberg (2007)
3. Boyapati, C., Khurshid, S., Marinov, D.: Korat: automated testing based on Java predicates. In: Proceedings, International Symposium on Software Testing and Analysis, Roma, Italy, pp. 123–133. ACM, New York (2002)

[4] But it should be noted that incorrectness proofs cannot detect bugs in other components like the compiler or the runtime environment, in contrast to testing.

4. Burstall, R.M.: Program proving as hand simulation with a little induction. In: Information Processing 1974, pp. 308–312. Elsevier/North-Holland (1974)
5. Chen, Z.: Java Card Technology for Smart Cards: Architecture and Programmer's Guide, June 2000. Java Series. Addison-Wesley, Reading (2000)
6. Cheon, Y., Kim, M., Perumandla, A.: A complete automation of unit testing for Java programs. In: Proceedings, Software Engineering Research and Practice (SERP), Las Vegas, USA, pp. 290–295. CSREA Press (2005)
7. Cheon, Y., Rubio-Medrano, C.E.: Random test data generation for Java classes annotated with JML specifications. In: Software Engineering Research and Practice, pp. 385–391 (2007)
8. Cook, B., Kroening, D., Sharygina, N.: Cogent: Accurate theorem proving for program verification. In: Etessami, K., Rajamani, S.K. (eds.) CAV 2005. LNCS, vol. 3576, pp. 296–300. Springer, Heidelberg (2005)
9. Detlefs, D., Nelson, G., Saxe, J.: Simplify: A Theorem Prover for Program Checking. Technical Report HPL-2003-148, HP Labs (July 2003)
10. Engel, C., Hähnle, R.: Generating unit tests from formal proofs. In: Gurevich, Y., Meyer, B. (eds.) TAP 2007. LNCS, vol. 4454, pp. 169–188. Springer, Heidelberg (2007)
11. Giese, M.: Incremental closure of free variable tableaux. In: Goré, R.P., Leitsch, A., Nipkow, T. (eds.) IJCAR 2001. LNCS (LNAI), vol. 2083, pp. 545–560. Springer, Heidelberg (2001)
12. Harel, D., Kozen, D., Tiuryn, J.: Dynamic Logic. MIT Press, Cambridge (2000)
13. Heisel, M., Reif, W., Stephan, W.: Program verification by symbolic execution and induction. In: Morik, K. (ed.) Proceedings, 11th German Workshop on Artificial Intelligence. Informatik Fachberichte, vol. 152, Springer, Heidelberg (1987)
14. Hoare, C.A.R.: An axiomatic basis for computer programming. Commun. ACM 12(10), 576–580, 583 (1969)
15. Larsson, D., Mostowski, W.: Specifying Java Card API in OCL. In: Schmitt, P.H. (ed.) OCL 2.0 Workshop at UML 2003. ENTCS, vol. 102C, pp. 3–19. Elsevier, Amsterdam (2004)
16. Leavens, G.T., Poll, E., Clifton, C., Cheon, Y., Ruby, C., Cok, D., Müller, P., Kiniry, J., Chalin, P.: JML Reference Manual. Draft Revision 1.200 (February 2007)
17. Parasoft. JTest manual (2004), `http://www.parasoft.com/jtest`
18. Rümmer, P., Shah, M.A.: Proving programs incorrect using a sequent calculus for Java Dynamic Logic. In: Gurevich, Y., Meyer, B. (eds.) TAP 2007. LNCS, vol. 4454, pp. 41–60. Springer, Heidelberg (2007)
19. Velroyen, H., Rümmer, P.: Non-termination checking for imperative programs. In: Meyer, B. (ed.) TAP 2008, Prato, Italy (to appear, 2008), `http://www.key-project.org/nonTermination/`
20. Warmer, J., Kleppe, A.: The Object Constraint Language: Getting Your Models Ready for MDA. Object Technology Series. Addison-Wesley, Reading (2003)

Author Index

Lecture Notes in Computer Science

Sublibrary 2: Programming and Software Engineering

For information about Vols. 1–4309
please contact your bookseller or Springer

Vol. 4989: J. Garrigue, M. Hermenegildo (Eds.), Functional and Logic Programming. XI, 337 pages. 2008.

Vol. 4966: B. Beckert, R. Hähnle (Eds.), Tests and Proofs. X, 193 pages. 2008.

Vol. 4954: C. Pautasso, É. Tanter (Eds.), Software Composition. X, 263 pages. 2008.

Vol. 4949: R.M. Hierons, J.P. Bowen, M. Harman (Eds.), Formal Methods and Testing. XIII, 367 pages. 2008.

Vol. 4906: M. Cebulla (Ed.), Object-Oriented Technology. VIII, 204 pages. 2008.

Vol. 4902: P. Hudak, D.S. Warren (Eds.), Practical Aspects of Declarative Languages. X, 333 pages. 2007.

Vol. 4899: K. Yorav (Ed.), Hardware and Software: Verification and Testing. XII, 267 pages. 2008.

Vol. 4888: F. Kordon, O. Sokolsky (Eds.), Composition of Embedded Systems. XII, 221 pages. 2007.

Vol. 4880: S. Overhage, C.A. Szyperski, R. Reussner, J.A. Stafford (Eds.), Software Architectures, Components, and Applications. X, 249 pages. 2008.

Vol. 4849: M. Winckler, H. Johnson, P. Palanque (Eds.), Task Models and Diagrams for User Interface Design. XIII, 299 pages. 2007.

Vol. 4839: O. Sokolsky, S. Taşıran (Eds.), Runtime Verification. VI, 215 pages. 2007.

Vol. 4834: R. Cerqueira, R.H. Campbell (Eds.), Middleware 2007. XIII, 451 pages. 2007.

Vol. 4829: M. Lumpe, W. Vanderperren (Eds.), Software Composition. VIII, 281 pages. 2007.

Vol. 4824: A. Paschke, Y. Biletskiy (Eds.), Advances in Rule Interchange and Applications. XIII, 243 pages. 2007.

Vol. 4807: Z. Shao (Ed.), Programming Languages and Systems. XI, 431 pages. 2007.

Vol. 4799: A. Holzinger (Ed.), HCI and Usability for Medicine and Health Care. XVI, 458 pages. 2007.

Vol. 4789: M. Butler, M.G. Hinchey, M.M. Larrondo-Petrie (Eds.), Formal Methods and Software Engineering. VIII, 387 pages. 2007.

Vol. 4767: F. Arbab, M. Sirjani (Eds.), International Symposium on Fundamentals of Software Engineering. XIII, 450 pages. 2007.

Vol. 4765: A. Moreira, J. Grundy (Eds.), Early Aspects: Current Challenges and Future Directions. X, 199 pages. 2007.

Vol. 4764: P. Abrahamsson, N. Baddoo, T. Margaria, R. Messnarz (Eds.), Software Process Improvement. XI, 225 pages. 2007.

Vol. 4762: K.S. Namjoshi, T. Yoneda, T. Higashino, Y. Okamura (Eds.), Automated Technology for Verification and Analysis. XIV, 566 pages. 2007.

Vol. 4758: F. Oquendo (Ed.), Software Architecture. XVI, 340 pages. 2007.

Vol. 4757: F. Cappello, T. Herault, J. Dongarra (Eds.), Recent Advances in Parallel Virtual Machine and Message Passing Interface. XVI, 396 pages. 2007.

Vol. 4753: E. Duval, R. Klamma, M. Wolpers (Eds.), Creating New Learning Experiences on a Global Scale. XII, 518 pages. 2007.

Vol. 4749: B.J. Krämer, K.-J. Lin, P. Narasimhan (Eds.), Service-Oriented Computing – ICSOC 2007. XIX, 629 pages. 2007.

Vol. 4748: K. Wolter (Ed.), Formal Methods and Stochastic Models for Performance Evaluation. X, 301 pages. 2007.

Vol. 4741: C. Bessière (Ed.), Principles and Practice of Constraint Programming – CP 2007. XV, 890 pages. 2007.

Vol. 4735: G. Engels, B. Opdyke, D.C. Schmidt, F. Weil (Eds.), Model Driven Engineering Languages and Systems. XV, 698 pages. 2007.

Vol. 4716: B. Meyer, M. Joseph (Eds.), Software Engineering Approaches for Offshore and Outsourced Development. X, 201 pages. 2007.

Vol. 4709: F.S. de Boer, M.M. Bonsangue, S. Graf, W.-P. de Roever (Eds.), Formal Methods for Components and Objects. VIII, 297 pages. 2007.

Vol. 4680: F. Saglietti, N. Oster (Eds.), Computer Safety, Reliability, and Security. XV, 548 pages. 2007.

Vol. 4670: V. Dahl, I. Niemelä (Eds.), Logic Programming. XII, 470 pages. 2007.

Vol. 4652: D. Georgakopoulos, N. Ritter, B. Benatallah, C. Zirpins, G. Feuerlicht, M. Schoenherr, H.R. Motahari-Nezhad (Eds.), Service-Oriented Computing ICSOC 2006. XVI, 201 pages. 2007.

Vol. 4640: A. Rashid, M. Aksit (Eds.), Transactions on Aspect-Oriented Software Development IV. IX, 191 pages. 2007.

Vol. 4634: H. Riis Nielson, G. Filé (Eds.), Static Analysis. XI, 469 pages. 2007.

Vol. 4620: A. Rashid, M. Aksit (Eds.), Transactions on Aspect-Oriented Software Development III. IX, 201 pages. 2007.

Vol. 4615: R. de Lemos, C. Gacek, A. Romanovsky (Eds.), Architecting Dependable Systems IV. XIV, 435 pages. 2007.

Vol. 4610: B. Xiao, L.T. Yang, J. Ma, C. Muller-Schloer, Y. Hua (Eds.), Autonomic and Trusted Computing. XVIII, 571 pages. 2007.

Vol. 4609: E. Ernst (Ed.), ECOOP 2007 – Object-Oriented Programming. XIII, 625 pages. 2007.

Vol. 4608: H.W. Schmidt, I. Crnković, G.T. Heineman, J.A. Stafford (Eds.), Component-Based Software Engineering. XII, 283 pages. 2007.

Vol. 4591: J. Davies, J. Gibbons (Eds.), Integrated Formal Methods. IX, 660 pages. 2007.

Vol. 4589: J. Münch, P. Abrahamsson (Eds.), Product-Focused Software Process Improvement. XII, 414 pages. 2007.

Vol. 4574: J. Derrick, J. Vain (Eds.), Formal Techniques for Networked and Distributed Systems – FORTE 2007. XI, 375 pages. 2007.

Vol. 4556: C. Stephanidis (Ed.), Universal Access in Human-Computer Interaction, Part III. XXII, 1020 pages. 2007.

Vol. 4555: C. Stephanidis (Ed.), Universal Access in Human-Computer Interaction, Part II. XXII, 1066 pages. 2007.

Vol. 4554: C. Stephanidis (Ed.), Universal Acess in Human Computer Interaction, Part I. XXII, 1054 pages. 2007.

Vol. 4553: J.A. Jacko (Ed.), Human-Computer Interaction, Part IV. XXIV, 1225 pages. 2007.

Vol. 4552: J.A. Jacko (Ed.), Human-Computer Interaction, Part III. XXI, 1038 pages. 2007.

Vol. 4551: J.A. Jacko (Ed.), Human-Computer Interaction, Part II. XXIII, 1253 pages. 2007.

Vol. 4550: J.A. Jacko (Ed.), Human-Computer Interaction, Part I. XXIII, 1240 pages. 2007.

Vol. 4542: P. Sawyer, B. Paech, P. Heymans (Eds.), Requirements Engineering: Foundation for Software Quality. IX, 384 pages. 2007.

Vol. 4536: G. Concas, E. Damiani, M. Scotto, G. Succi (Eds.), Agile Processes in Software Engineering and Extreme Programming. XV, 276 pages. 2007.

Vol. 4530: D.H. Akehurst, R. Vogel, R.F. Paige (Eds.), Model Driven Architecture - Foundations and Applications. X, 219 pages. 2007.

Vol. 4523: Y.-H. Lee, H.-N. Kim, J. Kim, Y.W. Park, L.T. Yang, S.W. Kim (Eds.), Embedded Software and Systems. XIX, 829 pages. 2007.

Vol. 4498: N. Abdennahder, F. Kordon (Eds.), Reliable Software Technologies - Ada-Europe 2007. XII, 247 pages. 2007.

Vol. 4486: M. Bernardo, J. Hillston (Eds.), Formal Methods for Performance Evaluation. VII, 469 pages. 2007.

Vol. 4470: Q. Wang, D. Pfahl, D.M. Raffo (Eds.), Software Process Dynamics and Agility. XI, 346 pages. 2007.

Vol. 4468: M.M. Bonsangue, E.B. Johnsen (Eds.), Formal Methods for Open Object-Based Distributed Systems. X, 317 pages. 2007.

Vol. 4467: A.L. Murphy, J. Vitek (Eds.), Coordination Models and Languages. X, 325 pages. 2007.

Vol. 4454: Y. Gurevich, B. Meyer (Eds.), Tests and Proofs. IX, 217 pages. 2007.

Vol. 4444: T. Reps, M. Sagiv, J. Bauer (Eds.), Program Analysis and Compilation, Theory and Practice. X, 361 pages. 2007.

Vol. 4440: B. Liblit, Cooperative Bug Isolation. XV, 101 pages. 2007.

Vol. 4408: R. Choren, A. Garcia, H. Giese, H.-f. Leung, C. Lucena, A. Romanovsky (Eds.), Software Engineering for Multi-Agent Systems V. XII, 233 pages. 2007.

Vol. 4406: W. De Meuter (Ed.), Advances in Smalltalk. VII, 157 pages. 2007.

Vol. 4405: L. Padgham, F. Zambonelli (Eds.), Agent-Oriented Software Engineering VII. XII, 225 pages. 2007.

Vol. 4401: N. Guelfi, D. Buchs (Eds.), Rapid Integration of Software Engineering Techniques. IX, 177 pages. 2007.

Vol. 4385: K. Coninx, K. Luyten, K.A. Schneider (Eds.), Task Models and Diagrams for Users Interface Design. XI, 355 pages. 2007.

Vol. 4383: E. Bin, A. Ziv, S. Ur (Eds.), Hardware and Software, Verification and Testing. XII, 235 pages. 2007.

Vol. 4379: M. Südholt, C. Consel (Eds.), Object-Oriented Technology. VIII, 157 pages. 2007.

Vol. 4364: T. Kühne (Ed.), Models in Software Engineering. XI, 332 pages. 2007.

Vol. 4355: J. Julliand, O. Kouchnarenko (Eds.), B 2007: Formal Specification and Development in B. XIII, 293 pages. 2006.

Vol. 4354: M. Hanus (Ed.), Practical Aspects of Declarative Languages. X, 335 pages. 2006.

Vol. 4350: M. Clavel, F. Durán, S. Eker, P. Lincoln, N. Martí-Oliet, J. Meseguer, C. Talcott, All About Maude - A High-Performance Logical Framework. XXII, 797 pages. 2007.

Vol. 4348: S. Tucker Taft, R.A. Duff, R.L. Brukardt, E. Plödereder, P. Leroy, Ada 2005 Reference Manual. XXII, 765 pages. 2006.

Vol. 4346: L. Brim, B.R. Haverkort, M. Leucker, J. van de Pol (Eds.), Formal Methods: Applications and Technology. X, 363 pages. 2007.

Vol. 4344: V. Gruhn, F. Oquendo (Eds.), Software Architecture. X, 245 pages. 2006.

Vol. 4340: R. Prodan, T. Fahringer, Grid Computing. XXIII, 317 pages. 2007.

Vol. 4336: V.R. Basili, H.D. Rombach, K. Schneider, B. Kitchenham, D. Pfahl, R.W. Selby (Eds.), Empirical Software Engineering Issues. XVII, 193 pages. 2007.

Vol. 4326: S. Göbel, R. Malkewitz, I. Iurgel (Eds.), Technologies for Interactive Digital Storytelling and Entertainment. X, 384 pages. 2006.

Vol. 4323: G. Doherty, A. Blandford (Eds.), Interactive Systems. XI, 269 pages. 2007.

Vol. 4322: F. Kordon, J. Sztipanovits (Eds.), Reliable Systems on Unreliable Networked Platforms. XIV, 317 pages. 2007.